The Self-Fashioning of Disraeli, 1818–1851

Benjamin Disraeli remains a commanding figure in the history and ideology of the British Conservative party, and a remarkable example of ascent to high office from outside the traditional elite. This is the first book to bring together specialists in history, literary studies and psychiatry to show how he successfully fashioned his personality in the formative years up to his emergence as Conservative leader in the House of Commons.

The analysis of this process of self-fashioning – the situation to which it responded, the problems of an outsider's integration and advancement in British society, the goals it sought to reach, the techniques which it employed, and the sources on which it drew – offers fresh insight into Disraeli's character and career. Vital aspects of his personality and outlook discussed here include his education, Jewishness, romanticism, orientalism, historical scholarship and political ideas, and the psychiatric disorder of his mid-twenties, which is examined seriously for the first time.

CHARLES RICHMOND has practised law in New York and London, and is a member of the New York Bar and of the Institute of Historical Research, University of London.

PAUL SMITH was formerly Professor of Modern History, University of South-ampton. His books include *Disraelian Conservatism and Social Reform* (1967), *Disraeli: A Brief Life* (1996) and, as editor, *Lord Salisbury on Politics* (1972).

THE SELF-FASHIONING OF DISRAELI 1818–1851

EDITED BY
CHARLES RICHMOND
AND
PAUL SMITH

CAMBRIDGE
UNIVERSITY PRESS

PUBLISHED BY THE PRESS SYNDICATE OF THE UNIVERSITY OF CAMBRIDGE
The Pitt Building, Trumpington Street, Cambridge CB2 1RP, United Kingdom

CAMBRIDGE UNIVERSITY PRESS
The Edinburgh Building, Cambridge, CB2 2RU, United Kingdom   http://www.cup.cam.ac.uk
40 West 20th Street, New York, NY 10011–4211, USA   http://www.cup.org
10 Stamford Road, Oakleigh, Melbourne 3166, Australia

© Cambridge University Press 1998

First published 1998

Printed in the United Kingdom at the University Press, Cambridge

Typeset in Janson 10/13pt [CE]

A catalogue record for this book is available from the British Library

Library of Congress Cataloguing in Publication data

Disraeli: The Fashioning of the Self / edited by Charles Richmond and Paul Smith.
p.   cm.
Includes bibliographical references and index.
ISBN 0 521 49729 9 (hb)
1. Disraeli, Benjamin, Earl of Beaconsfield, 1804–1881.
2. Disraeli, Benjamin, Earl of Beaconsfield, 1804–1881. – Criticism and interpretation.
3. Conservatism – Great Britain – History – 19th century. 4. Great Britain – Politics and government – 1830–1837. 5. Great Britain – Politics and government – 1837–1901.
6. Conservative Party (Great Britain) – Biography. 7. Prime ministers – Great Britain – Biography. 8. Legislators – Great Britain – Biography. 9. Identity (Psychology) 10. Self in literature. I. Richmond, Charles. II. Smith, Paul, 1937–   .   I. Title.
DA564.B3D54   1998
941.081'092–dc21   97–52756   CIP

ISBN 0 521 49729 9 hardback

Contents

Contributors

PATRICK BRANTLINGER is Professor of English at Indiana University and a former editor of *Victorian Studies* (1980–90). His recent books include *Rule of Darkness: British Literature and Imperialism, 1830–1914* (Ithaca, NY, 1988), *Crusoe's Footprints: Cultural Studies in Britain and America* (New York, 1990) and *Fictions of State: Culture and Credit in Britain* (Ithaca, NY, 1996).

TODD M. ENDELMAN is William Haber Professor of Modern Jewish History at the University of Michigan. He is the author of *The Jews of Georgian England, 1714–1830: Tradition and Change in a Liberal Society* (Philadelphia, 1979) and *Radical Assimilation in English Jewish History, 1656–1945* (Bloomington, IN, 1990) and the editor of *Jewish Apostasy in the Modern World* (New York, 1987) and *Comparing Jewish Societies* (Ann Arbor, 1997).

PETER JUPP is Professor of Modern British History in the Queen's University, Belfast. His publications include a biography of *Lord Grenville* (Oxford, 1985), *The Letter-Journal of George Canning* (London, 1991) and *British Politics on the Eve of Reform: The Duke of Wellington's Administration, 1828–1830* (London, 1998).

JERROLD M. POST is Professor of Psychiatry, Political Psychology and International Affairs at the George Washington University. He founded and led for twenty-one years the US government's Center for the Analysis of Personality and Political Behavior. He is the co-author of *When Illness Strikes the Leader* (New Haven, 1993) and *Political Paranoia: The Psychopolitics of Hatred* (New Haven, 1997).

CHARLES RICHMOND is a member of the New York Bar and has practised securities and banking law in New York and London. He took his first degree in history at the University of Toronto and wrote an Oxford University M.Litt. thesis (1982) entitled 'Benjamin Disraeli: A Psychological Biography, 1804–1832'. He is currently engaged in research on the life of the fifth earl of Rosebery.

DANIEL R. SCHWARZ is Professor of English at Cornell University. His books include *Reconfiguring Modernism: Explorations in the Relationship between Modern Art and Modern Literature* (New York, 1997), *Narrative and Representation in Wallace Stevens* (New York, 1993), *The Case for a Humanistic Poetics* (Philadelphia, 1991), *The Transformation of the English Novel, 1890–1930* (New York, 1989; rev. edn 1995) and *Disraeli's Fiction* (London, 1979).

PAUL SMITH, formerly Professor of Modern History in the University of Southampton, is the author of *Disraelian Conservatism and Social Reform* (London, 1967) and *Disraeli: A Brief Life* (Cambridge, 1996).

Preface

We express our gratitude to the Canadian Publishing Foundation and its Research Director, Marion Ruth Tapper, for their support for the compilation of this volume, and to William Davies of Cambridge University Press for his encouragement and patience. We must thank the National Trust for permission to use and quote from the Disraeli Papers in the Bodleian Library, which are referred to herein as the Hughenden Papers; and we would like to thank the owners of copyright in other materials which contributors have been permitted to consult and to cite. We must also express our gratitude to Dr Harold Merskey for his generous assistance with the chapter on Disraeli's illness. Like all students of Disraeli's career, we must acknowledge a special obligation to the Disraeli Project at Queen's University, Kingston, Ontario. Its edition of *Benjamin Disraeli Letters* has been a fundamental source.

In order to allow consultation of any edition, Disraeli's novels, together with *Lord George Bentinck*, are normally cited by reference to book or part (large roman) and chapter number (small roman) (in the case of *Hartlebury*, the large roman numerals denote the volume number). Letters are cited by reference to their serial number and volume and page number in *Benjamin Disraeli Letters*.

Introduction

PAUL SMITH

There has been something like a new wave of study of Disraeli in the last decade and a half, in which much attention has been paid to aspects of his personality and *œuvre* inadequately recognized or analysed in the standard accounts, especially his social and political ideas, his style of self-presentation, and the significance of his Jewish origins and his assumption of the romantic mode.[1] This volume tries to deepen and expand those explorations for the most formative period of his life, up to about 1850, in the belief that Disraeli sought strenuously to construct the persona with which he confronted the world, and that the analysis of that process of construction – the situation and the stimuli to which it responded, the goals it sought to reach, the materials which it employed, and the manner in which it was pursued – offers the best prospect that we have of advancing our understanding of his character.

For this purpose, we need to escape from the historiography which treats Disraeli, perhaps unconsciously, as an aberrant Victorian, judging him, often in highly moralistic terms, by the standards of an age in which he was already an anachronism and a culture to which he only partially belonged, and therefore seeing him as a deviant from a norm he did not acknowledge. The studies here collected attempt to see him as himself – a product of Jewish origins and European intellectual strains which made him in some sense and degree a stranger and a sojourner in England, and obliged him to pursue in society, literature and politics an intense effort of denization, through which his 'genius' could be materialized in terms appropriate to its physical location and to its need to dominate. The task involves giving careful scrutiny to Disraeli's sensibility and ideas both in their derivation and in their adaptation to the necessities of his progress in an often unsympathetic environment. Disraeli was a highly derivative thinker, and as we locate the springs of his inspiration in a wide spectrum of European thought, literature, and social and aesthetic consciousness, so it becomes possible to set him in a firm context of the cultural development of his age. Related to European trends in, for example, Jewish emancipation and assimilation, or romantic self-formation, he appears less isolated and strange than when viewed against a purely English background. In placing him in his proper cultural context, we may better understand not only Disraeli himself, and the nature of the transaction between his 'genius' and the society with which it had to negotiate, but also the forms of expression and action of some of the more important European intellectual and social tendencies of his age.

The process of self-fashioning reached its public apogee in the creation of the political persona with which Disraeli mounted to the leadership of the Conservative party and the prime ministership of England, and engaged in the contest with Gladstone which forms a convenient focus for those who like to take their Victorian politics in the form of dramatic antithesis between personalities apparently at opposite poles of temperament and belief. Here, however, Disraeli's early life is considered not as a prologue to, nor a preparation for, nor an explanation of, the ascent to high office, but rather as a struggle to materialize and exhibit his 'genius', in which politics was one of several forms of expression and fields of action, alongside literature, social climbing, and the effort to seize and guide the mind of the age on such topical and exploitable themes as the determining force of race in history, the advance of the democratic at the expense of the aristocratic spirit, the social and political implications of capitalist industrialism, and the nature and destiny of English nationhood.

Disraeli's preoccupation with 'genius' is the main connecting thread through these chapters. Like much else, it suggests the influence of his father. If he was not quite, as he would put it, 'born in a library',[2] he was certainly largely formed as a boy by reading in his father's. Isaac D'Israeli's inability to produce a convincing demonstration of high literary talent of his own had early led him to specialize in fluttering round the flame of other people's. In successive editions (1795–1840) of what was originally titled *An Essay on the Manners and Genius of the Literary Character*, he pottered to provide an anatomy of 'genius', considered first as the characteristic disposition of writers, but increasingly also as the phenomenon of supreme intellectual power.[3] Benjamin Disraeli grew up in an environment strewn with anecdotes of genius and much exercised about the mechanism of being or becoming a genius. It was natural for a boy of talent and ardour to infer that the materialization and demonstration of genius was what life was about.

As Charles Richmond demonstrates, however, in his study of Disraeli's education, the examples of preternatural ability and dazzling achievement that first appealed to the young Disraeli were men who had gained power rather than written books. From the first, Disraeli was contemplating the contrast between the life of action and the life of artistic creation, between the corruption which seemed to be involved in success in the one and the purity which seemed to attend dedication to the other. It was clear that in either case the individual genius could not impose itself, indeed could not even form itself, except in interaction with, and adaptation to, the genius of the age in which it lived and the genius of the place which it inhabited, modify the terms of the problem in its favour though it might by asserting the definition of the two last which offered it the best opportunities. The negotiations and transactions involved in this relationship run through all these chapters, as they ran constantly in Disraeli's mind. To recognize, define and sharpen your genius was useless unless you could also recognize the point and method of its successful insertion into its environment. 'Spirit of the Times. To know it & one'self the secret of success', he entered in his commonplace book in 1842.[4] What he hankered after was what he called, in acknowledging his father's lack of it, 'that rare creative power, which the blended and simultaneous influence of the individual organisation and the spirit of the age, reciprocally acting upon each other, can alone, perhaps, perfectly develop'.[5]

In gauging the character of, and working out the relation between, his 'individual organisation' (that is, his psychological make-up) and the spirit of the time and place, Disraeli had more incentive and more latitude than many of his contemporaries. Without assured station in English society (if with some *entrée* through his father to the world of *belles lettres*), and without inherited standpoint in English politics, he was less directed than they by conventional social patterning or traditionary prejudice. He was not pressed in the mould of public school and university education, but left to the free range of his father's shelves. He was left more than most to invent himself, and even to invent the world he wished to conquer, with the aid of the romantic idealism which he caught at secondhand from Germany via Madame de Staël. The Kantian lesson he wrote down, that it was the power of the understanding 'which gives laws to exterior nature and not exterior nature to it',[6] was one which he did not forget. The conviction which sustained him in the struggles of his early career was that the force of individual genius could shape the terms of its reception into the world by imposing upon contemporaries its own reconceptualization of that world. It was that power which made it possible for the 'destiny' in which Disraeli so strongly believed to be accomplished. If his notion of the superiority of mind over the obdurate density of matter did not extend quite to the transcendentalism which he noted down from Madame de Staël's characterization of Fichte,[7] he evidently sensed the application to his needs of that philosopher's doctrine that 'every human being ... is alike in this, that underlying the various manifestations of his life, there is one impulse, which amid all change persists unchanged ... Incidentally, the self-comprehension of this impulse and its translation into ideas creates the world, and there is no other world but this world, which is created thus in thought, not freely but of necessity.'[8]

The imperious necessity of realizing the true nature of his genius and translating it into mastery over his environment drove the young Disraeli through the hectic endeavours to create great works of literature and thought, conquer polite, or for that matter impolite, society, make love and money, and mount the ladder of political power (sometimes all in the same week), which supply the subject matter of this volume. There was a good deal of coxcombry in these efforts. To get a footing, a young man without fortune or assured social position had to grab attention. 'I have to make a noise because I'm poor', was the young Evelyn Waugh's reply when Cyril Connolly asked him why he was making a row outside Balliol.[9] Disraeli's ringlets, and dandified costumes, and affected manners, and purple passages, and ferocious invectives, sought notice. But they did not entirely convey his character. However flippant and flamboyant, however ironic or fantastical, he was entirely serious, and intense in application, in the purpose of being a great man.

Much though Disraeli relished the theatre of the salon or the hustings, his main avenue of self-realization and self-assertion in his early years lay in the ventures in literature that came naturally enough to the son of a minor literary celebrity. Daniel Schwarz's chapter demonstrates the instrumentality of his novels in exploring the possibilities of being that tempted him, testing out the shapes his identity might assume and the roles he might play. The limitations of the young Disraeli's knowledge of life, and a certain lack of real creative imagination in the depiction of character, would perhaps have been enough to ensure that his first novels would be about himself, but in any case it was about himself that he wanted to write. It was a self in course of evolution and definition by the very act of writing about it. Disraeli's novels are autobiographical, not in the sense that they furnish a simple record of feelings and events, but in the sense that they exhibit a process of self-fashioning of which they themselves form a vital part. In that, they do no more than follow the normal pattern of autobiography as an activity of self-development, exemplifying P. J. Eakin's argument 'that autobiographical truth is not a fixed but an evolving content in an intricate process of self-discovery and self-creation, and, further, that the self that is the center of all autobiographical narrative is necessarily a fictive structure'.[10] The self, however, could not be a subject of free invention: it could not easily be conceived apart from the models made available by the culture of the age. For Disraeli, as Schwarz explains, the romantic mode supplied the pattern of thought and feeling and the technique of expression appropriate to his nature and needs. Romanticism incorporated into a self-electing European elite the young man hovering on the fringes of social and political acceptance at home, and offered him the reassurance of the preternatural artistic vision that could discern beneath the surfaces of mundane reality the true nature and ultimate meaning of things. In the superiority of that special insight lay the chief moral justification of his claim to play a leading role in a country where he had no unimpeachable native antecedents or automatic membership of the governing class.

Disraeli savoured to the full the dramatic poses and rhetorical flights of romanticism and its sanctioning of theatrical self-indulgence as an avenue, even a condition, of moral authenticity. But it was the moral authenticity as much as the self-indulgence with which he was concerned. Daniel Schwarz points out the extent to which his earliest novels were an anxious weighing and balancing of the moral merits, and faithfulness to his nature, of the impulses which drove him and the courses of life which they seemed to dictate: they were 'moral parables told by himself for himself about ambitious egoists'.[11] Schwarz notes also how the early fiction represents for Disraeli 'the means of ordering and controlling his personality', as he judges his leading characters by the measure of 'traditional values and the community's interest', displaying even in the almost *Sturm und Drang* wildness of his first novel, *Vivian Grey*, his 'sense of propriety and a respect for moderation in passions'.[12] Beneath the strutting sense of supreme powers and boundless ambition lay the reticences of a moralist and the hesitations of a *parvenu*. Perhaps we have given too little credence to what Disraeli wrote in 1833 in the 'Mutilated Diary': 'The world calls me *"conceited"*. The world is in error ... When I was considered very conceited *indeed*, I was nervous, and had self confidence only by fits.'[13]

Perhaps, too, the truth was that Disraeli as a romantic was not altogether to the manner born. Behind the 'continental' and 'revolutionary' mind with which he credited himself,[14] and the eastern exoticism he came to affect, the Bloomsbury boy was not hard to discern. There is something in Jonathan Parry's observation that Disraeli was a case of 'Venice, Constantinople or Jerusalem on the surface, but Holborn beneath'.[15] Expansiveness of ambition was not matched by expansiveness of circumstances or of opportunities. The high aristocratic tone of the romanticism exemplified by the Byronic model which Disraeli so much admired was not one he was well placed to emulate. He might learn to be scornful of the dullness of the English bourgeoisie ('For the middle class', he would note waspishly, 'marriage often the only adventure of life'[16]) but he belonged to it. The urge to heroic deeds was tempered by shortage of funds and by conspicuous attachment to the domestic comforts financed by his father, first in the modest confines of the family home in Bloomsbury Square and then in the more spacious surroundings of Bradenham, the country house which Isaac rented from 1829, 'most of the rooms 30 and 40 feet long, and plenty of servants, horses, dogs, and a library full of the rarest books' as Mrs Wyndham Lewis found it.[17] Disraeli needed this kind of support structure. On the eastern tour of 1830–1, the only long period he ever spent away from home, he leaned on one of his travelling companions, James Clay, writing to Sarah: 'You know that tho' I like to be at my ease, I want energy in those little affairs of which life greatly consists.' Clay's comment was that he was the sort of person who 'ought never to travel without a nurse'.[18] In England, most of the nursing services were supplied by the succession of older women whom Disraeli induced to mother him, from his sister, the prime confidante of his early days, to the Holborn solicitor's wife Sara Austen, and Clara Bolton, the wife of a fashionable West End doctor. With Lady Henrietta Sykes, from the spring of 1833, he was able to try his hand at a grand passion with a woman of fashion and beauty, but even with Henrietta he was no more than clinging to the skirts of the *beau monde* – she was the illegitimate offspring of a gentleman brewer and a horse dealer's daughter, married to a baronet struggling to conserve the remnants of an East India Company fortune.

Yet Holborn habits and Holborn friends could be shaken off, and even the more raffish fringe of society represented by Henrietta or by the Blessington–D'Orsay *ménage* was a start. The main obstacle to a heroic career was the lack of scope offered by a settled and self-complacent society with a stable political system. The rapid satisfaction of Disraeli's ambition required change and motion. But the era of the French Revolution and Napoleonic upheaval in Europe was over by the time he began the world, and so was much of what Eric Hobsbawm has described as 'the typical revolutionary struggle of the Restoration period, all dashing young men in guards or hussar uniforms leaving operas, soirées, assignments with duchesses or highly ritualized lodge-meetings to make a military coup or place themselves at the head of a struggling nation; in fact the Byronic pattern'.[19] Disraeli was an apprentice solicitor in a London office when Byron died in the service of the Greek struggle for independence. England did not offer those avenues of heroic endeavour and prospects of cataclysmic upheaval that would allow youthful genius to rush to the fore, though the crisis of parliamentary reform in 1831 caused Disraeli to hope for a moment that it might.[20] Its intellectual life did not engender the kind of passionate public confrontation between old values and new that in February 1830 enabled the nineteen-year-old Théophile Gautier to stamp his image unforgettably on the minds of his contemporaries by wearing his red waistcoat like a banner of revolution at the tumultuous first night of Hugo's *Hernani*. Disraeli, at that period, was scraping together the money for his eastern tour and worrying about his greying hair.[21] His waistcoats were equally striking, but less fortunate in their opportunities.

The frustrations of his situation were much increased by the alarming sensation that he was running out of time. It was characteristic of the great romantic talents to produce masterpieces in their twenties, and to avoid anti-climax by dying in their thirties, if not before. By the time his attempt to secure political influence through the establishment of the *Representative* newspaper had collapsed, and his first novel, *Vivian Grey*, had failed to conquer the critics, Disraeli was falling behind schedule. The effect was to make him doubt, first the possibility of realizing his genius, and then its very existence. Turning experience into saleable goods in his habitual manner, he described both terrors in *The Young Duke*, published in 1831:

> View the obscure Napoleon, starving in the streets of Paris! What was St. Helena to the bitterness of such existence? ... to be conscious that his supernatural energies might die away without creating their miracles – can the wheel, or the rack, rival the torture of such a suspicion?
>
> To doubt of the truth of the creed in which you have been nurtured, is not so terrific as to doubt respecting the intellectual vigour on whose strength you have staked your happiness (II, vii).

To such fears the illness which almost removed him from circulation between the summer of 1827 and the latter part of 1829 owed much of its origin. Charles Richmond and Jerrold Post supply in this volume the first full examination of the psychiatric character of what the patient described as 'one of those tremendous disorganisations which happen to all men at some period of their lives'.[22] Nervous breakdown could at least be interpreted as a reinforcement of Disraeli's credentials – the almost inevitable response of the artist to a world in which, increasingly deprived of recognized public function, of sustaining patronage and of an assured public, he was, as Eric Hobsbawm has put it, 'left to cast his soul as a commodity upon a blind market, to be bought or not'.[23] Hobsbawm's image of the artist standing alone, 'shouting into the night, uncertain even of an echo',[24] evokes Disraeli's reminiscence (for it is surely that) in *Contarini Fleming*: 'I was not always assured of my identity or even existence, for I sometimes found it necessary to shout aloud to be sure that I lived' (IV, v).[25] The notion that wild, exalted, desperate states of mind might unlock the door to truth not revealed to normal consciousness, hence that they might be a sign of the supreme insight of the genius, was hardly invented by the romantics – Dryden observed that 'Great Wits are sure to Madness near alli'd / And thin Partitions do their Bounds divide'[26] – but it was a frequent component of their experiential/experimental technique. Disraeli's illness was real, but it was surreal also, a fascinated, perhaps half-willed dabbling in that state of mind akin to a waking dream which Isaac in the *Literary Character* had selected as one of the marks of men of genius.[27]

Whether or not his illness served to reassure Disraeli of his membership of the geniuses' club, he emerged from it to a sustained period of creative activity, in which *The Young Duke* (completed in 1830) was followed by *Contarini Fleming, Alroy* and *The Revolutionary Epick* within the space of four years. In that period, too, he began to add new dimensions to the fashioning of the self. Patrick Brantlinger shows how he followed the current fashion (of which his father had been a precursor)[28] for turning the East into a resource of the western imagination, and in so doing embarked on the romanticization of his own Semitic origins in a way which would turn them from a source at best of embarrassment, at worst of self-hatred, into the membership card of a racial and intellectual aristocracy effortlessly superior to anything that had emerged from the primeval forests of northern Europe. Following close upon the awakening of interest in the Jewish past that had set him to work on the history of David Alroy,

Disraeli's health-restoring tour of the Near East in 1830–1 was the making of him in more senses than one.

Perhaps the most important single contribution of recent writing on Disraeli has been to re-establish the centrality to any interpretation of his character and career of his Jewishness and the way in which he chose to understand and to utilize it. That Jewishness was a principal determinant both of his situation and of his mode of response to it has been clear enough to students like Israel Zangwill, Philip Rieff and Isaiah Berlin; but full recognition and exploration of its significance was set back by Robert Blake's virtual dismissal of the issue, first in his observation that 'England at the beginning of the nineteenth century was a tolerant place, and its Jewish inhabitants were numerically far below the figure at which, sociologists tell us, an alien minority risks becoming the object of hatred to their fellow citizens', and second by his contention that 'it is not so much the Jewish as the Italian streak in Disraeli that predominated'.[29] Lord Blake, all the same, acknowledged Disraeli's own interest in his Jewishness, 'to the point of being something of a bore on the subject', and his need, as evinced in *Tancred* and *Lord George Bentinck*, to find a form of composition between pride in Jewish ancestry and adherence to the Christian religion.[30] Disraeli was, in fact, as Stanley Weintraub and Anthony Wohl have recently been at pains to illustrate,[31] operating in a context often more tolerationist than tolerant, in which anti-Semitic prejudice of a racial as well as a religious kind was commonplace, even if discrimination did not boil into persecution. That he had been a baptized Christian since the age of twelve made little difference to the way in which he was identified by many of his contemporaries, not only by critics and enemies eager to characterize him in terms which they assumed would heap him with contempt, but by friends and supporters too. The Salford Conservative who, at the end of his career, praising his ascent from humble origins, described him as 'the son of an outcast' betrayed not only ignorance but a common popular recognition both of his Jewishness and of the handicap which it imposed.[32]

The handicap was not very great in the making of a literary reputation or the achievement of a certain level of acceptance in society – indeed, a touch of strangeness might add spice to a novel or a fashionable party – but, as Todd Endelman points out in this volume,[33] the case was different when Disraeli started to climb the political ladder and to assert a claim to prominence in what was still a specifically Christian legislature, part of an avowedly Christian polity. Anything that could be used by his opponents to impugn his credentials for such a role would be. Weintraub believes that already with *Alroy* in 1833, at the very beginning of his struggles to enter parliament, he was adopting the tactic of aggressively anticipating slurs about his origins by defiantly celebrating 'that sacred and romantic people from whom I derive my blood and name'.[34] Certainly by the 1840s, as Endelman shows, he was devoting much energy and ingenuity to demonstrating the aristocracy and the spiritual genius of his race, in order to establish his membership of it as a source of pride and a title to that objective external vision – that 'absolute freedom from prejudice which was the compensatory possession of a man without a country', credited to Sidonia in *Coningsby* (IV, x) – which, in giving him the insight into English history, character and destiny that only an outsider of superior formation and understanding could possess, authorized his claim to lead. The readiness of opponents to exploit anti-Semitic feeling against him left him little option but to counter-attack in the most vigorous way possible. Todd Endelman believes that he could have chosen, as did other Jewish aspirants to political leadership, to play down his Jewish identity,[35] but no amount of reticence would have spared him from anti-Semitic shafts, and reticence in any case was not his nature. Moreover, set up as a country gentleman at Hughenden and a Buckinghamshire county member by Bentinck money, so that he could give the protectionists the debating power in the House of Commons which they conspicuously lacked, he felt an imperious need to show that, if he was being hired, he was taking service on his own terms, without denial of any aspect of his identity or concealment of any article of his beliefs. With *Tancred* in 1847 and the biography of *Lord George Bentinck* in 1851, he defied the prejudices of the bigoted Protestant party for which he spoke with an assertion of Jewish racial pride rendered only slightly less risky by the unlikelihood that it would catch the attention of many of his not very bookish backbenchers.

In so utilizing his Jewishness to situate himself more rather than less comfortably in English society, indeed to place himself in the saddle, Disraeli exhibited the technique of thought with which he characteristically transcended, at least in idea, all the difficulties in his path. It was a form of romantic transfiguration of the real in the light of the ideal, achieved through the supposed ability of the man of exalted intellect to discern a deeper reality beneath the banalities of conventional wisdom. It operated largely by the mechanism of radical inversion, at its simplest asserting the precise opposite of what was generally believed to be the case. No wonder that in 1833 Disraeli could retail to Sarah as a joke a journalist's assertion that he had replied to a question as to what he intended to stand on in the Marylebone election with the words: 'On my head.'[36] His treatment of Jewishness was the prime example. On the broadest front, he simply reversed the relations of superiority and inferiority between East and West, dilating sardonically on the high civilization achieved by the former when the latter was still sunk in savagery and swamps, and ascribing to the influence and action of Jews, or supposed Jews, most of the overt achievements of western civilization and most of the secret history of western states. Even Napoleon was half assimilated to the Jewish genius.[37] In the local English context, this approach enabled Disraeli to reverse the positions of host nation and alien minority by turning the former into the religious and intellectual pupil and tributary of the latter. It was possible even to reverse the relations of patronage between himself and the aristocracy on which his political progress depended, but for the intellectual qualities of which he felt limited respect: the super-Jew figure of Sidonia not only undertakes the political education of the young nobleman, Henry Coningsby (as Disraeli was undertaking the political education of his Young England associates) but condescends to accept him as a fellow Caucasian whose race is 'sufficiently pure' (*Coningsby*, IV, xv).[38] The same technique was applied, as the chapters by Peter Jupp and me illustrate, to upending conventional views of English history and politics and reversing the stereotypes of the 1820s and 1830s by presenting the Tories as the national and popular, the Whigs as the sectional and oligarchic, party.

Disraeli's arguments, or, often, simply pronouncements, on these themes tended to be expressed in a fashion sufficiently ornate, fantastical and mocking to make it difficult to be sure that he was not speaking with his tongue in his cheek, and both the sincerity and the substance of his views were, and are, frequently doubted. It would be absurd to suppose that he believed in the literal truth of everything that he said, but dangerous also to deride the aspiration with which Contarini Fleming emerges from his spiritual formation, to be remembered 'as one who devoted himself to the amelioration of his kind, by the destruction of error and the propagation of truth' (*Contarini Fleming*, VII, ii). There was a strong didactic bent in Disraeli, and it is clear that he had, or thought he had, substantial authority for most of his views. He seldom attempted to offer detailed substantiation: he supplied few footnotes and rarely gave a reference, as opposed to an allusion. Yet that was probably the result more of a regard for literary form (most of his ideas being broached in his

novels), and of a desire to appear original, than of an inability to cite
sources and evidence. He dwelt with approval on his father's contribution
to the development of serious literary and historical research.[39] Very
occasionally opposition would goad him to give his authorities. It was
criticism in the *Morning Post* of the racial assertions of *Coningsby* that led
him to cite the late count of Toreno, a Spanish statesman and scholar, and
Ranke's *History of the Popes* in support of his contention that many of the
first Jesuits were christianized Jews, and, more importantly, to reveal that
he derived his classification of races from the work of the Göttingen
anthropologist J. F. Blumenbach, as developed in J. C. Pritchard's
Researches Into The Physical History of Mankind ('a work of the highest class'),
and embellished by his own gloss that the Jews were the only Caucasian
race that had remained 'pure and unmixed'.[40]

Usually, any indication of sources is less precise. He told Henry
Lennox in 1852 that observations in *Lord George Bentinck* 'denounced as
heterodox by English clergymen, who are more ignorant of theology than
any body of men in the world (the natural consequence of being tied
down to 39 articles, and stopped from all research into the literature
which they are endowed to illustrate), are only reproductions from St
Augustine and Tertullian'.[41] But he did not say which patristic passages he
was drawing on, though for Tertullian at least we can surmise that he had
in mind the argument that Christianity was the true spiritual heir of
Israel.[42] Often his sources can only be glimpsed through such occasional
remarks in his correspondence or requests for information and books to
his sister or to Sara Austen, whom he used as research assistants, or
inferred from lists of the books in his possession, like that printed by Todd
Endelman in this volume or that which appears in the 1842 inventory of
the Disraelis' London home printed in the *Letters*.[43] What is evident,
however, is that sources there always were. The fashioning of background
and context, spiritual, racial and historical, which was a necessary and
integral part of Disraeli's fashioning of self, used a considerable range of
materials. Peter Jupp's study of Disraeli's version of English history shows
how much can be done to recover them, and in so doing to relate Disraeli
to contemporary thought and scholarship in a way which may make some
of his views appear less startling in content than they were made to seem
by his deliberately provocative way of presenting them. Sometimes,
however, it is a matter of conjecture where and how Disraeli picked up his
ideas. Felix Gilbert suggested that *Contarini Fleming* showed the influence
of the newly translated work of the German historian of ancient Greece,

Carl Otfried Müller, whose development of ideas of immutable tribal character and *Volksgeist* might have contributed to the formation of Disraeli's view of history as a drama of racial development.[44] Disraeli's anatomy of the social, political and spiritual 'condition of England' in *Coningsby, Sybil* and *Tancred* employs metaphors of crowd as opposed to community, notions of social cleavage in industrial and urban society, and views about the need for a reinvigorated monarchy as the only possible arbitrator between the claims of conflicting classes, which strongly suggest that he must have heard in some form of the ideas expounded by Hegel, especially in the *Philosophy of Right* (1821), and by those on the continent, like Lorenz von Stein, who were developing Hegel's social analysis in the 1840s.[45] He did not read German, and if he knew of these authors it was presumably via reviewers and popularizers (as he knew of Kant and Fichte from Madame de Staël) or, most likely, from the conversation of friends and acquaintances. He was, as Patrick Brantlinger puts it,[46] a 'superb *bricoleur* of the conventional ideas of his era', good at catching on the wing whatever was exercising the serious minds as well as the polite society of the day.

Much of his knowledge was superficial and glancing, but it should not be underestimated. He was acute in seizing the essentials of a topic, and he spent more time in reading and reflection than is always appreciated. Contemporaries might sometimes find him shallow, but seldom ignorant or obtuse. At Lady Blessington's in February 1837, Henry Crabb Robinson met 'a stranger whose conversation interested and even pleased me till I knew he was young Disraeli. He talked with spirit on German literature.'[47] Disraeli had access to German literature only in translation, but he evidently knew enough to pass muster with a leading English authority on the subject. The best witness to the range and seriousness of his intellectual pursuits is perhaps his friend and political pupil, Edward Henry, Lord Stanley, son and heir of the Conservatives' leader, the fourteenth earl of Derby. Despite a degree of intimacy, Stanley found Disraeli no less the man in the ironic mask than did most people, and was uncomfortable with what he felt to be his lack of genuine principle, yet he freely credited him with 'such intellectual powers as not one human being among a million can lay claim to', and relished their talks on literature and thought, discovering that Disraeli's favourite topic after politics was 'the origins of the various beliefs which have governed mankind, their changes at different epochs, and those still to come. This was common ground to us both: of the new German school of criticism I had perhaps read more than my friend, but his acquaintance with the earlier phases of the great controversy much exceeded mine.'[48]

Disraeli lacked inclination, and perhaps capacity, for the elaboration of systematic argument. He preferred throwing off ideas to constructing theses. He was an intellectual of the dinner table and the debating chamber, not of the academy. Nonetheless, his ideas have received closer attention and more careful analysis in recent writing. That is partly a result of their 'modernity': if the racial ideas seem hopelessly marooned in their age, many of the others, bred out of the great European debates sparked by the French and Industrial Revolutions, relate to problems of the nature and conduct of politics and the conditions of social and political stability which are perennial, and they have a recurrent role in attempts to define and refine the Tory ideology of which they are conventionally considered to be a vital inspiration. In this volume, however, they are discussed principally in their functional role as components of the persona Disraeli created for himself. The intricate web – it could hardly be called a system – of racial, religious, historical and political ideas which Disraeli spun was the necessary construction of a world his genius could comfortably inhabit, and this was a part of the definition and realization of that genius itself.

In this earnest exercise in self-fashioning, Disraeli was in large measure talking to himself. His scheme of thought answered to personal needs that few could share or even understand.[49] Designed to integrate his genius into English society on the plane of action and power, it nevertheless, and necessarily, left him standing spiritually aloof, since detachment from the common origins and prejudices of the English was the source of the superior insight into their nature and destiny that gave him his title to counsel and to lead them. A more intimate belonging would have had to be on their terms, not his. He could root himself physically at Hughenden, but not in intellectual sympathy with his contemporaries. Until Derby relinquished the Conservative leadership to him in 1868, the consciousness of superiority had to co-exist painfully with the reality of long and gruelling subaltern service to the party which he had made the vehicle of his career, and of dependence on the patronage of an aristocratic class which he was often moved to despise. The grand romantic grasp for power and fame faltered in the prosaic business of leading the Conservatives in a seemingly permanent minority in the House of Commons, night after night, often into the small hours, amid what his most acid aristocratic critic, Lord Robert Cecil, called 'those dreary, dreary green benches ...

that odoriferous library ... that compound of human carbon and Thames exhalations ... that greasy gutta-percha which Mr Bellamy dignifies with the name of beef'.[50] It faltered, too, in the routine of bourgeois domesticity with Mary Anne – whose fortune had turned out to be less than he had supposed – in the Grosvenor Gate house in which she had only a life interest. The operational identity which Disraeli had brought fully into being by the beginning of the 1850s was compressed into a narrow and frustrating course of life. It is a question whether it was ever able to stretch its limbs. Between the self Disraeli had so strenuously fashioned and his subsequent career as a Conservative leader and, ultimately and very late, prime minister, it is sometimes hard to discern any intimate correspondence, despite the continuity which marked the expression of his ideas. The fundamental impulse of man, exalted to self-knowledge, was concerned, Fichte had said, 'with a world that is to be, an *a priori* world that exists in the future and ever remains in the future'.[51] The self-consciousness of genius had to be its own reward.

1

___

Disraeli's education

CHARLES RICHMOND

'A sneer! Oh! Ladylove, do I ever sneer?' (Vivian Grey)

I

In 1852, one month after Disraeli became chancellor of the exchequer, Heinrich Heine wrote: 'A singular phenomenon in England – a novelist becoming a minister.'[1] Disraeli was not the first public man with literary inclinations; but the romantic and imaginative quality of his writing makes him unique. This anomalous combination of romantic artist and practical politician, together with the apparent disjunction between what he wrote in his books and what he did in political life, has caused his biographers to comprehend him either as actuated by a mere vulgar ambition to climb, or as a far-sighted statesman, whose career was guided by transcendent ideas. If the former view is accepted, then a charge of insincerity must be sustained; if the latter is accepted then his opportunism is inexplicable. In this chapter, on the basis of an examination of his unconventional education, I explore whether or not it is possible to combine Disraeli's romantic ideas and cynical politics as an organic whole, without excluding either one or the other.

Little is known of Disraeli's education prior to his fourteenth year. At a very early age, he was sent to a school at Islington, which was kept by a Miss Roper. He was then moved to a boarding school at Blackheath, whose headmaster was a nonconformist minister named Potticary. Later in life Disraeli had little recollection of Blackheath but, according to one of his schoolfellows, Disraeli and another Jewish boy were required to stand at the back of the room during prayers. Once a week they received some sort of instruction in Hebrew.[2]

In the autumn of 1817, after his baptism in July of that year, Disraeli was transferred to a school kept by the Reverend Eli Cogan at Higham Hill, Walthamstow called Higham Hall. Later in life Disraeli said that he had been 'intended' for Winchester; and it is unclear why he was sent to Higham Hall when his 'younger and duller' brothers both attended the former institution, one of England's greatest public schools.[3] Higham Hall was not a backwater; and Cogan – a self-educated classicist and liberal utilitarian with a considerable reputation as a schoolmaster – placed some emphasis on English and modern subjects, which was by no means common then.[4] Gladstone, for example, who like other public school boys was stuffed full of Latin and Greek, complained that an Eton education had left him 'wretchedly deficient in the knowledge of modern ... literature and history'[5] – a defect that his future rival would never feel. Cogan's openness to modern subjects may have influenced Isaac D'Israeli's decision to send his son to Higham Hall – for he was himself an original, and a student of modern letters. He was evidently impressed by Cogan. 'My father made his acquaintance in a bookseller's shop', Disraeli wrote later in life in a memorandum on his education, '[and] assumed for a long time that he was a clergyman. When he discovered that he was a school-master, he thought I should be his pupil.'[6]

At any rate, the decision to send Benjamin to this school rather than to Winchester – for whatever reason it may have been made – was momentous. His career was, in a sense, diverted from the stream of public life; and the availability of modern books, both at Higham Hall and in his father's library, was to exercise a curious influence upon his mind. His sense of being an outsider was forged during these years: for he missed the 'blithe and congenial comradeship'[7] which John Morley asserts was prevalent in public school society. His boyhood was filled with solitude, reading and introspection instead of sport, friendship and debating clubs. However, the outcome at Winchester would probably have been worse. A young Jew of Disraeli's looks and temperament might have been treated to that 'torture', which, in a public school, Thackeray wrote, 'is as much licensed as the knout in Russia'.

Disraeli may have suffered some sort of rebuff at Cogan's school. The eponymous heroes in *Vivian Grey* – the 'seditious stranger' (I, iv) – and *Contarini Fleming* – the 'Venetian countenance' (I, ii) – are involved in schoolboy fights, with the majority of their schoolfellows arrayed on the side of their opponents. There is no direct evidence that Disraeli endured anti-Semitism at school but he would have been unusual to have avoided it.[8] It is evident from autobiographical fragments left by Jewish boys who attended public schools that many of them were tormented because they were Jews. For example, after leaving Harrow, Charles de Rothschild (1877–1923) told a friend that, 'If I ever have a son he will be instructed in boxing and jiu-jitsu before he enters school, as Jew hunts such as I experienced are a very one-sided amusement, and there is apt to be a lack of sympathy between the hunters and the hunted.'[9] Moreover, boys with Jewish antecedents, who were baptized and had a foreign name, were 'due for hell' at English schools, according to the Jewish poet E. H. Meyerstein (1889–1952), who suffered on this account at Harrow. A boy from a solidly Jewish background, who was proud of his religion 'got through school just fine' in Meyerstein's experience.[10]

There is also indirect evidence that Disraeli may have suffered at school because he was Jewish. It is evident from the diaries and memoranda that he wrote in or about 1821 (he left Cogan's school late in 1819 or early in 1820) that he was concerned with the subject of religious persecution. In one hitherto unpublished memorandum he wrote:

> bold spirits if not allowed to vent themselves in the court will explode in conspiracy. To debar the follower of ano[the]r faith from partaking of the benefits of the constitution to keep them from the senate because you fear that they may change that senate & that constitution seems to me both impolitic & improv[iden]t. If they can follow their faith and yet enjoy the high[es]t political privileges they have little temptation to attempt any revolution. If you argue on the contr[ary] that the followers of a diff[eren]t faith [?] political privileges they have great opportunities by their influence in the state to cause a revolution in the existing constitution, it must then be asked and examined what is the spirit of the religion which they profess and what power and what wish they may have to restore it.[11]

In a diary entry dated January 1821, he writes: 'In talking of the Unity of Religion this mighty spirit [Francis Bacon] strongly blames Religious Persecution and in his essay on that subject has this beautiful Passage "Surely this is to bring down the Holy Ghost, instead of the likeness of a Dove, in the shape of a Vulture or a Raven." '[12] This was also the basis of his identification with David Alroy, who championed the oppressed Jews of Persia against the Moslems. He probably began reading about Alroy in 1824; and in the novel which he devoted to Alroy he causes him to exclaim:

The world goes well with thee, my Lord Honain. But if, instead of bows and blessings, thou like my brethren, wert greeted only with a cuff and curse, if thou didst rise each morning only to feel existence a dishonour, and to find thyself marked out among men as something foul and fatal; if it were thy lot, like theirs, at best to drag on a mean and dull career, hopeless and aimless, or with no other hope or aim but that which is degrading, and all this too with a keen sense of thy intrinsic worth, and a deep conviction of superior race; why, then perchance you might discover 'twere worth a struggle to be free and honoured (V, iv).

It is difficult to say why Disraeli was not more explicit about his Judaism in his autobiographical novels, diaries and memoranda in the 1820s; but it is probable that he himself was confused. Born a Jew and baptized at the age of twelve with a father who was, if anything, an eighteenth-century deist, and a grandmother who would not consort with other Jews, it is only natural that he suffered from a crisis of identity in the 1820s.[13] Was he a Jew or a Christian; and what was his relation to English society? Contarini Fleming reflects that, 'I was not always assured of my identity, or even existence; for I sometimes found it necessary to shout aloud to be sure that I lived' (IV, v). Disraeli did not invent the role of the 'aristocratic Jew' for himself until after his illness and trip to the East. Until that time, he may have suffered from a lingering doubt as to who and what he was. In any case, as a consequence of what may have been rebuff at school, Disraeli's ambition,[14] which was given its initial impetus by a feeling that he had been neglected by his mother, was both darkened and intensified.[15]

Disraeli's ambition was probably conditioned by schoolboy slights. They created dichotomous humours in him: vengefulness and the desire for love and acceptance. When his longing to be loved met with jealousy and hatred, he became ambitious 'with a vengeance'. Emma Lazarus thought Disraeli shared with Shylock, as a representative Jew of the Diaspora, 'the rebellion of a proud heart embittered and perverted by brutal humiliations, and the consequent thirst for revenge'.[16]

It is true that Disraeli was not known for vengefulness in his later career. He was regarded by many as a man of magnanimity, strong loyalties and party spirit. But this was later in life – after 1852, at any rate – when he had attained power and partial acceptance. Between 1820 and 1846 his career was repeatedly stained with this passion. He was always more ready to repay an injury than a benefit: for, as Tacitus asserts, 'gratitude is a burden and revenge a pleasure'. The reader is invited to test this judgement of Disraeli by comparing his treatment of Benjamin Austen and Daniel O'Connell in the 1830s. He befriended the former and received his loans but dropped him as he began to make his way in the *beau monde*; and he responded ferociously to the anti-Semitic attack of the latter, swearing to 'pursue his existence' with an 'unextinguishable hatred'.[17]

Vivian Grey, the book which Disraeli regarded as a portrayal of his 'active and real ambition',[18] breathes a ferocious spirit of revenge. When Vivian becomes the manager of some clandestine theatricals at the Reverend Everard Dallas' school, an usher called Mallet becomes envious. He glares at Vivian (who treats him as a sort of 'upper servant') 'with eyes gloating with vengeance' (I, iv). Mallet draws the proscribed theatricals to Dallas' attention, and the latter indirectly denounces Vivian as a 'seditious stranger' (I, iv). Vivian's schoolfellows, including his erstwhile friends, join in the chorus of denunciation. The chorus is led by an older boy named St Leger Smith, whom Vivian proceeds to thrash in a fight. After this, Vivian is universally shunned and is warned not to return. 'Not return, eh! but that will I though', he growls, 'and we shall see who, in future, can complain of the sweetness of my voice! Ungrateful fools!' (I, iv). When he returns he cronies (for he is charming) with Mallet, whom he causes to rule over the school tyrannically. Thus the first revenge is exacted. St Leger Smith and the schoolboys, incensed at the injustice, attack Mallet and Vivian. The latter pulls out a pistol:

> 'Not an inch nearer, Smith, or – I fire. Let me not, however, baulk your vengeance on yonder hound [Mallet]: if I could suggest any refinements in torture, they would be at your service.' Vivian Grey smiled, while the horrid cries of Mallet indicated that the boys were 'roasting' him (I, v).

This theme continues later in the novel in connection with Vivian's attempt to organize a political party for the marquess of Carabas and his friends. Mrs Felix Lorraine (a distant relation of the marquess), whose love for Vivian has become jealousy, poisons the minds of the Carabas men, whose allegiance Vivian has endeavoured to win. She also attempts physically to poison Vivian. In response, Vivian informs her that her scheme has failed (prior to her learning of its success), and this intelligence causes her blood vessel to burst. The result is more than satisfactory: 'Had Vivian left the boudoir a pledged bridegroom, his countenance could not have been more triumphant' (IV, vi). Then he writes to his confederate:

'We have been betrayed – and by a woman; but, there has been revenge! oh! what revenge!' (IV, vi).

However, it is true that a generalized humour of revenge was not the only motive for Disraeli's prodigious feat of climbing in the 1830s and 1840s. After his illness and travels in the East, he was impelled by the conviction that he was a superior man as both a genius and an 'aristocratic Jew'. The desire to vindicate these qualities in himself was probably something akin to pride. 'Alas I struggle from Pride', he wrote in his 'Mutilated Diary' in 1833.[19] There was also a longing for fame for its own sake. 'To create a sensation', Robert Blake writes, 'to occupy the limelight, to act a part on the greatest stage in the world, these were the springs of action that thrust Disraeli onward.'[20]

The corrupt character of Disraeli's ambition at the age of fourteen is demonstrated by the historical types to which he gravitated. There is a diary in his papers,[21] hitherto unpublished, and entitled 'The Reign of Henry the Eighth', which sheds some light on this subject. It is well to note that Disraeli began to imbibe 'the new, ruthless political ideas of Renaissance Europe'[22] at this early age. The 'immense series of historical reading' which comprised Vivian Grey's early education may have been commenced by the author of that work while he was still under the tuition of Eli Cogan. Disraeli's career was distinguished by a knowledge of modern history, despite the fact that his view of the past was sometimes more imaginative than rational. It is probable that he laid the foundation for this knowledge in or about 1818 and in the early 1820s. However, it is clear that the young Disraeli was repeatedly fascinated by the same kind of historical figure. Most of his heroes rise by cunning from mean origins to immense power; some are not born in the countries in which they rise, and all express their wills in foreign affairs.

Cardinal Wolsey (whom Vivian Grey wishes to 'act') was the chief among these (I, ix). The son of an Ipswich butcher, Wolsey rose by cunning, deceit, wit and personal charm, effectively to rule England for fourteen years. His vast wealth and immense power, which were expressed both in foreign politics and spiritual affairs, evidently fascinated Disraeli. In his diary, he focuses upon Wolsey's ambition and perfidy: 'The object of Wolsey's early ambition was the papacy. He would not have hesitated to commit any action inimical to the influence of Rome and favourable to his own views.'[23] Paraphrasing Lord Herbert, he concludes: 'He got a kind of absolute power in spiritual matters at home, and during his favour with the King, all things succeeded better than afterwards, tho' yet it may be doubted whether the impression he gave, did occasion diverse irregularities which were observed to follow.'[24]

In another diary Disraeli draws biographical sketches of a similar kind:

> *Craut* – who from a boy behind y counter raised himself by his industry to y post of Paymaster General of y army, and at length to that of Minister of State. He was to have been called to account in his last stage of life but he cunningly diverted that storm by feigning himself lunatic.[25]
>
> *M. d'Ilgen* – revengeful, crafty, a master of his temper, tongue, countenance eyes. As by his parts he raised himself, so by them he supports himself. He is the repository of his own secrets, hav[in]g no confidant nor favourite to share them ... He has so little scruple in point of oaths, that he takes & breaks them with equal indifference ... That which ... proves his genius, is that he has supported himself a long time without kindred, friends or creatures.[26]

Disraeli was also fascinated by Marshal Dorfling, Cardinal Alberoni and Baron Ripperda. The first of these heroes was a seventeenth-century field marshal in the Brandenburg army. He was the son of Bohemian peasants, and began life as a tailor's apprentice – which facts Disraeli notes in his diary. However, for Alberoni and Ripperda he reserved a special affection. 'Often', Contarini Fleming says of his boyhood, 'had I been an Alboroni [*sic*], a Ripperda' (II, xi). Cardinal Alberoni (1664–1752) was the son of an Italian gardener. From an itinerant priest he became cardinal and minister of state in the Spain of Philip V. He rose and fell in virtue of a love of intrigue. Baron Ripperda (?–1737), enjoyed a similar fate in the same country. One historian has written of him: 'Few more unconscionable liars and intriguers are recorded in history than this audacious courtier.'[27] It is as if Disraeli is reassuring himself in these diaries that it is always possible to rise. He seems also to embrace the lesson that much cunning, fraud and deceit are necessary in order to do so. In light of the above examples, it can be said that his ambition was conditioned by his perception of the obstacles in its path.

In one sense these obstacles were real, and in another sense they were imaginary. As F. M. L. Thompson demonstrates, the caste attitude in England became more pronounced between Pitt's expansion of the peerage and the first Reform bill. The old aristocracy endeavoured to strengthen class lines in order to differentiate itself from the newly ennobled and from the wealthy middle class.[28] Their grasp upon the reins of the two great political parties was firm, if not absolute, prior to 1832; and this monopoly was based upon control of the electoral system. Even after the 1832 Reform, over forty peers remained who could 'virtually nominate'[29] a representative to the Lower House; and usually these seats were placed at the disposal of a member of the family. There were few patrons; and the price of politics was, very often, prohibitive.[30]

However, as Robert Blake has shown, Disraeli's 'point of departure, though low by the standards of nineteenth century Prime Ministers, was neither as humble nor as alien as some people have believed'.[31] His father was neither a gardener nor a peasant, but a literary man of some eminence and private means. In view of the fact that Disraeli could have studied at Oxford, it must be said that the obstacles in his path were, to some extent, self-imposed. Had he distinguished himself in the debating club, as for example George Canning had done, there is no reason to believe that his talent would have gone unnoticed. But this was not Disraeli's understanding. It is clear that when he left Cogan's school, he believed himself to be socially inferior and an outsider. However, he would not, as Contarini Fleming declares, 'sink into my innermost self' (I, vii). He would show them all. The recurrent lesson in his diaries is that, in order to escape from low origins, low arts must be employed.

II

Disraeli's formal education ended when he left Higham Hall. Having missed both Winchester and Oxford, he had failed to follow the educational course that was becoming customary for the country's political elite; which contributed both to the somewhat oblique character of his relation to British society, and to his own acute sense of that obliqueness. While there are rather wistful references in *Hartlebury* (I, ii) and *Coningsby* (I, viii–xi) to Eton and the benefits of a 'crack college', on the other hand he seemed to glory in his own superiority in 'general knowledge',[32] acquired from his modern and cosmopolitan education. He regarded men like Gladstone as 'overgrown schoolboys'[33] who, as he wrote in *Endymion*, had read 'very little more than some Latin writers, some Greek plays, and some treatises of Aristotle. These with a due course of Bampton Lectures and some dipping into the "Quarterly Review"... qualified a man ... not only for being a member of Parliament, but becoming a candidate for the responsibility of statesmanship' (iii). In the end, he derived from his education a form of self-knowledge based more upon a comprehension of his own subjectivity and vocation than upon a knowledge of Man's limitations in the cosmos;[34] and a view of heroic morality rooted more in the idea of self-realization than self-sacrifice.[35]

Disraeli spent 1820 and the greater part of 1821 at home reading in his father's library. In the memorandum on his education already alluded to, Disraeli said that he never reached the first class, 'and was not even eminent in the second'[36] in the study of classics at Cogan's school. At home, and so far as we know on his own, he now contrived to make himself a scholar of Greek and Latin. Disraeli is excessively generous to himself when he causes Vivian Grey to boast that 'twelve hours a day, and self-banishment from society, overcame, in twelve months, the ill-effects of his imperfect education' (I, vi). It is apparent from the diaries which Disraeli kept in 1820 that, although he made himself a passable scholar of Latin, he never gained a firm grounding in Greek. However, 'the frequent blunders in Greek accidence' which 'disfigure' his diaries[37] do not concern us here – except insofar as they tended to set him even further apart from the classically educated politicians who were graduates of Eton and Christ Church. It is of more interest to contrast the reverent tone of Disraeli's 'classical diaries' with the corruption and cunning of his diary in or about 1818. For example, he finds the conduct of Admetus worthy of blame. 'Eurip. Alcest.', he notes, 'the character of Admetus is most detestable, he first suffers his wife to die for him and then abuses his father for not dying for her. He is a faithless husband, and an undutiful son.'[38] But he admires Pericles: 'In my opinion & most humbly do I advance it (at the same time exulting to find the sagacious Mitford on my side) Pericles is the greatest and most accomplished of the characters of Antiquity.'[39] He seems also especially to have revered Homer and Plato. There are two memoranda devoted to them in his papers.[40] Of Vivian Grey's admiration for Plato, Disraeli wrote:

> Wonderful is it that while the whole soul of Vivian Grey seemed concentrated and wrapped in the glorious pages of the Athenian; while, with keen and almost inspired curiosity, he searched, and followed up, and meditated upon, the definite mystery, the indefinite development; while his spirit alternately bowed in trembling and in admiration, as he seemed to be listening to the secrets of the Universe revealed in the glorious melodies of an immortal voice (I, vi).

This does not seem to be a very classical formulation. Indeed, Disraeli's 'classic reverie' probably has more to do with romanticism. Scholars of European romanticism attribute to Plato and the latter Platonists (especially Plotinus) a crucial formative influence upon the early romantic theorists: directly on Novalis and Schelling, and through them on the Schlegels. The German theorists wished to bypass Plato's derogation of the arts; and they found in his disciples a justification for the deviation of art from reality. Plotinus taught that art must imitate the permanent Platonic Forms which transcend the impermanent visible world.[41] Vivian Grey's father attempts to dissuade him from reading the latter Platonists. 'Pray, tell me my dear boy, what possible good your perusal of the latter Platonists can produce?' (I, vi).

Vivian Grey's reverence is also apparent, in muted form, in Disraeli's classical diaries, as we have seen. This surely constitutes a remarkable contrast to Cardinal Wolsey and M d'Ilgen. In fact, it is the first real sign of that elaborate romantic faculty which exerted so much influence upon his life. In a sense, this faculty is common to humanity. Illusions are necessary for life. The necessary corruption that attends most human life produces a concomitant longing for purity. But in Disraeli's case the degree of his corruption and the height of his longing far surpass those of the generality of men. This psychological paradigm of romance and corruption, it will be evident, deepened and intensified between 1821 and 1824. In the latter half of the 1820s Disraeli endeavoured to purge himself of the excesses of his imagination; but throughout his life he remained subject to its effect.

It may also have been during 1820 that Disraeli became the object of his father's desultory guidance. Much of what is Toryish and old-fashioned in Disraeli's outlook is attributable to this guidance. Vivian Grey undergoes 'a prodigious change' as a result of 'constant communion with a mind highly refined, severely cultivated, and much experienced' (I, ii).[42] Isaac D'Israeli may well have inspired in his son a romantic reverence for the traditions of the Tory party. In the general preface to the 1870 edition of his novels, Disraeli asserts that he derived his 'Tory theory of history', which is set out in *Coningsby* and *Sybil*, from the reading which he did in his father's library.

> Born in a library, and trained from early childhood by learned men who did not share the passions and prejudices of our political and social life, I had imbibed on some subjects conclusions different from those which generally prevail, and especially with reference to the history of our country. How an oligarchy had been substituted for a kingdom, and a narrow-minded and bigoted fanaticism flourished in the name of religious liberty, were problems long to me insoluble, but which early interested me. But what most attracted my musing, even as a boy, was the elements of our political parties, and the strange mystification by which that which was national in its constitution

had become odious, and that which was exclusive was presented as popular.[43]

This account was written half a century after the period it claims to describe. Doubtless it is coloured by much of what subsequently occurred. For example, there is no sign in his diaries and memoranda of a theory of a national party. However, much of this reminiscence is accurate. In light of the assertion that he pondered how an 'oligarchy had been substituted for a kingdom', and in light of the argument for a revived monarchy in *Coningsby* and *Sybil*, the following memorandum is of much interest. Written in or about 1820, it is entitled 'The Constitution'. It is in fact an argument in favour of a mixed constitution, in which the power of the Crown is given full scope. 'The influence of the Crown is acknowledged and intended by the constitution as much as the influence of the aristocracy and the influence of the people.' The future Radical candidate proceeds, on the basis of tradition, to refute the views of parliamentary reformers:

> At no period of English history can the house of commons be found correspond[in]g to the idea entertained of it by the reformers. There have always been 'boros' and always what they term corruption and from this I conceive that those 'boros' and that influence was an acknowledged and intended influence. What is ye influence of the King supposing that the house of commons sho[ul]d be that which ye reformers wish it? – it would not exist. Yet the kingly power is of equal authority and of equal importance in the ancient constitution as the Lords or the Commons. Our ancestors would not have endowed the kingly power with an equal authority if they had intended him not to exercise it. Where then is the kingly power to be found, in its influence in the councils of the nation.[44]

It need hardly be said that, prior to 1832, it was a major tenet of the Tory party that franchise reform would vitiate the influence of the Crown and destroy the balance of the constitution. The Whigs, from the first, were opposed to the king's prerogative.

This inchoate royalism was probably derived from his father. His influence provided Disraeli with a bridge into the Tory party fourteen years later. Isaac D'Israeli's political opinions inclined to be Toryish for most of his life; and he devoted two of his works to the vindication of James I and Charles I. He wrote in the final chapter of his work on the latter: 'his devotion to the institutions of his country ... his magnanimity, and the unsubdued spirit, were more peculiarly his own ... his virtues and his genius alone triumphed over his fate'.[45]

In questions of foreign policy (which were always his primary interest), Disraeli's opinions seem also to have coincided with those of the Tories. He neither understood nor sympathized with liberalism. The struggle of weak nations against the strong left him cold. This view was in reality the natural extension of his view of domestic politics. The guiding principle of individuals (at least individuals like Wolsey) was power and self-interest, and the same principle governed nations. Like most men of the 'right', he believed in a natural hierarchy based upon power, and in *Realpolitik*. He believed in conservatism and expansion not in liberal magnanimity. To this view Disraeli adhered throughout his life: he was as much of an 'imperialist' at sixteen as at seventy.

There is a memorandum in his papers, written in or about 1820, which is devoted to the question of Greek liberty. The issue at the time was whether the English should interfere on behalf of the Greeks in their struggle against the Turks. The Whigs, and much of the country, answered in the affirmative; but the Tories preferred to defend the English alliance with the Turks. In this spirit, Disraeli closes his memorandum:

> Thus the argument is brought to this point whe[the]r we are entitled by the law of nations to assist the subjects of the Turkish Empire in the revolt and struggle for independence. The inhabitants of Greece would be contented with our portion of Liberty. Some spirits at home ask for more. This leads me to ask what you mean by LIBERTY.[46]

Ten years later, it is interesting to note, he agreed with Wellington and the Tories in condemning Sir Edward Codrington's destruction of the Turkish fleet at Navarino.[47] To the Whigs the Turks were wholly distasteful. In Lord John Russell's scale of civilized nations they represent darkness and tyranny.[48] Disraeli, however, was always an ardent Turkophile.

Disraeli's 'classic reverie' did not last for long. In 1821 there is decided change in the tone of his diaries. It is interesting to note that Vivian Grey undergoes a similar change when he discovers 'the futility of that mass of insanity and imposture – the Greek philosophy', and begins to read the moderns. Under their influence 'the mind of Vivian Grey recovered ... a great portion of its original freshness and primal vigour' (I, vii). Then he begins to study politics:

> having now got through an immense series of historical reading, he had stumbled upon a branch of study certainly the most delightful in the world

– but, for a boy, as certainly the most pernicious – THE STUDY OF POLITICS.
And now everything was solved! ... He paced his chamber in an agitated
spirit, and panted for the Senate (I, viii).

There is reason to believe that such a transformation actually occurred
sometime in 1821. In November of that year he was articled to Swain,
Stevens, Maples, Pearse and Hunt, a firm of solicitors; and in the
memorandum on his education he wrote that he 'had some scruples' about
this employment: 'for even then I dreamed of Parliament'.[49]

However, there is more convincing evidence of this change in the
diaries which he kept in 1821. One of these is entitled 'A Study of Lord
Bacon's Essays',[50] and in it Disraeli collected the 'pernicious' political
doctrines of the sixteenth century. He took a number of notes verbatim
from the *Essays*; and it is well to observe the tone and character of the
maxims which attracted him. 'The Rising unto place', he notes from Essay
XI, 'is Laborious, and by pains men come to greater pains; and it is
sometimes base, and by indignities men come to dignities.'[51] And he
embraces the following notion of self-interest:

> Wisdom for a man's self, is in many branches thereof, a depraved thing; it is
> wisdom of rats, that will be sure to leave a house before it fall; it is the
> wisdom of the fox, that thrusts out the Badger, who digged and made room
> for him; it is the Wisdom of Crocodiles, that shed tears, when they would
> devour.[52]

Friendship is also considered in this light: 'The Parable of Pythagoras is
dark, but true, "cor ne edito". Certainly, if a man would give it a hard
phrase, those that want friends to open themselves unto, are cannibals of
their own hearts.'[53]

It may have been at this time that Disraeli read Bolingbroke. We cannot
be sure about the extent of his reading but it does not seem to have been
very deep. Vivian Grey quotes 'a whole passage of Bolingbroke' (II, i) in
order to vindicate the opinions of the marquess of Carabas; but there is
only a fragmentary reference to Bolingbroke in one of Disraeli's diaries.
'The true point of political wisdom', he notes, 'consists in distinguishing
justly, between what is absolutely best in Speculation, and what is the best
of things practicable in particular conjunctures.'[54] Although Bolingbroke
exerted a far greater influence upon his future career, Disraeli was
probably more familiar with the precepts of Bacon in 1821.

Bacon and Bolingbroke are similar in a fundamental respect: they are
two of Machiavelli's greatest English disciples. Bacon shared with Machia-

velli an essentially secular approach to politics.[55] One scholar has written that 'Bacon is more Machiavellian than Machiavelli.'[56] Bolingbroke, whom Herbert Butterfield calls 'the most remarkable of Machiavelli's disciples',[57] modelled his Patriot King after the Prince with *virtù*. The influence of Machiavelli on all modern thought has been enormous. Felix Raab did not exaggerate when he wrote that 'as far as the modern world is concerned, Machiavelli invented politics'.[58] It is not my purpose to discuss the importance of Machiavelli in the history of political thought. However, suffice to say that he was the first political philosopher to suggest that statesmen *ought* to do bad things.[59] He lowered the ends of politics by rejecting the 'imaginary principalities' of the ancients and Christianity and replaced them with a politics of this world. In Machiavellian thought, politics and conventional morality do not mix; and it is upon this fundamental point that Disraeli is in agreement with him. Perhaps this is why Disraeli has often been called 'the most modern of all Victorian statesmen'.[60]

It is improbable that Disraeli read Machiavelli in the 1820s. He was evidently familiar with him, insofar as Vivian Grey, before his first meeting with the statesman Beckendorff, exclaims, 'what I would give now to know by rote only one quotation from Machiavel!' (VI, vi). Among Disraeli's miscellaneous memoranda, there is a biographical note which identifies 'Machiavel' as a 'Politician, Historian, General, dramatist, Poet & novelist'.[61] It is possible that Disraeli found reference to that 'doctor of Italy' in the writings of Bacon and Bolingbroke and wished to satisfy his curiosity. But there is no real evidence that he knew Machiavelli's writings intimately. However, there are many similarities between Disraeli's conception of politics in the 1820s (as expressed in *Contarini Fleming* and *Vivian Grey*) and the political philosophy of Machiavelli. It is true that much of what Disraeli wrote about politics can be ascribed to natural prudence; but some of his similarities with Machiavelli may be attributable to the influence of Bolingbroke and Bacon.

There is a striking prefiguration of one of these similarities in the diary devoted to Bacon's *Essays*. From the essay on 'Great Place', Disraeli notes: 'Reduce things to the first institution, & observe wherein and how they have degenerated; but yet ask counsel of both times; of the ancient what is best; of the latter time what is fittest.'[62] This notion conditioned much of Disraeli's future political practice. From 1834 to 1846 he viewed himself as a prophet of 'reinvigorated toryism'. He believed that, like Bolingbroke, he lived in an age corrupted by a 'factious aristocracy' which led the

country away from the salutary principles of 'Primitive Toryism'.[63] Even
in his first attempts to be elected at High Wycombe, he spoke of
'regenerating'[64] that borough. The role of the great man in this dilemma is
to purge the nation of the present corruption, and restore it to its original
principles.

This conception of the great man as one who purges the state of its
corruption and causes its return to first principles (in order to ensure
survival) is fundamental in the thought of Bolingbroke and Bacon.[65] It is
derived from book III, chapter 1 of Machiavelli's *Discourses*:

> For, as all religious republics and monarchies have within themselves some
> goodness, by means of which they obtain their first growth and reputation,
> and as in the process of time this goodness becomes corrupted, it will of
> necessity destroy the body unless something intervenes to bring it back to
> its normal condition. This [may be caused by] some man of superior
> character.[66]

Disraeli's politics were characterized by Machiavellian flexibility in
conjunction with an overriding belief in the power of the individual will.
He was always 'ready to trim his sails';[67] he did not, for example, cling to
Protection when he perceived that it was 'dead and damned' in the late
1840s. Disraeli revered historical examples and traditions; but he did not
scruple to commit any act which broke with precept and ensured survival
in the future. It is this concentration upon survival that is peculiarly
modern. In the ancient theoretical tradition, civil society existed in order
to make men good; the theoretical purpose of civil society in modernity is
continued survival. Disraeli's treatment of the Tory party was informed
by this attitude. Perhaps more than any other statesman he ensured the
survival of an essentially aristocratic party in a democratic age. In a sense,
of course, this was only prudence. Statesmen must be sufficiently flexible
to meet the exigencies and shifting circumstances of political life, or they
become, as Robert Blake puts it, 'antediluvian survivals'.[68] But Disraeli
possessed this subtlety in an uncommon degree. Both Gladstone and Peel
were more willing than Disraeli to sacrifice survival on the altar of
morality. The latter never swerved from the Machiavellian teaching that
'he errs least and will be most favoured by fortune who suits his
proceedings to the times'.[69]

Like Machiavelli, Disraeli thought of politics as the conquest of *fortuna*.
In *Lord George Bentinck*, he acknowledges the shocking extent to which
fortune decides the outcome of political battles: 'there is nothing in which
the power of circumstances is more evident than in politics. They baffle

the forethought of statesmen, and control even the apparently inflexible laws of national development and decay.'[70] But Disraeli had a preponderant belief in the power of the will. Beckendorff in *Vivian Grey* – Disraeli's ideal creation of a statesman – possesses the *virtù* that Machiavelli attributes to Moses, Cyrus, Romulus and Theseus. In chapter 6 of *The Prince*, Machiavelli writes: 'And in examining their life and deeds [Moses *et al.*] it will be seen that they owed nothing to fortune but the opportunity which gave them matter to be shaped into what form they thought fit.'[71] This conquest of fortune has been the object of Beckendorff's life. When Vivian Grey tells him that he recognizes 'in every contingency the preordination of my fate', Beckendorff responds:

A delusion of the brain! Fate, Destiny, Chance, peculiar and special Providence – idle words! Dismiss them all, Sir! A man's Fate is his own temper; and according to that will be his opinion as to the particular manner in which the course of events is regulated. A consistent man believes in Destiny – a capricious man in Chance … Man is not the creature of circumstances. Circumstances are the creatures of men. We are free agents, and man is more powerful than matter. I recognize no intervening influence between that of the established course of Nature, and my own mind (VI, vii).

And Beckendorff, who depends 'only upon himself', concludes: 'No conjuncture can possibly occur, however fearful, however tremendous it may appear, from which a man, by his own energy, may not extricate himself' (VI, vii).

The essence of *virtù* is boldness. Boldness is the principal instrument with which fortune is conquered. 'Fortune is a woman', Machiavelli wrote, 'and it is necessary, if you wish to master her, to conquer her by force; and it can be seen that she lets herself be overcome by the bold rather than by those who proceed coldly.'[72] Disraeli illustrates this precept – probably more for his own edification than for the reader's – in his depiction of the secret conference of European ambassadors in *Contarini Fleming*. Contarini and his father attend the conference on behalf of their king, whose succession is opposed by three of the ambassadors who favour the interest of the abdicated dynasty. Contarini's father, the prime minister, hopes that the issue will be resolved by negotiation, since no appeal to force is possible. However, when the negotiations founder, Baron Fleming makes a timorous appeal to his two allies for support, but they are reticent. Then the young Contarini takes the initiative without prior authorization. He disarms the absolutist ambassadors, who are hostile to his king, with the threat that he will institute a popular election of the monarch. The possible spread of democratic tendencies causes the ambassadors to relent. 'I was astounded by my audacity', Contarini exclaims, 'It is difficult to convey any idea of the success of my boldness' (II, xiii).

But *virtù* is not virtue: flexibility presupposes an indifference to morality. The lesson to which Disraeli seems to return again and again in the 1820s is that good and evil arts must be employed in order to conquer fortune. Both Beckendorff and Baron Fleming (the practical statesmen who appear in Disraeli's novels in the 1820s) are alike in this respect. They have risen from lower-class and middle-class origins respectively to become the prime ministers of their countries; and they have, in turn, both made their countries powerful. Like Baron Fleming, 'Beckendorff has not scrupled to resort to any measures, or adopt any opinions in order to further the interests of his monarch and his country' (VI, iv).[73] There is a striking similarity between this ostensible patriotism and 'the end justifies the means'[74] teaching of Machiavelli.

The truth is that, in the 1820s, Disraeli had a deeply cynical view of politics. He shared with Machiavelli the fundamental view that moral considerations are inimical to the practice of politics. Machiavelli believed that Christian morality and the concern with heaven had led to the neglect of this world. If men are permanently self-interested and niggardly, then statesmen must not act as if they are altruistic and liberal. Adherence to principle limits the statesman's vision and flexibility; and it is impossible to make men moral.

There is an illustration of this conviction in *Vivian Grey*. Young Vivian, while travelling through the German countryside, happens to kill a wild boar which is about to gore the prince of Little Lilliput. This prince, formerly the king of 50,000 subjects, has been 'mediatised', and has come under the suzerainty of the duke of Reisenberg and his prime minister, Beckendorff. After about an hour of conversation, Vivian is enlisted to restore the prince's power (at least this is Vivian's understanding). For this purpose, a meeting between the prince, Vivian and Beckendorff is arranged at the latter's house. Upon their arrival, the prince harangues Beckendorff with an anti-slavery speech, in which he asserts that 'the Divine Author of our religion was its decided enemy', and that he is speaking 'as I have felt it my duty to do, as the advocate of popular rights and national privileges' (VI, vii). He represents himself as the defender of the liberties of his people. The prince is confused by Beckendorff's eccentric response. Beckendorff, who neither eats nor sleeps and tucks perfumed handkerchiefs in his sleeve, leaves his guest and rides off in the middle of the night. The prince confuses this simulation of folly with madness. In fact, while the prince has been espousing popular rights, he has missed the play of power politics which is carried on beneath the surface by Beckendorff. The latter's plan has been to wean the prince away from his recalcitrant independence with an offer of a Grand Marshallship in the duke of Reisenberg's government. Beckendorff's midnight ride is occasioned, not by madness, but by a sudden desire of the duke to revoke the offer. Of these designs the prince is entirely ignorant; although they do not escape the shrewd and discerning Vivian. The upshot of these machinations is that the champion of the liberties of his kingdom relinquishes his independence for a post in the duke's imperial government. Thus the moralist's vision is obscured; and, in the crisis, he acts solely on the basis of self-interest. Mr Sievers, Vivian's confidant, assesses the actions of the prince, and political practice in general:

> And yet [he observes to Vivian] without the slightest compunction, has this same man [the prince] deserted the party of which, ten days ago, he was the zealous leader. How can you account for this, except if it be, as I have long suspected, that in politics there positively is no feeling of honour? Every one is conscious that not only himself, but his colleagues and his rivals, are working for their own private purpose; and that however a party may apparently be assisting in bringing about a result of common benefit, that nevertheless, and in fact, each is conscious that he is the tool of another. With such an understanding, treason is an expected affair; and the only point to consider is, who shall be so unfortunate as to be deserted, instead of the deserter (VII, ii).

The statesman must always be ready to act basely; although he must be capable of dissembling his baseness. Beckendorff dissembles his designs by feigning himself 'a frivolous creature' (VI, vi). The narrator in *Vivian Grey* asserts that 'our wisdom must be concealed under folly' (I, ix). This notion of appearances is fundamental in Machiavellian thought. To a man who wishes to rise from low origins, Machiavelli recommends that 'it may at times be the highest wisdom to simulate folly'.[75] Disraeli's dandyism in the 1830s was surely, to some extent, a calculated folly. In a fascinating passage in *Vivian Grey*, the narrator likens the hero of that book to the god Jupiter, who came to earth in the form of a herdsman. 'For, to govern man, even the god appeared to feel as man; and sometimes as a beast, was apparently influenced by their vilest passions' (I, ix). Contarini Fleming is described as a 'wild beast' (II, xii) when he enters politics. At the

conference which takes place in the same book, and which has been
alluded to, Contarini observes that 'the great diplomats appeared to me so
many wild beasts ready to devour our innocent lamb of a sovereign' (II,
xiii). Their practical mode is 'compressed in two words – subtlety and
force' (I, xxi). These passages are redolent of chapter 18 of *The Prince*, in
which the statesman is enjoined to imitate Severus: 'a Prince being thus
obliged to know well how to act as a beast must imitate the fox and the
lion'.[76]

III

Disraeli worked as a solicitor's clerk from November of 1821 until July of
1824. In May of 1824 he submitted his *Aylmer Papillon* to the publisher
John Murray, with whom he was becoming more intimate. The work is a
light satire on English society; but it is more interesting as a manifestation
of his restlessness than as a serious literary effort. It is impossible to say
precisely when, but it was probably sometime in 1824 that Disraeli read
Madame De Staël's *Germany*. There are two hitherto unpublished diaries
in Disraeli's papers containing copious notes from that work, which attest
to this fact.[77] *Germany* had been published in an English translation from
the French by Murray in November of 1813,[78] when the latter became
friendly with its author. It is not unreasonable to surmise that Disraeli
learned of the existence of this book through Murray. Moreover, in July of
1824, Disraeli made a trip to Belgium and the Rhine; and it is clear from
the diaries which he kept during his travels, and from his letters, that he
became fascinated by Germany in 1824.[79] This interest was apparently
sustained throughout the 1820s. The second part of *Vivian Grey*, it will be
remembered, is set in that country; and one of Disraeli's other autobiographical novels, *Contarini Fleming*, was written under the influence of
Goethe's *Wilhelm Meister*.[80]

Germany made a great impression in England both at the time of its
publication and in the 1820s, when it was read, for example, by William
Hazlitt. Carlyle called *Germany* 'the parent of whatever acquaintance with
the German literature which exists among us'.[81] It was also much admired
by Byron, who wrote: 'What the devil shall I say about D'Allemagne? I
like it prodigiously.'[82] The book is informed by a cloudy and sentimenta-
lized version of the early romantic theorists – especially August Schlegel.
Madame De Staël may be said to have been an advocate of German
romanticism. The final chapter of the book is an exhortation to the

enthusiasm which was deplored so much by the thinkers of the eighteenth century: 'The meaning of this word [enthusiasm] among the Greeks is the noblest definition of it: enthusiasm means *God in us*. Indeed, when man's life is emotionally overflowing it has something of the divine.'[83]

Disraeli may have read this work as a kind of reaction against his political and historical studies – although it is uncertain whether he did so consciously at the time. It is difficult to avoid the impression that he felt himself to have been corrupted. Like the German romantics he became a hard student of mysticism; and he was evidently transfixed by the idea of purity. In 'an essay on the soofees' he writes:

> The Oabitan mentions these opinionists by y name of Suffi, Soofee, Sefi, Sephi. The Arabic term which bears all these spellings means wise, holy, & is supposed to be derived from a word signifying *pure, clean*. The distinct & finite nature of y human soul being denied & man declared an [*sic*] pure emanation or ray from the divine essence ... the best life imitates the celestial purity.[84]

Disraeli may have felt that he had been corrupted by his early education. Contarini Fleming declares: 'Blessed by nature with a heart that is the shrine of sensibility, my infamous education had succeeded in rendering me the most selfish of my species' (II, xii). Thus he sought in romanticism a mode of purification and a means of transforming his view of himself and the world. Friedrich Nietzsche observed this phenomenon in artists like Byron, Poe, Musset and Kleist. He believed them to be men with 'souls in which they usually try to conceal some fracture; often taking revenge with their works for some inner contamination, often seeking with their high flights to escape into forgetfulness from an all-too-faithful memory'.[85] Disraeli was also afflicted with this 'inner contamination'; and, like many of the continental romantics, he sought with his 'high flights' to escape to a transcendent purity.

There is an illustration of this psychological inversion in *Vivian Grey*. After Mrs Felix Lorraine attempts to poison him, Vivian sees his own corruption in her; which corruption is intolerable to him.

> I fancy [he exclaims] that in this mysterious foreigner, that in this woman, I have met a kind of *double* of myself ... Yet do I find her the most abandoned of all beings: a creature guilty of that which, even in this guilty age, I thought was obsolete. And is it possible that I am like her? that I can resemble her? ... Oh, God! the system of my existence seems to stop: I cannot breathe ... It is not so – it cannot be so – it shall not be so! (III, v).

This passage is immediately followed by a lyrical outburst, the object of which is the 'Sultana of the soul' – the moon. In one of the Byronic digressions in *The Young Duke*, the narrator succumbs to an access of remorse when he realizes that he is 'infinitely corrupt'. 'My thousand errors, my ten thousand follies, my infinite corruption', he says, 'have well deserved a bitterer fate than this' (III, xviii). By reaction, he flies to the greatest ideal of all romantics: his own soul. 'Must we, then, part, indeed, my delicate Ariel! and must thou quit this earth without a record! Oh! Mistress, that I have ever loved! oh! idol, that I have ever worshipped!' (III, xviii). But, as so often is the case with Disraeli, this sudden access of genuine emotion is succeeded by humour and wit. 'Where are we?' he continues, 'I think I was saying, that 'tis difficult to form an opinion of ourselves. They say it is impossible ... And yet, I sometimes think I write a pretty style, though spoiled by that confounded puppyism; but then mine is the puppy age, and that will wear off' (III, xviii).[86]

Wit is a fixture in Disraeli's career: he was 'one of the wittiest men that ever lived'.[87] In view of the peculiar collocation of corruption, romance and irony in Disraeli, he can be comprehended in relation to the German romantics.[88] It is true that Disraeli read Burke, probably in 1825, and that he resembled Coleridge and Carlyle in some respects. He shared their Burkean contempt for theory, and for the utilitarians. But there are elements in Disraeli's romanticism that are clearly foreign to the essence of English romanticism – rather, they are distinctly German. The characteristic experience of the German romantics is of a tension between the real and the ideal (or of polarities in general – the inward 'fracture') which is reconciled by irony. Novalis, for example, strove to idealize vulgar physical reality, but could not finally believe in his imaginative creations. The romantic generation in Germany, Raymond Immerwahr asserts, 'could never take its romanticism in deadly earnest, never quite pretend to eliminate the chasm separating life and literary imagination. This gap, which it knew it could not close, it chose to bridge with conscious irony.'[89] Friedrich Schlegel actually posited a doctrine of *romantische Ironie*. He saw 'two antagonistic powers within the creative process: creative enthusiasm counteracted by skeptical irony'. Irony enables the mind 'to mediate between two opposing aesthetical systems'.[90] The essence of German romanticism, and its uniqueness, consists in its concentration upon the synthesis of paired opposites; and the failure of this synthetic process is manifest in irony.

The English romantics differ from the Germans in this respect. Wordsworth, Coleridge, Shelley and Keats abandoned the satiric tradition of the

eighteenth century; and consequently they are devoid of wit.[91] It would
be difficult, for example, to imagine Keats declaring at the end of his 'Ode
on a Grecian Urn': 'But what the deuce is death, when dinner is waiting all
this time!' (*The Young Duke*, II, viii). There is a heaviness and earnestness
in the English that is foreign to the German romantics, who are distinguished by either daemonic humours or lightness and the play of intellect.
The exception to this rule is Byron; but Byron was an uncharacteristic
English romantic. He was essentially a man of the eighteenth century who
wrote for fame in the nineteenth century; and, having spent most of his
adult life on the continent, his affinities, such as they were, were with the
continental romantics.

It is true that Byron exerted an immense influence on Disraeli; and it is
probable that Disraeli's irony is in part attributable to this influence, as it
was also to his status as a Jewish *étranger*. But it is a mistake to regard
Disraeli's romanticism solely as the sort of fashionable affectation of youth
which was prevalent in the generation which followed Byron. Disraeli was
not, as David Cecil wrote of Byron's lover, Lady Oxford, 'a professional
romantic', who adopted a 'fashionable pose'.[92] Most of the positive
emotion that historians identify in Disraeli's career – his admiration for
the English aristocracy; his pride in himself as an 'aristocratic Jew'; and his
belief in the greatness of England – is connected with his romanticism. It
served his deepest needs, by providing him with a redeeming vision of the
world, which permitted him to transcend the limitations and frustrations
of his own situation through the power to transform the external world.[93]
In or about 1824, German romanticism, with its concentration upon
mysticism and the supernatural, served as a vehicle for an inner purification. But it is his ironical relation to reality that seems to place him in the
German camp. Much of his foreignness and ostensible insincerity become
comprehensible when Disraeli is understood in these terms.

What ideas of the German romantics were imparted to Disraeli by
Madame De Staël? It must be said that Disraeli shared, to some extent, the
understanding of reality which was peculiar to the post-Kantian idealists.
Later in the 1820s, when he discovered that their excessively imaginative
world view had in part been the cause of his nervous collapse, and
interfered with his prospects for a political career, he endeavoured to
restrain the flights of his imagination. He appears to have passed through a
sort of anti-romantic phase, and approached the more extreme claims of
his romanticism in a spirit of satire and inquisition. In the second part of
Vivian Grey, for example, a pupil of Fichte's is depicted at a literary *soirée*

stuffing *kalte Schale* into his mouth (VII, iii); and Contarini Fleming's father advises him, 'I think if you could control your imagination you might be a great man' (II, ix). But Disraeli was never able wholly to purge himself of the effect of his imagination – indeed, he never wished to, for he always considered it the noblest virtue of a statesman.[94]

Disraeli was familiar with the ideas of Kant and his 'disciples'. Kant made an overwhelming impression on German romantic philosophy. He argued that the mind is not simply a passive recipient of the world around us, but that it is also to some extent the creator of knowledge. He denied the possibility of absolute knowledge, for the mind is a mechanism which acts upon the impressions it receives. Thus we do not know reality as it is in itself, but only as it appears to us. This notion had a liberating effect upon the romantic theorists who followed him. If reality is finally unknowable, they asserted, then man is free to 'think-create'[95] the world. 'The organs of thinking', Novalis wrote, 'are the creative organs of the world.'[96] In an extensive essay on part III, chapter 6 of *Germany* (which is devoted to Kant), Disraeli notes the Kantian idea that the mind is, in part, the creator of reality.

> Kant and the Idealists are for re-establishing primitive truths and a spontaneous action in y soul – Thus far for the understanding – in morality they preach conscience in the arts – the ideal ... Kant endeavoured to trace the limits of the two empires, *of the senses & of y soul* – of *nature exterior*, and *nature intellectual*. They call, in German philosophy ideas *subjective* those which spring from ye nature of our intelligence and its faculties, & ideas *objective* all those which are excited by y [senses?]: that is by external objects. Kant takes nothing *a priori*. He believes in no innate knowledge ... But he believes that the power of understanding is innate – that this power cannot be brought into action unless it is exercised – that its exercise is the acquisition of knowledge, but that it is this understanding which gives laws to exterior nature and not exterior nature to it.[97]

The post-Kantian idealists accepted the liberating elements of this philosophy. They were also influenced by the Platonic view (through his latter disciples) that the sensible physical world half-reveals or disguises the Forms or Ideas, and that, consequently, the physical world is not ultimately real. The post-Kantians posit a dim conception of ultimate reality;[98] but their primary concern is with avoiding reality and not finding it. The post-Kantians deprecate the physical world, but their conception of ultimate reality is open ended. The German romantics engaged in a quest for wonders, and in a constant endeavour 'to seek strange truth in undiscovered lands'. This quest derived from the post-Kantian belief that the physical world is pervaded and surrounded by mysteries which man might sense and art adumbrate. Their thought concentrates upon the mystical, the supernatural, the unconscious and the invisible. They shared the deprecatory view of reason that is common to all romanticism. Thus they stood in an ambiguous relation to reality. 'The most characteristic art of German romanticism', Siegbert Prawer writes, 'transports reader, viewer and listener to a frontier between the visible and the invisible, the tangible and the intangible.'[99]

The desire to be free of vulgar physical reality led the German romantics to concentrate upon mysticism in thought and music in art. Mysticism was believed to be the most transcendent form of thought, and music the most transcendent art. Disraeli shared this German inclination. It will be remembered that Disraeli familiarized himself with mysticism while reading about the East and David Alroy, in conjunction with Madame De Staël. In his diary he writes: 'Life is a miracle & death a mystery. Nothing is extrord[inar]y for everything is extraordinary.'[100] To this mystical view he adhered throughout his life; and his politics were full of the symbols of mysticism when he attained power. He wrote in *Lothair* at the age of seventy: 'Can there be anything more miraculous than the existence of man and this world? anything more literally supernatural than the origin of things?' (xxxviii).

The concentration upon music is also peculiar to German romanticism. 'In England', M. H. Abrams asserts, 'the lyrical poem seems to have been the root consideration out of which developed the concept that all art is emotional expression. In Germany, on the other hand, music came to be regarded as the art that is most purely expressive.'[101] Music was regarded as the most transcendent art and the purest expression of spirit because of its remoteness from the demonstrable logic of rational experience. It is the art which is most free of physical reality. 'The musician', August Schlegel averred, 'has a language of feeling independent of all external objects; in verbal language, on the contrary, the expression of feeling always depends on its connection with the idea.'[102] The German romantics also had a preference for instrumental music, because of its freedom from the earthly association of words.

Disraeli's education in music was probably advanced by his reading of Madame De Staël. Disraeli's 'champagne-like sparkle' can be understood in light of this education: Lothair admires 'no one so much as Mozart' (xx). In his diary on *Germany*, he writes:

effect of music – See Mad De Stael theory written in the 2nd vol. of her
Germany ... Music: It can speak to the secrets of a man's heart as if by
divination ... We cannot express the inexpressible. The Musician can make
us feel what the Poet cannot. He creates secret sympathies by melodious
mysteries.[103]

It is clear from *Contarini Fleming* that Disraeli was familiar with German
music and that he had 'a passion for instrumental music' (III, viii).[104]

The basis of Disraeli's fascination with music and mysticism was
probably the same as that of the post-Kantian idealists – disdain for
reality. In his diary he notes Madame De Staël's characterization of
perhaps the most extreme idealist, Johann Gottlieb Fichte:

A German Philo. Mad. d. S. vol.3. 107. Idealists. The character of Fichte
p.110–11. He despised particularly all expressions w[hi]ch inclined in y
slightest degree to substantiality: *existence* was a word in his opinion too
absolute. *Being, principle, essence* were words scarcely sufficiently etherial to
indicate the subtile shadowings of his opinions. On dit that he dreaded the
contact of real things, & that he endeavoured to avoid them. When you talk
with him, you lose all conscience of this world.[105]

It is not suggested that Disraeli was transformed into an idealist after
reading Madame De Staël. He was, as he probably would have said
himself, 'predisposed' to that philosophy. It is apparent that Disraeli was
aware, or became aware, of his tendency to dissociate from reality, which
was one of the symptoms of the neurotic illness to which he succumbed
between 1827 and 1832.[106]

While the German romantics despised reality they glorified imagination. They arrogated to the great man the power to make or remake
reality. This transformational faculty – the compulsion to transform
vulgar physical reality – is fundamental to the romantic vision. M. H.
Abrams likens the romantic mind to 'a radiant projector which makes a
contribution to the objects it perceives'.[107] Transformation of the world is
effected by the imagination. 'Imagination is the highest and most original
part of man', Friedrich Schleiermacher wrote, 'and everything outside it
only a reflection upon it.'[108] The German romantics admired, above all,
the naive poetical imagination of Homer, which created the horizon of a
whole civilization, and a complete world view. But the Germans were not
naive: they were self-conscious creators; and consequently they were
ironic. They sought to defy the dictation of reality; and this defiance they
believed to be heroic. Novalis maintained that romance is a kind of
discipline: 'By giving a high meaning to what is ordinary, a mysterious

aspect to what is commonplace, the dignity of the unknown to the familiar, a semblance of infinity to the finite, I romanticize it ... Life itself should be a *Roman*, not one given us but one made by us.'[109] When Contarini Fleming is asked by his cousin Alceste why he wishes to undertake the impossible task of restoring his family's fortune in Rome, he responds: 'I have no sympathy with reality. What vanity in all the empty bustle of common life! ... It develops all the lowering attributes of my nature' (III, ix).

In a sense, Disraeli's life was a sustained effort to live a fiction. 'Poetry', he wrote in his diary in 1833, 'is the safety valve of my passions, but I wish to *act* what I *write*.'[110] It was indeed necessary for him to invent a role for himself, for circumstances had denied him one. His early autobiographical novels were a sort of workshop of the self,[111] in which he invented, tested and often abandoned tentative models for possible selves,[112] using fiction as a means to attain self-knowledge. Having defined his essential character, the 'self-discoverer'[113] progressed to his political apprenticeship, during which he sought to integrate his personality with English political life. In his first efforts on the hustings, he reached into the theatrical properties box and found the costume of Bolingbroke, and with it the pose of a prophet of reinvigorated toryism. This impersonation eased his way into the Tory party. But in order to meet the aristocratic rulers of England on equal terms he was obliged further to transform his vision of himself. 'Unable to function in his proper person as a man of dubious pedigree in a highly class-conscious society', Isaiah Berlin writes, 'Disraeli invented a splendid fairy tale.'[114] In his own eyes he was not the middle-class Jew who had been tormented at school, and whose first attempts to make his fortune had ended in ruin – he was a member of the most aristocratic branch of the most aristocratic race. By the end of the 1840s, when this elaborate fiction had been fully articulated, both Disraeli's political persona and his education were essentially complete.

2

Disraeli's romanticism: self-fashioning in the novels

DANIEL R. SCHWARZ

I

Disraeli tells us something about the history of taste in the nineteenth century. His early novels – *Vivian Grey* (1826–7), *The Young Duke* (1831), *Contarini Fleming* (1832) and *Alroy* (1833) – met the middle-class desire for revelations of aristocratic life, for romances about bizarre characters in strange lands, and for extreme behaviour on the part of wilful egoists posing as latter-day Byrons. As an outsider, as a man who savoured his own feelings and sought unusual sensations, the youthful Disraeli saw himself as an heir to Byron and Shelley.

Disraeli's career as artist and politician should be seen in the context of the romantic movement. As Harold Fisch has remarked:

> Insofar as his novels are the expression of his personal life, his feelings, his scarcely avowed hidden ideals, he achieves an appropriately resonant statement. His novels have the subtle egoism of all true romantics, of Shelley, of Wordsworth, of Milton. His subject is himself: he is Coningsby; he is Contarini Fleming; he is Alroy; he is Tancred; and he is the Wandering Jew, Sidonia. From these varied characters we are able to reconstruct the inner vision of Disraeli, the rich landscape of his dreams, his irrepressible vision of grandeur, of power, but power used for glorious and elevating ends ... Disraeli is certainly an egoist, but if that means that he is impelled by a sense of personal dedication, of election, of being favoured and gifted to an almost unlimited degree, and of being charged with grand tasks and opportunities, then it is the sort of egoism which finds its parallel in the lives of the great romantic poets and dreamers, of Milton, Words-worth and Shelley.[1]

In the early novels he could play the role of the romantic figure that tantalized his imagination without sacrificing the public image that he wished to cultivate. To be sure, he might dress unconventionally and play the dandy, but that kind of socially sanctioned rebelliousness was different in kind rather than degree from the imagined social outlawry of Vivian Grey, Alroy and Contarini.

Contarini Fleming and *Alroy* are meant as visions rather than restatements of known truths. Disraeli tries to extend into prose the fusion of politics and philosophy – as well as the range and imaginative energy – of the Miltonic epic and the romantic masterworks such as Blake's prophecies, *The Prelude*, *Prometheus Unbound* and *Don Juan*. While Disraeli's works at times seem bathetic when viewed in the context of this tradition, there can be no doubt that he saw himself in the line of romantic visionaries that M. H. Abrams has described:

> The Romantics, then, often spoke confidently as elected members of what Harold Bloom calls 'The Visionary Company', the inspired line of singers from the prophets of the Old and New Testament, through Dante, Spenser, and above all Milton ... Whatever the form, the Romantic Bard is one 'who present, past and future sees'; so that in dealing with current affairs his procedure is often panoramic, his stage cosmic, his agents quasi-mythological, and logic of events apocalyptic. Typically this mode of Romantic vision fuses history, politics, philosophy and religion into one grand design, by asserting Providence – or some form of natural teleology – to operate in the seeming chaos of human history so as to effect from present evil a greater good.[2]

Describing the process of writing *Death in Venice*, Thomas Mann recalled, 'Originally the tale was to be brief and modest. But things or whatever better word there may be for the conception *organic* have a will of their own, and shape themselves accordingly ... The truth is that every piece of work is a realization, fragmentary but complete in itself, of our individuality; and this kind of realization is the sole and painful way we have of getting the particular experience – no wonder, then, that the process is attended by surprises.'[3] Mann reminds us that the author both creates a text and discovers an aspect of him or her self during its creation. In Disraeli's first four novels, *Vivian Grey* (1826–7), *The Young Duke* (1831), *Contarini Fleming* (1832) and *The Wondrous Tale of Alroy* (1833), he 'realized' aspects of his individuality. Not only did he create imagined worlds in his novels, but the novels played a crucial role in creating his character and personality. In discussing Disraeli's first four novels, I shall argue that understanding the symbiotic relationship between author and text is an essential condition to appreciating his art.

An 1833 entry in Disraeli's 'Mutilated Diary' shows that the novels compensate for his failure to excel even as they protest against accepted English conventions and manners:

> The world calls me "*conceited*". The world is in error. I trace all the blunders of my life to sacrificing my own opinion to that of others. When I was considered very conceited *indeed*, I was nervous, and had self confidence only by fits. I intend in future to act entirely from my own impulse. I have an unerring instinct. I can read characters at a glance; few men can deceive me. My mind is a continental mind. It is a revolutionary mind. I am only truly great in action. If ever I am placed in a truly eminent position I shall prove this. I co[ul]d rule the House of Commons, altho' there wo[ul]d be a great prejudice against me at first. It is the most jealous assembly in the world. The fixed character of our English society, the consequence of our aristocratic institutions renders a *career* difficult.[4]

The subsequent passage in the diary makes it clear that literature is a compensation for the frustration he feels at not being given the opportunity to play a major role in public events.

Vivian Grey is about the precocious and ambitious eponymous hero's efforts to attain political influence through Machiavellian manoeuvres that ultimately fail. If Vivian portrays Disraeli's 'active and real ambition', it was because Disraeli recognized that one aspect of himself savoured power for its own sake. Vivian's sensational and erratic school career has striking parallels to Disraeli's. Vivian's dependence on the co-operation of others reflects Disraeli's own view, in 1826, that a man without wealth, family and power required help to rise to a position of responsibility.

Beckendorff, the major figure in books VI and VII, has a philosophy that Disraeli himself might have articulated at most stages of his career.[5] Beckendorff believes a man may shape his own destiny by the sheer force of his will and personality. Beckendorff is the successful version of the egoistic alternative that Vivian, but not his creator, had put behind him. While the melancholy, disillusioned Grey sees Beckendorff's philosophy as a version of the false principles he once held, Disraeli's narrative voice is impatient with Vivian's ennui and is sympathetic with the bold, idiosyncratic minister.

Disraeli's fiction is never inhibited by those aesthetic conventions that stipulate that differing kinds of mimesis cannot co-exist in the same work. The reader's aesthetic pleasure derives in part from the dextrous movement from one kind of narrative to another, and the arousing of expecta-tions that are not fulfilled in the expected way. *Vivian Grey* does not always benefit from its hodgepodge of genres, but in it Disraeli shows how the picaresque tale and romance form need not be incompatible with scenes of psychological realism. An example is the scene in which Mrs Felix Lorraine tries to poison Vivian. Gothic melodrama presents the occasion for exploring psychological complexity in a way that recalls Jacobean tragedy. Disraeli may have lacked the vocabulary of modern psychology, but he knew how obsessions, fixations, and darker impulses determine human behaviour. In this important regard, Disraeli parted company with the novels of manners and morals that Austen and Fielding had written and put himself in the tradition of Richardson, Emily Brontë and Hardy.

Despite his flamboyant personality (embodied within the text in the narrative voice), Disraeli is quite a conventional moralist in *Vivian Grey*, particularly for one who speaks in the guise of a Byronic iconoclast. Even in this early novel the voice of the unconventional dandy and the passionate romantic is restrained by Disraeli's sense of propriety and a respect for moderation in passions. The early novels show hints of the self-control, intellectual discipline, pragmatism and deference to historical traditions that characterized Disraeli's behaviour in political circles.

In 1826 Disraeli considered himself as Byron's heir, and he wished to be thought of as the new Byron. However, in the 1853 edition of his novels, Disraeli sought to emphasize his condemnation of Vivian by stressing the ironic distance between the narrator and Vivian. Part of Disraeli's embarrassment with *Vivian Grey* derives from Vivian's abuse of political power and his subsequent disgust with public life. Yet Disraeli is indebted to Byron's *Don Juan* for his eccentric, arrogant and delightful narrator.

In *The Young Duke*, again we see Disraeli, the dandy and self-styled heir to Byron, imposing traditional standards upon his hero. In *The Young Duke*, Disraeli dramatizes a rebellious temperament only to show that such a temperament must adjust to community standards and renounce some of its individuality. In temperament as well as in politics, the man who first ran as a Radical before converting to toryism was even in the early 1830s far more conservative than he thought himself.

While Disraeli did not regard *The Young Duke* as part of 'the secret history of his feelings', it is difficult to separate Disraeli from the young duke's conflict between self-indulgence and responsibility. Disraeli's surrogate, the narrative voice, vacillates revealingly from a worldly jaded tone to a self-consciousness about his own situation. Even if he was not always familiar with the *beau monde* he purported to describe, his strong capacity for self-fashioning enabled him to believe he knew that world. Thus it may have been crucial to Disraeli's own self-image to show that the duke's inherent quality protected him from permanent corruption. In any case, the duke's real self seems immune to the effects of drinking, gambling and adultery. The narrator's self-denigration may be related to Disraeli's disgust with the vapid social world in which he has been living, a world to which Disraeli's narrator implies that he, to his regret, belongs. Disraeli's chameleonic speaker is alternately performer, virtuoso and Byronic hero; we attend to his presence and ventriloquism as surely as we do to Thackeray's puppeteer in *Vanity Fair*.

As Jerman has remarked, *Contarini Fleming: A Psychological Romance* is Disraeli's *A Portrait of the Artist as a Young Man*. 'Disraeli's fictionalized autobiography ... reflects his own reveries, doubts, miseries, failures and despair, dredged up out of the past and only slightly disguised.'[6] Disraeli's third novel, published in 1832 when he was still only twenty-seven, mimes his poetic and psychological development. In *Contarini*, external events are a correlative to Contarini's state of mind. Yet, Disraeli is most concerned with creating words and images that reflect his own inner feelings.

Contarini may nominally have an independent existence but he is inseparable from Disraeli's own complex personality and character. Disraeli does not succeed in creating a sufficient distinction between himself and his character. While Contarini is meant to be Disraeli's version of the poetic personality, he is really a representation of Disraeli's own psyche. Disraeli the romantic uses Contarini to dramatize how his own imagination will free his soul from conventions, traditions, systems and false knowledge.

What Disraeli has done is to create a persona whose superficial social circumstances and biography differ from his own, but whose subjective life mirrors his own life. Contarini is born with the advantages Disraeli lacked: nobility, wealth and a politically prominent family. Visions, dreams and fictions occupy young Contarini's mind. In a passage that echoes the preface to the *Lyrical Ballads*, Contarini says that he writes in search of 'relief from the overwhelming vitality of thought in the flowing spirit of poetic creation' (I, i). Just as he now finds an outlet for his feelings in creative activity, throughout his life his imagination provides him with solace from stress and turmoil.

In *Contarini Fleming* Disraeli divides himself into two characters: Contarini, the imaginative man who responds to impulses, passions and unacknowledged psychic needs, and Contarini's father, Baron Fleming, the pragmatic, rational self who commits himself to public affairs despite his cynical view of mankind. If Disraeli objectified his imagination in the son, he transferred his will for power to the father. He himself believed in the ability of a forceful individual to shape his own destiny and the course of external events. Disraeli's political philosophy was often based less upon principles than upon the belief that he could act in the best interest of those less perspicacious, intelligent and informed than himself. He believed that the 'natural aristocracy' of ability had the responsibility to lead and to do so in ways that served the interests of the entire people rather than the special interests of privileged classes.

The plot dramatizes, to quote from Contarini's concluding homily, that 'Circumstances are beyond the control of man; but his conduct is in his own power' (VII, ii). But Disraeli really believed that circumstances could be significantly influenced by character. The novel's last paragraphs make clear that creativity is not necessarily limited to poetry and may include unspecified activities relating to 'the political regeneration of the country to which I am devoted' (VII, ii). For Contarini that is Italy; but within the novel Disraeli uses Italy as a metaphor for England. Disraeli's prophetic tone is an outgrowth of a strain of moral seriousness. Nor must we forget that the 1830s were the period when Browning and Carlyle were self-appointed legislators for the world, a view that owed much to the influence of Shelley. Finally, Disraeli understood that the Reform act of 1832, which extended the franchise to the middle class, opened the door to people of ability and energy like himself.

The novel is built upon the romantic premise that is voiced to Contarini by the oracular figure Winter: 'Never apologize for showing feeling ... when you do so you apologize for truth' (I, xiii). Disraeli may have set the novel in Europe to place it in the tradition of European novels (including Goethe's *Werther* and *Wilhelm Meister* and the works of Chateaubriand and Senancour) where feeling has epistemological value as the avenue to truth. Indeed he may have tentatively modelled himself on Goethe who had recognized Disraeli's genius.[7] Disraeli implies that each man has the capacity to discover his own truth by means of experience, if he is aided by an active imagination. Speaking through Contarini, Disraeli reaffirms the romantic view that a major source of knowledge is an individual's experience; Truth is not in the world outside, but within the self:

I am desirous of writing a book which shall be all truth; a work of which the
passion, the thought, the action, and even the style, should spring from my
own experience of feeling, from the meditations of my own intellect, from
my own observation of incident, from my own study of the genius of
expression ... When I search into my own breast, and trace the development
of my own intellect, and the formation of my own character, all is light and
order. The luminous succeeds to the obscure, the certain to the doubtful,
the intelligent to the illogical, the practical to the impossible, and I
experience all that refined and ennobling satisfaction that we derive from
the discovery of truth, and the contemplation of nature (I, i).

Contarini's therapeutic and expressive theory of art shows a rare but acute
recognition on Disraeli's part of the reasons he wrote fiction. Fiction
became for Disraeli the means of ordering and controlling his personality.
As he wrote, he rescued what he believed were his real values and
emotions from a host of contradictory roles he played as political aspirant,
dandy, scandalous novelist, Byronic iconoclast – to say nothing of his
private relationships.

For Disraeli, the Jews were a romantic and spiritual people unlike the
pragmatic and utilitarian British. *Alroy* is Disraeli's ultimate heroic fantasy.
He uses the figure of the twelfth-century Jewish prince, Alroy, as the basis
for a tale of Jewish conquest and empire. Disraeli found the medieval
world in which Alroy lived an apt model for some of his own values. He
saw in that world an emphasis on imagination, emotion and tradition;
respect for political and social hierarchies; and a vital spiritual life. *Alroy*
anticipates Disraeli's attraction to the Middle Ages in Young England.
Writing of the flowering of medieval Jewry under Alroy enabled him to
express his opposition to rationalism and utilitarianism.

In fact, the historic Alroy was a self-appointed messiah in Kurdistan
during a period of severe tribulation and unusual suffering for the Jews.[8]
Alroy's father claimed he was Elijah and that his son was the Messiah.
Although his actual name was Menahem, young Alroy took the name
David, the appropriate name for a king of the Jews, and promised to lead
his followers to Jerusalem where he would be their king. Apparently
learned in Jewish mysticism, Alroy managed to convince his followers that
he could perform supernatural acts. While he scored some victories before
he was murdered, probably by his father-in-law, his successes were hardly
of the magnitude of his victories in Disraeli's romance.

Since completing *Vivian Grey*, Disraeli had been fascinated by Alroy, the
Jew who had achieved power and prominence during Jewish captivity. But

perhaps he needed the inspiration of his 1831 trip to Jerusalem to finish *Alroy*. Disraeli wrote in the preface to *The Revolutionary Epick* (1834) that the purpose of *Alroy* was 'the celebration of a gorgeous incident in the annals of that sacred and romantic people from whom I derive my blood and name'.[9]

Doubtless Disraeli's journey to Jerusalem stimulated his fantasies of revived Jewish hegemony. Moreover, he believed that the Jews are not only an especially gifted race but the most aristocratic of races.[10] He also believed that the Jewish race is the source of all that is spiritual in European civilization, most notably Christianity. Disraeli's only historical romance, except for *The Rise of Iskander* (1833), resulted from his desire to depict Jews on a heroic scale. But it also derives from the discrepancy between his aspirations and his position in the early 1830s. In Alroy's hyperbolic self-dramatization is the thinly disguised voice of the young frustrated Disraeli who has not yet begun to fulfil the 'ideal ambition' of which he wrote in his diary. Yet with typical Disraelian – and Byronic – emotional resilience, Alroy's early self-pity and ennui give way to the vision of a transformation of his condition: 'I linger in this shadowy life, and feed on silent images which no eye but mine can gaze upon, till at length they are invested with all the terrible circumstance of life, and breathe, and act, and form a stirring world of fate and beauty, time, and death, and glory' (I, i).

In *Alroy* the evolving pattern of events and circumstances depends upon Alroy's moral health, whereas we have seen in *Contarini Fleming* that the character's visions and dreams, and on occasion actual events, depend on his psychological life. Alroy's moral status *determines* the action. Such a pattern, in which a man's behaviour shapes the world, enables Disraeli to reconcile the conflict between his own poetic and political ambition. If Contarini vacillates erratically between imagination and action, Disraeli shows in *Alroy* that the life of action is not incompatible with the imaginative life. For Alroy's political success is dependent upon visions that show how a life of action need not exclude poetic and imaginative impulses. Alroy uses his imagination in the service of his political goals. For example, the catalyst for his original act of rebellion is his insight that, as 'the descendant of sacred kings', he is not suited for a life of activity (I, i). His imagination creates the fiction of Jewish and personal glory. Killing the city governor Alschiroch who harassed his sister, his *alter ego* throughout the novel, is the necessary heroic action which takes Alroy from the imaginative world into the public world. We recall that Disraeli's sister Sarah was often his *alter ego*.

Disraeli wants to create a context where the marvellous is possible. Moreover, he wishes to present himself as an original artist and to flout conventional expectations as to what a work of prose fiction should be. His use of rhythm and rhyme is part of his rebellion against artistic captivity, a captivity created by standards he did not recognize and by what he felt was failure to appreciate his genius. In the original preface to *Alroy*, Disraeli stressed the genius of his achievement, particularly the prose-poetry. To stress his kinship with the visionary tradition of the Bible, *Alroy* is written in a prophetic tone and biblical rhythms as if Disraeli were proposing this text as his contribution to Jewish lore.

Disraeli's first four novels mime his psyche. His emotions, fantasies, aspirations and anxieties become fictional names, personalities and actions. These novels are moral parables told by himself for himself about ambitious egoists. He dramatizes the political rise and setbacks of an unscrupulous young man; the moral malaise and subsequent enlighten-ment of a young English duke; the flamboyant career of a young count who is torn between politics and poetry as well as between feeling and intellect; and finally the biography of Alroy, a Jewish prince who conquers much of Asia only to lose his kingdom and his life as he compromises his principles.

Disraeli uses his early novels, in particular *Alroy* and *Contarini*, as a means of controlling himself, of understanding himself, and of exorcizing flamboyant postures and forbidden emotions. For example, Alroy reflects Disraeli's fantasies of conquest and his will to power. In his early novels, the distinction between the external events and the interior visions of the eponymous character blurs. The reason is that both are reflections of the author's subjective life and both are dramatizations of his evolving imagination. In *Alroy*, both the divine machinery and the eponymous character's adventures are the metaphorical vehicles for Disraeli's atti-tudes and states of mind, and have as little to do with the phenomenal world as William Blake's prophecies.

Like a later self-defined dandy, Oscar Wilde, Disraeli used his literary creations as masks to disguise his wounded sensibilities and as devices to objectify aspects of himself that society would not tolerate. In his fiction, he freed himself from conventions and traditions, from priggishness and condescension, and found room for his fantasies. He discovered an alternative to the turmoil of his personal life in the *act* of creating the imagined worlds of his novels. But Disraeli's early novels are more than the creations of an egoistic, ambitious, but frustrated young man who found a temporary outlet for his imagination in the fictions he created. For the roles one imagines are as indicative of one's real self as supposedly 'sincere' moments, intense personal relationships, or daily routines. In the early novels the title character and the narrator represent the two sides of Disraeli. While the title character embodies Byronic fantasies of passionate love, heroism and rebellion against society's values, the narrator judges him according to standards that represent traditional values and the community's interest. In the first four books of *Vivian Grey* and in *The Young Duke* the narrator represents the political and social health of England; in *Alroy*, the narrator speaks for the interest of the Jews even after Alroy has betrayed them. In *Contarini* and in the later books of *Vivian Grey*, Disraeli speaks for a commitment to public life based on ideals rather than cynical self-interest.

II

Venetia (1837) is a thinly disguised novel about fictional versions of Shelley and Byron: Disraeli was in desperate financial straits when he wrote *Venetia*, in part because *Henrietta Temple*, although his most successful novel since *Vivian Grey*, did not produce anything like the revenue he required to pay his debts. He chose for his subjects England's most unconventional recent poetic geniuses, Shelley and Byron, because they gave him an opportunity to embody in fiction his pique that major artists, like himself, were unappreciated, if not ostracized. Disraeli saw himself as heir to the tradition of genius which those figures represented to him. By creating fictional versions of Byron and Shelley, he was reaffirming his ties to the romantic tradition. Because Shelley and Byron were both regarded as disreputable and immoral geniuses by the early Victorian establishment, his choice of subject was both a ploy to attract a voyeuristic audience and a statement about the kind of imaginative and personal life that intrigued him. His major figures, Lord Cadurcis and Marmion Herbert, are modelled respectively on Byron and Shelley. (In the novel Shelley is a generation older, although he was actually three years younger.) The novel fuses the melodrama of the Gothic plot with Disraeli's intensifying interest in the inner workings of the psyche.

Deserted by her husband and living in self-imposed seclusion in Cherbury, Lady Annabel Herbert (modelled on Byron's wife who was called Annabelle) devotes her life to her child, Venetia. Cadurcis and his mother come to live at the nearby Abbey. Because his mother is emotionally erratic if not mentally ill, Cadurcis becomes increasingly dependent on the affection of Lady Annabel and Venetia. When his mother abuses him without provocation, he runs away; during his flight, his mother dies of heart failure. Subsequently Cadurcis leaves the Abbey to continue his education. Only the local vicar, Dr Masham, knows the secret of Venetia's paternity or the reasons for her mother's seclusion. One day Venetia discovers that a closed-off room contains her father's portrait and his poems which she reads. In true Gothic fashion, she becomes ill; while delirious, she reveals to her mother what she has seen.

In the guise of his fictional counterparts, Herbert and Cadurcis, Disraeli presents both Shelley and Byron as sympathetic figures and extenuates their unconventional conduct. Of course, by giving them other names, Disraeli could have it both ways; Herbert and Cadurcis do not parallel Shelley and Byron, except in the broad outlines of their careers.[11] While it adds a dimension to the novel, it is doubtful whether a modern reader requires the identification to find the novel interesting. While Herbert is nominally Shelley after he finally emerges late in the novel, his energies are rather reduced. He becomes both the typical Disraeli wisdom figure and the surrogate father who fulfils the emotional needs of Cadurcis. Cadurcis may be based on Byron, but he is also a recognizable successor to the tempestuous, impulsive, passionate hero of Disraeli's prior novels, the man whose energies are never fully controlled and threaten to under-mine their possessor; I am thinking of Contarini, Alroy, Vivian Grey and even Ferdinand. Shelley and Byron provide Disraeli with models of the rebellious over-reacher to whom he was attracted, without exposing him to possible criticism for creating dissatisfied social misfits. They do so at a time when he was gaining increasing political recognition and when he knew that he was close finally to gaining the seat in parliament that he had sought and which, after a number of setbacks, he won in 1837. These poets dramatize the direction that he was turning his back upon. Herbert and Cadurcis are the literary and imaginative *Übermenschen* of his imagination. Their lives are ways in which Disraeli tests the premise articulated by Annabel's sister-in-law: 'Everything is allowed, you know, to a genius!' (IV, vii).

Both the younger Herbert and Lord Cadurcis, prior to meeting Herbert, represent the self that Disraeli, rather reluctantly but quite consciously, is in the process of putting behind him, while the mature Herbert represents the idealized philosophic, mature man that Disraeli is trying to become. After the most tumultuous, unconventional life, Herbert discovers that human happiness resides in family ties. The dialogue between Disraeli's two surrogates, Cadurcis and Herbert, is really a dialogue between two aspects of himself. Cadurcis' iconoclastic view, that 'men have always been fools and slaves, and fools and slaves they always will be' (VI, iv), parallels one strand of Disraeli's own thinking. Yet, like his character, Disraeli had experienced the erratic fluctuation of public opinion and knew what it was to be in public disfavour (for example, when *Vivian Grey* was ridiculed and lampooned). Herbert, the man who carried individualism to an extreme, renounces his Byronic quest and speaks for Disraeli's commitment to community values: 'Love ... is an universal thirst for a communion, not merely of the senses, but of our whole nature, intellectual, imaginative and sensitive. He who finds his antitype enjoys a love perfect and enduring; time cannot change it, distance cannot remove it; the sympathy is complete' (VI, vi).

The ambitiousness of Herbert's vision, if not its profundity, testifies to the kind of cosmic and prophetic view to which Disraeli aspired in the 1830s. If the younger and unseen Herbert is Shelley, the rebel and iconoclast, the mature Herbert gives us an insight into the visionary and imaginative pretensions of Disraeli's mind at this time. Like the descent of the angel in *Tancred*, the actual details are unimportant as predictions, but illustrative of the kind of fantasy that Disraeli could articulate and temporarily believe. Yet, as Blake writes, Disraeli was 'one of those actors who enter so deeply into their role that for the time being they suspend disbelief and really live the part which they enact'.[12]

It is extremely significant that Disraeli has the mature Marmion Herbert quote Shelley's famous statement that 'poets are the unacknowledged legislators of the world' (VI, viii). Self-conscious about his failure to make any mark as a poet, after the first three books of *The Revolutionary Epick* (1834) had been unenthusiastically received, Disraeli wished to establish the legitimacy of his novels. His original preface to *Alroy* in 1832, which boasted of an innovative merging of prose and poetry based on the use of rhyme and rhythm in his romance, reflected his desire that he be taken seriously as an artist, even though he was writing prose.[13] Disraeli evokes Shelley's words to convince both his father and himself of the importance of his creative endeavours. When Herbert says of Cervantes' work, '[Cervantes] is the same to this age as if he had absolutely wandered over the plains of Castile and watched in the Sierra Morena', he is applying Shelley's words that only a poem is 'universal, and contains within itself the germ of a relation to whatever motives or actions have place in the possible varieties of human nature' (IV, i).[14] Through his character, Disraeli is claiming the same position for prose as Shelley did for poetry.[15] When Herbert quotes Shelley, Disraeli the novelist includes himself in the vast claims for imaginative literature implied by the invocation of Shelley's spirit. Nor is it accidental that Herbert is moved, not by a poet's, but by a novelist's vision of the golden age. It is Disraeli's position that the *imaginative writer*, not merely the poet, combines the roles of legislator and prophet. He would certainly have insisted on the inclusion of novelists in the following statement that Shelley made of poets in *A Defence of Poetry*: 'For he not only beholds intensely the present as it is, and discovers those laws according to which present things ought to be ordered, but he beholds the future in the present, and his thoughts are the germs of the flower and the fruit of latest time.'[16]

Yet in *Venetia* and *Henrietta Temple* (1836), more conventional artistic control and a more consistent point of view are achieved at the sacrifice of the double focus upon the teller as well as the tale that was so prominent a feature of the early novels. In the mid-1830s Disraeli moved from rewriting Byron in prose to more traditional concepts of prose fiction. Disraeli was influenced by the eighteenth-century novel with its uneasy balance between romance and realism, between comedy and tragedy, between seriousness and burlesque, between satire and sentimentalism. The *artistic* influence of Byron, particularly *Don Juan* with its undisciplined and extravagant speaker and impulsive and uninhibited energy, virtually disappears (although that influence had played a much lesser role in *Contarini Fleming* and *Alroy* than in *Vivian Grey* and *The Young Duke*). In these middle novels Disraeli wanted his narrator to assume the stance of worldliness and urbanity that he now thought appropriate for tales of aristocratic manners and passions. Such a stance contrasts with the passionate excesses of Lord Cadurcis, Marmion Herbert and Ferdinand Armine, and of course implicitly comments on their extravagant behaviour until each of these characters is modified by experience to conform to the narrator's values. On occasion, Disraeli's former propensity to present himself in his novels as a dramatized personality and performer overwhelms the ironic detachment that he sought.

III

Disraeli's romanticism deeply influenced his political fiction. Writing on Disraeli's imaginary voyage *Popanilla* (1828), Lucien Wolf has remarked:

Indeed, it is in the anti-Benthamism and anti-Ricardoism of *Popanilla* that we have the first glimpse of the Romanticism which afterwards inspired the 'Young England' party, and was turned into channels of practical politics by the struggle against Peel's surrender to Free Trade. There are whole pages of *Popanilla* – especially Chapter IV – which are clearly the raw material out of which was ultimately evolved the anti-Utilitarianism preached by Sidonia in *Coningsby* and by Gerard in *Sybil.*[17]

Although later Disraeli became an advocate of particular positions that he satirizes in *Popanilla* such as the Corn Laws and the colonial system, this early novella foreshadows many of Young England's values, especially its dislike of materialism and expedience. For example, *Tancred* develops *Popanilla's* disdain for a culture that reduces man to a machine and that glorifies reason and logic at the expense of mystery and imagination.

As Blake has remarked, Young England was 'a sort of nostalgic escape from the disagreeable present to the agreeable but imaginary past'.[18] Young England was a movement in the early 1840s which despised utilitarianism, middle-class liberalism and centralized government. It sought to return England to the feudal and monarchal antecedents of its national youth. While its other two leaders, George Smythe and Lord John Manners, were primarily young aristocrats, Disraeli was the central figure. Now close to forty, Disraeli for the first time had some political importance. George Smythe was a man of great gifts, but uncertain judgement, who was at least in part the model for Coningsby. Lord John Manners lacked Smythe's extraordinary potential and scintillating intellect, but he was a kindly, high-principled man who epitomized the integrity and idealism of Young England. Manners was the model for Lord Henry Sidney in *Coningsby.* Alexander Baillie-Cochrane, the next most prominent figure after Disraeli, Smythe and Manners, was the model for Buckhurst in *Coningsby.* A Scotsman of Disraeli's age, Baillie-Cochrane played a lesser role but was the fourth member of the founding group. Although Disraeli wrote that he was 'the leader of a party-chiefly of the youth, & new members',[19] Young England was never a numerical factor in parliament, only including about a dozen at best; even Disraeli, Smythe, Manners and Baillie-Cochrane, the four central members, did not always agree on major issues.

They sought to form a party composed of the younger, more vigorous members of the Tory party, but Young England never became more than a small group of like-minded Tories who, as Disraeli put it in the 1870 general preface to the collected edition of his novels, 'Living much together, without combination ... acted together'.[20] Although on occasion some of Peel's supporters voted with them on certain issues, Young England never achieved a specific legislative programme. For example, Young England stood firmly for the Corn Laws, even after Peel had begun to waver. As Stephen R. Graubard has written, 'Young England took upon itself the task of bringing the party back to a greater consciousness of its historic traditions.'[21] Typical not only of the kind of community for which Young England longed, but of the romantic nostalgia that formed the basis of their political programme, are the following lines by Manners:

> Each knew his place – king, peasant, peer, or priest –
> The greater owned connexion with the least;
> From rank to rank the generous feeling ran
> And linked society as man to man.[22]

Young England argued that the poor should be cared for by conscientious aristocrats and a responsive Church rather than administrative structures created by Poor Laws. They idealized the role of the pre-Reformation Catholic Church in creating community ties and in fulfilling community responsibilities.

For Disraeli, Young England was a sustaining personal fiction, a political programme that provided an alternative not only to Chartism and utilitarianism, but to the practical considerations of advancing his position. Like Disraeli's dream that a coterie of youth would revive England, *Coningsby* reflects a mixture of idealism, fantasy and escapism. But in *Sybil* Disraeli comes to grips with the economic deprivation experienced by the rural and urban poor and seems to be ambivalent about the notion that one heroic man can make a substantive difference.[23]

By the time Disraeli wrote *Tancred* in 1846, Young England had virtually disintegrated following the controversy over funding the Maynooth Seminary in late 1845. Disraeli sharply disagreed with Peel's proposal to increase the government grant to Maynooth, whose purpose was the education of Catholic priests. Influenced by the Oxford Movement and their family ties to Ireland, Smythe and Manners supported Peel. Disraeli took the opposing position but used the debate as the occasion for a devastating attack on Peel, whom he had never forgiven for passing him over for office in 1841 and whose conduct and politics he attacked in *Coningsby* and *Sybil*. Disraeli's Young England novels – *Coningsby, or The New Generation* (1844); *Sybil, or The Two Nations* (1845); *Tancred, or The New Crusade* (1847) – are a radical departure from his earlier fiction. Politics were more than a vocation for Disraeli. In the 1840s, his political life seemed to fulfil for him what George Eliot speaks of in *Scenes of Clerical Life* as 'that idea of duty, that recognition of something to be lived for beyond the mere satisfaction of self'. For the first time since he began his parliamentary career in 1837, he returned to fiction because he understood the potential of presenting his ideas in an imaginative framework.

Disraeli's general preface to his novels, written in 1870, should be understood as a retrospective statement of intention, not as a substantive critical commentary. In that preface, he writes:

> The derivation and character of political parties; the condition of the people which had been the consequence of them; the duties of the Church as a main remedial agency in our present state; were the principal topics which I intended to treat, but I found they were too vast for the space I had allotted to myself.
>
> They were all launched in 'Coningsby' but the origin and condition of political parties, the first portion of the theme, was the only one completely handled in that work.
>
> Next year (1845), in SYBIL, OR THE TWO NATIONS, I considered the condition of the people ... In recognizing the Church as a powerful agent in the previous development of England ... it seemed to me that the time had arrived when it became my duty to ... consider the position of the descendants of that race who had been the founders of Christianity. Familiar as we all are now with such themes, the House of Israel being now freed from the barbarism of mediaeval misconception, and judged like other races by their contributions to the existing sum of human welfare, and the general influence of race on human action being universally recognized as the key of history, the difficulty and hazard of touching for the first time on such topics cannot now be easily appreciated. But public opinion recognized both the truth and sincerity of these views, and, with its sanction, in TANCRED OR THE NEW CRUSADE, the third portion of the Trilogy, I completed their development.

Disraeli's trilogy presents both a political geography and a historical survey of England, and simultaneously suggests how England could experience a political and moral rebirth.

Despite the 1870 preface, we should not forget the intensely personal tone of his later letters. The following comment is quite typical: 'My books are the history of my life – I don't mean a vulgar photograph of incidents, but the psychological development of my character.'[24] Like Tennyson, Carlyle, Mill and Newman, Disraeli responded with a desperate search for absolutes to a world of moral turmoil. That Disraeli's narrators and major characters speak *ex cathedra* in generalizations and abstractions may derive from his desire to emulate in the fabric of his fiction the scope and seriousness of Victorian philosophical and religious tracts. The trilogy of the 1840s is his *Apologia*. Behind the dramatization of the education of Tancred, Coningsby and Egremont lies Disraeli's quest for the principles with which he could structure his public life. He continually asserted dogma to convince himself of its value although, as with Newman, the nature of the dogma was continually in flux. The political ideals discovered by his Young England heroes became, for a time, the tenets of his own political and moral creed.

Disraeli's motives for writing the trilogy were complex. He undoubtedly wanted to articulate political and moral principles, in part no doubt to erase the notoriety that he had acquired, owing to, as Blake puts it, 'the continued refusal of the *Quarterly Review* even to mention his name, the alleged tergiversations in his early political career, his rickety finances, the extravagancies of his novels ... his mysterious half-foreign appearance, and the virulent abuse, much of which stuck, hurled at him by malignant journalists'.[25] He also wanted to establish the importance of Judaism to western civilization.[26] He created Sidonia as a mouthpiece to *argue* for the historical significance of the Jewish people in *Coningsby* and in the first two books of *Tancred*. But it is Tancred's pilgrimage to Jerusalem for 'Asian spirituality' and his discovery of the Hebraic basis of Christianity that *dramatize* Disraeli's intense personal need to reconcile his Jewish origins with the Christian religion. He believed that Christianity was completed Judaism, although he may have unconsciously taken this position because of his need to justify his own conversion. He argued in *Lord George Bentinck* (1852) that a Jew converted to Christianity professes the 'whole Jewish religion and believes in Calvary as well as Sinai'.[27] In his study of Disraeli's Jewish aspect, Cecil Roth writes:

> But it seems as though the Christianity which he professed, quite sincerely, in his own mind was not that of the established Church, but a Judaic ethical monotheism, of which the Jew Jesus was the last and greatest exponent. As he put it, Christianity was a developed Judaism and Judaism a preparation for Christianity. Jesus was the ideal scion of the Jewish people ... in whose teachings the Mosaic faith received its culmination, the New Testament being the perfection, and climax, of the Old.[28]

Disraeli's self-confidence in part depended upon his belief that the Jews deserved esteem as an especially gifted *race*. Often, and with considerable justification, Disraeli is accused of political expedience and intellectual legerdemain. But the defence of Jews was an article of faith. Disraeli risked his chances for leadership when he insisted in 1847 that his friend Baron Lionel de Rothschild be allowed to take his seat in parliament without taking the parliamentary oath 'on the true faith of a Christian'.[29] On that occasion, he invoked arguments similar to those that appeared both in *Tancred* and later in *Lord George Bentinck* to support the Baron's position.

The trilogy explored the possibilities of heroism in an age which is epitomized for Disraeli by Vavasour, a secondary character in *Coningsby*, who 'is the quintessence of order, decency, and industry' and who complacently expresses the Benthamite creed that civilization is 'the progressive development of the faculties of man' (*Tancred*, II, xiv). Coningsby's ambition is admirable and necessary because the adult world into which he is born is corrupt and hypocritical. For Disraeli, as for Carlyle, ambition is not self-intoxication, but a noble quality that directs a man to follow in the heroic footsteps of the great men of history.[30]

In each novel of the trilogy, Disraeli's persona speaks not as a member of parliament, which Disraeli had been since 1837, but as an enlightened and perceptive aristocrat. One implicit premise of the trilogy is that a prophetic voice could arouse the sensibilities of his fellow aristocrats to the spiritual and economic plight of the people and to the need for restoring the monarchy and the Church to their former dignity. Disraeli's surrogate self, the narrator, is implicitly one of those 'primordial and creative mind[s] ... [that could] say to his fellows: Behold, God has given me thought; I have discovered truth; and you shall believe!' (*Coningsby*, II, iii). The comprehensive political consciousness of the speaker is the intellectual and moral position toward which the hero of each volume of the trilogy finally develops. The narrator empathetically traces the quest of the potential hero (Egremont, Coningsby and Tancred) to discover the appropriate values by which he can order his own life and fulfil the prominent public role that he feels himself obliged to play. (The complete absence of irony toward the protagonist occasionally has the negative effect of neutralizing Disraeli's wit and vivacity.)

According to Disraeli's intended argument, each of the protagonists overcomes dubiety and anxiety because he convinces himself that he possesses the unique intellectual and moral potential to shape not merely his own life but the very fabric of historical process. Each protagonist's quest is conceived as a heroic quest to discover the values essential for a new breed of political leaders who will recognize the supremacy of the monarchy and the importance of serving the common people. Coningsby's ambition and self-confidence, Egremont's compassion and consciousness of the miseries of others, and Tancred's spiritual faith and willingness to act on behalf of his beliefs are the ideals to which others (and *others* for Disraeli meant his aristocratic audience and hence potential political leaders) must strive. The quest for values takes place against the background of Tadpole's and Taper's political expedience; the self-indulgence and arrogance of such aristocrats as Marney and Monmouth; the spiritual emptiness of entire communities such as Wodgate; and the recurring periods of poverty. The trilogy satirizes a decadent aristocracy lacking in vitality and a sense of responsibility, and a parliamentary system that seems divorced from the people for whom it is responsible. The satire also focuses on those who, despite their pretensions, are without principles or faith: men like Rigby, Morley and Fakredeen, who betray the protagonists.

Tancred develops some of the social and political themes begun in *Coningsby* and *Sybil*. Tancred journeys to Jerusalem after convincing himself of the superficiality of contemporary English civilization and the futility of its politics. The political world of the Middle East parodies the intrigues of English politics; the major difference is that weapons rather than votes are the method of settling political disagreements. Syria's 'history' parodies England's: civil war followed the deposition of a strong monarch and, when the feudal (or territorial) system was endangered, monarchist sentiments revived. In the Lebanese mountains, Tancred discovers the mirror of Young England's dreams: 'a proud, feudal aristocracy; a conventual establishment ... a free and armed peasantry ... [and] bishops worthy of the Apostles' (*Tancred*, IV, xii). Predictably, the Young Syria Movement appeared in 1844 to 'profess nationality as their object' and to plead for 'the restoration of the house of Shehaab' (*Tancred*, V, i). And Fakredeen epitomizes the cynical aristocrats and hypocritical politicians of *Coningsby* and *Sybil* who, while espousing principles, practise self-interest. The narrator tells us that 'It was his profession and his pride to simulate and to dissemble' (III, vi). Although he is temporarily enraptured by Tancred's plans, Fakredeen lacks the moral energy to adhere to a consistent code of conduct, and once he considers the benefits of a dynasty founded on a marriage between himself and Astarte, he is not troubled by his betrayal of Tancred.

Tancred is a fictional version of the Victorian spiritual autobiography, epitomized by Newman's *Apologia*, Carlyle's *Sartor Resartus* and Tennyson's *In Memoriam*. Along with *Tancred*, several examples of the genre were published within a few years, including Charles Kingsley's *Yeast* (1848), James Anthony Froude's *Shadows of the Clouds* (1847), and Newman's *Loss and Gain* (1848). Mimesis in *Tancred* is based on entirely different assumptions from the rest of the trilogy. As in *Popanilla* and *Alroy*, verisimilitude of time and space is virtually absent. *Tancred* reflects Disraeli's continued admiration of romance plots. Like Byron's heroes, Childe Harold and Don Juan, or Scott's heroes in his historical romances, Tancred inhabits an imagined world where diurnal details rarely intrude into his quest.[31] An imaginary voyage, *Tancred* is loosely held together by the hero's physical journey which introduces him to incredible people and fantastic places. The novel begins in the present tense in England, but Tancred's crusade is virtually a journey backward in time; he discovers remote cultures which have religious beliefs and political customs that were in 1847 regarded condescendingly by Christian England: Judaism, pagan worship of the Greek gods and feudalism.

Disraeli may well have believed that the art of *Tancred* demonstrated the 'imagination' that was lacking in England. As Blake notes, 'Disraeli ... belongs to the same strand in nineteenth-century English thought as Coleridge and Carlyle, the romantic, conservative, organic thinkers who revolted against Benthamism and the legacy of eighteenth-century rationalism.'[32] As early as *Popanilla*, *Contarini Fleming* and *Alroy*, we can see his distrust of excessive logic and reason. In *Sybil*, Morley illustrates the emptiness of utilitarianism; once his own private designs are thwarted, the greatest good for the greatest number has little appeal, and repressed and unacknowledged atavistic impulses manifest themselves.

Tancred is the most introspective of the trilogy's heroes, a man who confides in no one and bears the burdens of self-consciousness most acutely; neither drawing room activities nor contemporary political issues of the day interest him. As a romantic hero, he pursues what Geoffrey H. Hartman calls 'the lure of false ultimates' in the expectation that he will find a 'final station for the mind'.[33] Tancred *never* finds the resting place he seeks. The process of searching for 'ultimates' is his consuming activity. Because he does not really find solace or direction from the angel's visitation, the novel's second half dissolves into a spiritual myth of Sisyphus where each new adventure puts him back at the start.

Disraeli's belief that a man could not fulfil himself in private life, but rather required a position with defined responsibilities to give life meaning, is contrary to the emphasis on private fulfilment through love or communion with nature that pervades nineteenth-century literature. As Robert Langbaum has written, 'The real man, the romanticist felt, was not to be got at through his social relations – his actions, his manners – there he was superficial, he was playing a role. The real man was to be got at when he was alone, in nature, when he was "musing" – thinking, that is, by free association – or when he was having visions or dreams.'[34] Egremont fulfils himself as a public man. Although not possessing the heroic potential or personal magnetism of Coningsby or Tancred, he is a more successful representative of the aristocratic resurgence for which Disraeli hoped, because he continually demonstrates his integrity, sympathy and judgement.

Within *Sybil*, we feel a narrowing of the distance between Egremont and the narrator, as Egremont develops into the kind of man the narrator admires. Egremont is at first an aristocratic spectator observing Sybil's world, a world from which he is excluded by virtue of class and sympathy. In the first stage of Egremont's metamorphosis after he assumes the identity of Franklin, he is rather like a Wordsworthian stereotype when he responds to the sublimity of rural life. But after his self-enforced rustication, he sympathizes with the physical conditions and psychological lives of others and does not, like Coningsby at times and Tancred always, seek refuge in vague abstractions. He develops a concept of self-responsibility that places service to the people before gratification of personal desires.

Sidonia – note the play on Disraeli's name – is a romantic version of the Jewish polymath: if Disraeli the man of action imagines himself as Coningsby, Disraeli the artist views himself as Sidonia, the Jewish polymath who sees more profoundly than his fellows. If Coningsby embodies the romance of youthful political success, Sidonia is the romance of the Jewish outsider who, despite having no position in government, is one of the most important, sophisticated and knowledgeable figures in all Europe. His role is the one that Disraeli most enjoys imagining. Brilliant, worldly and influential, he becomes Coningsby's intellectual guide.

Sidonia articulates Disraeli's creed; Coningsby evolves into the man who will carry it out. Often Coningsby articulates ideas that he has learned directly from Sidonia; in turn, they become the thoughts of Coningsby's friends and followers. Sidonia enables Disraeli to dramatize Coningsby's education within the novel's action; for Coningsby is profoundly affected by his conversations with a man who not only knows the history of civilization but is familiar with the intricacies and secrets of every European government. Moreover, Sidonia enables Disraeli to make provocative statements without fully committing himself to them.

Through Sidonia Disraeli not only establishes the position of Jews, but acknowledges his own Jewish heritage. His readers would have recognized immediately that the first three letters of Sidonia's name reversed the author's and that Sidonia, like his creator, had a three-syllable name with the accent on the second syllable. Disraeli describes Sidonia the way he himself might have been described by one who was favourably disposed to him: 'He was ... of a distinguished air and figure; pale, with an impressive brow, and dark eyes of great intelligence ... He spoke in a voice of remarkable clearness; and his manner, though easy, was touched by a degree of dignity that was engaging' (III, i). Sidonia instils in Coningsby the belief that a young man can be a great leader and that heroism and greatness are possibilities for him.

IV

Disraeli's ultimate romantic triumph was his political career. Before he was elected to parliament, he spoke of the day when he would become prime minister. His career was predicated on his ability to imagine himself in a position and then to find the resources to attain that position. Disraeli's career tells us something about the continuities between life and art. Disraeli used his novels not only to create the political figure he became but also to define his essential character and personality. His first six novels – *Vivian Grey, The Young Duke, Contarini Fleming, Alroy, Henrietta Temple* and *Venetia* – were outlets for his fantasies, fears, hopes and doubts. The novels provided him with the sense that he could impose an order on the recalcitrant flow of events. Were it not for his first six novels – his romances about young heroes – written prior to his election to parliament, he would not have discovered the self he wanted to be. Indulging his fantasy in heroic exploits and passionate love affairs provided a necessary outlet for his frustrated energies. Moreover, he objectified in his protagonists parts of himself that he wanted to exorcize, while creating in his more mature narrator the balance, judgement and character he required to fulfil his political and social ambitions. The early novels compensated for the disappointment at not achieving prominence. In the late 1820s and 1830s, he felt that, although he had aristocratic blood and deserved to be esteemed on the grounds of birth as well as merit, his heritage and accomplishments were patronized. As Paul Smith puts it:

> What relieved the tension between limitless aspiration and circumscribed prospects was the romantic mode of thought and feeling, whose cult of introspection, fascination with 'genius', and sense of preternatural vision presented Disraeli not simply with a handy set of stylistic conventions but with a pattern of self-realization and with the means to transcend the limitation and frustrations of his position through the power of the romantic imagination to transform the terms of relation to the external world. To Disraeli, with that sense of apartness from his fellows which he seems to have acquired very early in life, romanticism offered a home, membership of a European confraternity, a sense of special election and spiritual aristocracy which may have been a translation of the chosenness he felt, or came to feel, as a Jew.[35]

Dandyism was another kind of self-dramatization for Disraeli; it fulfilled his need for public attention at the same time as it enabled him to show himself that he was unique. His arrogance, self-assertiveness and flamboyance made him unpopular; yet his novels and his behaviour show that he needed to have love and companionship. When Disraeli created characters within fiction, he created, tested and often discarded tentative models for the various selves which he brought to the disparate social and private roles he was called upon to play.

Disraeli's compulsion for self-dramatization, extravagance and hyperbole finds an outlet in his political career. When, after he was first elected to parliament in 1837, he required a forum to articulate his social, political and spiritual principles, he returned to fiction and wrote the Young England trilogy – *Coningsby, Sybil* and *Tancred.* The trilogy was a testing ground for his political and moral philosophy. Young England itself was another of Disraeli's romantic fictions and, like his novels, enabled him to voice extravagant aspects of his complex and often contradictory political views. As the climax to the trilogy, *Tancred* emphasizes the need to discover faith and mystery as the bases for political health and proposes a theocracy as the way to reunite man with God and to make government 'again divine'. But *Tancred* is a fairy tale; even in the trilogy, except for most of *Sybil,* Disraeli is still using his novels as escapes from the frustrating world of responsibilities. When he actually achieved power, he ignored the romantic, visionary nostalgic tenets of Young England. Even in these final novels, his personality looms as larger than life. Just as he created a splendid public figure who lived a fantastic career, he created in all his novels characters who often play roles, adopt disguises, and undergo radical transformations of status and personality. His novels, like his public career, are about the *art* of creating life.

3

Disraeli's crucial illness

CHARLES RICHMOND AND JERROLD M. POST, MD

When every allowance is made for the good fortune Disraeli enjoyed, and the assets he possessed during his climb up the 'greasy pole', it remains one of the most remarkable phenomena of the nineteenth century that a Jewish, middle-class, literary *parvenu* became prime minister of Britain at the height of its imperial power. This was the achievement of a powerful man – Lytton Strachey called him 'formidable – one of the most formidable men who ever lived'.[1] Disraeli was a consummate politician; a superb debater, unrivalled as a manager of men; and even his enemy Gladstone recognized his 'strength of will; his long-sighted consistency of purpose ... his remarkable power of self-government; and ... his great parliamentary courage'.[2] But he was also debilitated by a nervous illness between the ages of twenty-two and twenty-seven, which has received scant consideration from his eighty or so biographers.[3] In this chapter, we hazard the first inter-disciplinary explanation.

Disraeli's illness is comprehensible in the context of his complex, narcissistic personality.[4] He aspired to greatness from an early age; and the foundations of his dreams of glory and grandiose aspirations can be traced to his childhood. His relations with his mother were apparently disturbed. The relative absence of her name from his private papers, correspondence and memoirs indicates, as Robert Blake puts it, that he almost 'wished to obliterate her memory'.[5] His sister noticed the omission from the essay on their father which Disraeli prefixed to the collected edition of the latter's works, and protested: 'I do wish that one felicitous stroke, one tender word had brought our dear Mother into the picture.'[6] Perhaps there is a hint in *Contarini Fleming*, Disraeli's 'Psychological Auto-

Biography', which he published at the age of twenty-seven, as to what went wrong in their relationship.

It is evident from Disraeli's so-called 'Mutilated Diary' that this novel, together with *Alroy* and *Vivian Grey*, was autobiographical. 'My works', he wrote, 'are the embodification [sic] of my feelings. In Vivian Grey I have pourtrayed [sic] my active and real ambition. In Alroy, my ideal ambition. The P. R. [Psychological Romance, the alternative title of *Contarini Fleming*] is a developmt. of my poetic character. This trilogy is the secret history of my feelings. I shall write no more about myself.'[7] In writing confessional and self-revelatory books, Disraeli was adopting a style which became the fashion after the publication of the autobiographical works of Goethe and Rousseau, the purpose of which was to attain self-knowledge. Scholars as acute as Daniel Schwarz and Robert Blake have noticed the close correspondence between Disraeli's life and fiction; and lacking real creative imagination and, necessarily in his twenties, experience, Disraeli was heavily dependent on recycling his inner life in the early novels. It will be seen that the trilogy and *The Young Duke*, another work of autobiographical import, are used here to add corroborative weight and colour to the analysis, and that the diagnosis can be made out on the basis of external evidence alone.

Contarini tells us that his stepmother treats him with 'the etiquette of maternal duty ... But for the rest, she was cold and I was repulsive, and she stole from the saloon, which I rendered interesting by no infantile graces'(I, ii). Her neglect causes serious depressive fits, during which he scarcely moves, speaks or eats for days (I, iv). Because he is unhappy and feels unloved he is 'sedentary and silent' and gains, as a consequence, 'the reputation of stupidity'(I, ii). Disraeli may have felt that his mother was cold, unreceptive and sceptical about his prodigious genius. '[T]ho' a *clever boy* ... no "prodigy"', was her assessment only months before he became ill; and it would appear that he never forgave her. Yet, as Robert Blake observes, the more Disraeli's personality, particularly in his relation with women, is scrutinized, the more clear it becomes that he felt the deprivation of maternal affection deeply.[8]

Crucial to the development of healthy self-esteem is the loving attention of the admiring mother who dotes on her child's achievements. The child raised by a cold mother so self-absorbed as to ignore the needs of her own progeny experiences a deep and profound wound to his self-concept, leaving him hungering throughout his life for the admiring adulation he did not receive as a child. This cold neglect may lead to a famished self that can entail a compensatory grandiose self. The trajectory of Disraeli's life suggests he was early set on this quest for compensatory adulation.

At a school in Epping Forest, at around the age of thirteen, Disraeli may have suffered some sort of rebuff on account of his foreign looks or experienced an isolation imposed by anti-Semitism.[9] A low, vengeful ambition emerged at this time, together with feelings of social inferiority,[10] and compensatory dreams of glory. In *Contarini Fleming* he writes:

> I entertained at this time a deep conviction that life must be intolerable unless I were the greatest of men ... Indeed ... I should have killed myself had I not been supported by my ambition, which now each day became more quickening, so that the desire of distinction and astounding action raged in my soul; and when I recollected that, at the soonest, many years must elapse before I could realize my ideas, I gnashed my teeth in silent rage and cursed my existence (I, viii–ix).[11]

After what may have been a rebuff, he left school to spend the next year or so in private study, and the following three years were spent as a solicitor's clerk. Shortly before his twentieth birthday, he became increasingly bored with the law, and decided to leave it. It is not quite true to say, as Disraeli suggests, that he entirely abandoned the law at this time – he attended Lincoln's Inn sporadically until around the age of twenty-six, when he petitioned to have his name removed. But his decision to abandon its settled study and practice brought him into conflict with his father.

> My father [Disraeli wrote later in life] was very warm about this business: the only time in his life in which he exerted authority, always, however, exerted with affection. I had some scruples, for even then I dreamed of Parliament ... I became pensive and restless, and before I was twenty I was obliged to terminate the dream of my father ... My father made a feeble effort for Oxford, but the hour of adventure had arrived.[12]

There is no doubt that Disraeli loved and admired his father. 'Kind soul!' he wrote of him in *The Young Duke,* 'beneficent, beloved friend! Oh! Let me die the traitor's death ... if ever I do love thee not; if I wear not thy image in my inmost core' (II, viii). He appears to have internalized much of his moral and philosophic outlook, as is manifest in the voices of Baron Fleming and Horace Grey in the autobiographical trilogy. Early on, he imbibed much of his father's view of history and politics.[13] He wrote in his

'Mutilated Diary' that his father was one of 'the few men from whose conversation I have gained wisdom'.[14]

Isaac had become famous as a literary anecdotalist, but had failed in the higher reaches of the world of letters. Perhaps this is why he insisted that his son become a man of business. He wrote in the *Literary Character* that, 'The career of genius is rarely that of happiness; and the father, who himself may not be insensible to glory, dreads lest his son be found among the obscure multitude … who must expire at the barriers of mediocrity.'[15] Perhaps he was concerned that his brilliant and veering son would be a drain on his fixed and limited income. Moreover, the educational theorists of the eighteenth century, with whom Isaac was more than familiar, advocated practical careers for their students: Emile is to be a carpenter, and Wilhelm Meister a doctor. But, for whatever reason he insisted upon the law, he created a conflict in his son which would soon have a deleterious effect.

In a hurry to become a conventional success, Benjamin now embarked on the 'hour of adventure'. In the memorandum on his legal career quoted above, he said that he 'dreamed of Parliament' at this time; and Vivian Grey, after studying politics, 'panted for the Senate'(I, viii). But rather than obtaining his 'magnificent ends' (I, ix) by the ordinary expedient of offering himself for election, as he did when he was 'cured' of his illness, he somehow saw possession of a fortune as a condition precedent to achieving his object. He began a series of wild, reckless and disastrous speculations in mining stocks, which loaded him with debts he bore for much of his life. He and two partners went 'short', or wagered that the stocks of companies created to exploit Latin American mines would fall in value. Their instinct was correct, because most of them were hollow concerns. But when Canning cleared the way for these companies to exploit the mines, in the prevailing mood of speculative mania, the value of their stocks in some cases quadrupled in a matter of days. Disraeli and his partners now went 'long' just as the shares achieved their optimum value; and over the next six months their prices steadily declined.

To recoup his losses, Disraeli wrote three long and mendacious pamphlets at great speed, puffing the worthless or fraudulent securities in which he had invested. The first of these pamphlets, which ran to nearly one hundred pages, was proffered for 'the benefit of the public';[16] and he described himself in the second as 'one whose opinions are unbiased by self-interest'.[17]

The pamphlets failed to sway investors; and Disraeli decided to establish a newspaper called *The Representative* with his father's publisher, John Murray. This also failed. But it is a measure of Disraeli's reckless state of mind – Murray complained about his 'unrelenting excitement'[18] – that he made himself liable for one quarter of the capital initially required. It fell to Disraeli to organize the paper, which involved a number of exhausting trips to Scotland to engage an editor, and frenetic correspondence with journalists, lawyers and architects. After four months he complained to his prospective editor, J. G. Lockhart, about being 'utterly exhausted in mind and body'.[19] But what is interesting is Disraeli's indulgence in power fantasies at this time. He told Murray, in a letter written partly in secret code, that Lockhart is 'not to be an Editor of a Newspaper, but the Directeur General of an immense organ' and is to be found a seat in parliament.[20] 'If this point could be arranged', he concluded, 'I have no doubt, that I shall be able to organise, in the interest, with which I am now engaged, a most IMMENSE PARTY, and MOST SERVICEABLE ONE.'[21] Disraeli appears to have envisaged the creation of some sort of Canningite faction, although this probably existed in his mind alone. But behind the facade of the man of business the ulterior ambition can be seen.

Disraeli's association with *The Representative* terminated coincidentally at the time he was to provide his share of the capital. A multiple failure and an insolvent, he began writing the first part of *Vivian Grey* – an 80,000 word novel, which Lucien Wolf speculates was written in around three weeks.[22] Whether or not it was written quite that rapidly, Disraeli called it, in the second part 'as hot and hurried a scetch [sic] as ever yet was penned'(V, i). What is certain is that he showed little sensitivity to the feelings of his former partner, Murray, who is viciously parodied as a 'tipsy nincompoop'.[23] Yet he was himself hypersensitive to the fierce and vituperative attacks on his novel in the press, and relived his mortification through Contarini Fleming's response to a damning review of his 'Manstein', in the 'great critical journal of the North of Europe':

> With what horror, with what blank despair, with what supreme appalling astonishment, did I find myself, for the first time in my life, a subject of the most reckless, the most malignant, and the most adroit ridicule. I was scarified, I was scalped … The criticism fell from my hand. A film floated over my vision; my knees trembled. I felt that sickness of the heart, that we experience in our first scrape. I was ridiculous. It was time to die (II, xv).

As if Disraeli were depleted by the extravagant expenditure of resources, the burst of frenzied activity was succeeded by an emotional breakdown. After completing part II of *Vivian Grey*, Disraeli collapsed at the age of twenty-two; and the next three years of his life were, as Monypenny puts it, 'almost a blank'.[24] He did not fully recover until the age of twenty-seven, just before he entered politics.

Disraeli was treated by a number of doctors, one of whom described his complaint as 'chronic inflammation of the membranes of the brain'.[25] This was a time when 'broad expanses of medical ignorance'[26] still obtained in the study of psychiatry, even though important discoveries were only decades away. In 1853, Robert Carter,[27] a British general practitioner, pointed out the significance of sexual repression in the aetiology of hysteria, anticipating Freud's findings by some forty years. But in the early nineteenth century, British psychiatry manifested a somatic bias;[28] and it was believed that, where the brain, as the neurological 'seat' of illness, became inflamed by 'the accelerated Motion of the Blood', a 'Phrensy'[29] occurred causing, 'acute pain in the head, with intolerance of light and sound; watchfulness, delirium, flushed countenance, and redness of the conjunctiva, or a heavy suffused state of the eyes; quick pulse; frequently spasmodic twitchings or convulsions, passing into somnolency, coma, and complete relaxation of the limbs'.[30] Although the term 'chronic inflammation of the membranes of the brain' has no modern application, and passed out of use long ago, many of the symptoms are consistent with some forms of meningitis – inflammation of the membranes covering the brain – or encephalitis – inflammation of the brain tissue.

'Chronic inflammation of the membranes of the brain' was a frequently diagnosed medical entity in the early nineteenth century – described in medical textbooks, recognized by lay people and dramatized in novels. Ruskin, Carlyle and Poe in reality, and Catherine Linton, Lucy Feverel and Emma Bovary in fiction (amongst others) all apparently suffered from 'brain fever', as it came to be called. William Buchan's popular reference book, *Domestic Medicine* described the causes of the illness as 'sedentary occupations', the most dangerous of which was study, leading to 'undue mental fatigue'[31] and severe emotional shock. For the latter reason the disease appealed to novelists, whose over-excited heroines fall down in dramatic fits when they are jilted in love. The treatments included blood-letting to draw pressure away from the blood-congested brain, ingestion of mercury and application of ammonia compresses to the head.[32]

Disraeli told his solicitor twenty years after the onset of the illness that his physicians had been 'quacks', in whose advice he had taken refuge out of desperation with his languishing condition.[33] Contarini Fleming has 'no confidence in medicine'(IV, iv), and looks upon his doctors 'with suspicion if not contempt'(I, v). Their treatments and prescriptions are unavailing. Contarini exclaims that he was 'bled, blistered, boiled, starved, poisoned, electrified, galvanised; and at the end of a year found myself with exactly the same oppression on my brain'(IV, vi). In the end, Disraeli became his own physician. Influenced by the late eighteenth-century proto-psychoanalytic strain in German literature and medicine while writing *Contarini Fleming*, he came to understand the causes of his illness in a manner very much analogous to that of a modern psychoanalyst.

Disraeli's illness therefore seems an appropriate subject for psychoanalytic treatment, not only because of its duration and severity, but also because, unlike most political men, who tend to be indifferent to their own psychology, he gave an explicitly psychological account of himself. It is true that our subject is an illness suffered 170 years ago by a great man who cannot be examined, and that the evidence is limited and the danger of reductionism great. But as historians we seek to discover the causes of events, using the tools at hand, knowing always that we are falling short of full comprehension. 'Investigations such as this' do not purport to 'explain' genius (as Freud put it),[34] or the extraordinary manner in which it transcends conflicts, only to show how it is shaped by psychological laws, to which even it is subject. Here, the analysis yields a political-psychological model which helps us to understand Disraeli's operative political personality.

The 'hour of adventure' and the collapse which followed need to be comprehended in the context of Disraeli's narcissistic personality. The power fantasies and longing for acclaim; the lies and moral flexibility; the belief that success could be achieved without patient application and the indifference to the feelings of others, yet hypersensitivity to criticism are all to be found in the narcissistic personality.[35] Because narcissists tend to be so self-absorbed, they are frequently unable to empathize with other people. Others are regarded as extensions of the self, who are there only to supply admiration. The undue need to be admired may betray an inner psychological wound caused by a lack of parental love and approval – in Disraeli's case from his mother. Behind the narcissist's grandiose facade is a foundation of doubt and low self-esteem which requires constant reassurance. It is this underlying doubt which makes the narcissist so sensitive to slight, and so vulnerable to reverses and failure.

Driven by dreams of glory, frustrated by the mundane tasks of the clerk, on leaving the practice of law Disraeli acted as if his brain were fevered; and there may well have been a pathophysiological aspect to his frenzied activity. His conduct during the 'hour of adventure' – with the reckless and impulsive nature of his investments, his rash judgement and the fevered pace and vast outpouring of his work – is strongly suggestive of a hypomanic episode, which has the qualities of the manic psychosis of manic-depressive illness but of lesser intensity.

Hypomanic episodes are often triggered by psychological events. Conflicts between Disraeli and his father may well have contributed to the débâcle. The son believed late in life that the 'hour of adventure' had terminated the father's dream. But where the son had been 'wounded' by the mother, retention of his father's love became essential. Contarini Fleming bursts 'into a wild cry' and rushes to his father's arms, after the latter comes into the room in which he has been locked by his stepmother. 'For the first time in my life I felt happy', Contarini exclaims, 'because, for the first time in my life I felt loved'(I, ii). Confrontation with, or resistance to, such a father would have been most difficult; and it is well known that Disraeli dreaded confrontations with Isaac – particularly over money.[36] It is possible that, rather than terminating the dream, he was subconsciously endeavouring to realize it during the 'hour of adventure'. The dream may well have extended beyond the law to something like a man of business. Isaac clearly approved of what 'the young plenipotentiary'[37] was doing during the *Representative* affair; and Disraeli may well have been predisposed to take the 'low path' by those feelings of social inferiority with which he left school. Guilt over terminating Isaac's dream that he become a lawyer, and a desire to retain his esteem, may have contributed to the frantic pace of Disraeli's commercial activities.

But there is perhaps a sense of a dissonance of Disraeli's inner voices during the 'hour of adventure': the daemonic 'grandiose self' demanding 'Napoleonic status', the contempt of his mother condemning him to mediocrity, and the voice of his father enjoining him to be a 'clerk'. As Murray's agent and partner during the *Representative* affair, the cacophony is audible when he closes the business letter quoted above with the exclamation that he is organizing 'a most IMMENSE PARTY, and MOST SERVICEABLE ONE'. Disraeli rationalized what he was doing in business as a step toward admission to parliament. He saw the course of action demanded by his father as condition precedent to what he really desired. Disraeli's father approved of the condition-precedent behaviour, while

Disraeli kept the illusion that he was pursuing his real aim. But by pursuing both, he pursued neither – he was no financier in any case – and this, in conjunction with the distorted judgement associated with hypomania, turned the enterprise into a disaster.

When dreams of glory are disappointed, the wounds to the fragile self-concept are deep; failure for the narcissist is intolerable. Disraeli's failure to achieve recognition and success during the 'hour of adventure' produced a profound narcissistic 'wound'. The resultant blow to his self-esteem precipitated a major clinical depression, characterized by weakness, fatigue, apathy, lack of volition, feelings of despondency and despair – all with a hysteroid flavour, very much the vogue in early Victorian England.

He was now a young man out of work and in debt, who had been held up to public contempt on account of *Vivian Grey*. A dark depression is evident in his writings during his illness, which are punctuated with references to death, and are darkened by doubt and hopelessness. The Vivian Grey of part II, who, like his author, is an enervated character, looks 'for death' (V, i), and speaks of 'a terrible consciousness of meeting death in the flush of life, a moment of suffering, which, from its intense, and novel character, may appear an eternity of anguish'(V, ix). The narrator in *The Young Duke*, written in the third year of his illness, exclaims, 'My life has been but brief, and in that brevity there has been enough of bitterness; yet I have not lived in vain, since I have learnt to die'(II, viii). Vivian Grey of the second part awakens 'to a conviction of the worthlessness of human fortunes', and 'doubting all things, he doubted himself'(V, i). Disraeli's own doubts were rooted in a sense of failure, and in the apprehension that his genius might not be equal to his ends. At their base was a horror of the mediocrity which he feared might be his fate. 'I am at present quite idle', Disraeli wrote during the second year of his illness to his father's friend Sharon Turner, 'being at this moment slowly recovering from one of those tremendous disorganisations which happen to all men at some period of their lives ... Whether I shall ever do anything which may mark me out from the crowd I know not. I am one of those to whom moderate reputation can give no pleasure, and who, in all probability, am incapable of achieving a great one.'[38] Robert Blake rightly says of this passage that 'scorn for a 'moderate reputation' is the quintessence of Disraeli, indeed the key to his character and career';[39] but it is also essential to the narcissistic personality, which, according to Otto

Kernberg, 'divide[s] the world into famous, rich and great people on the one hand, and the despicable, worthless "mediocrity" on the other'.[40] Disraeli now apprehended that he might belong to the latter category and, in short, must have feared that his 'grandiose' conception of himself would never become real. His self-doubt was profound:

> They know not ... [Contarini Fleming exclaims] the cold, dull world ... the agony of doubt and despair which is the doom of youthful genius. To sigh for fame in obscurity is like sighing in a dungeon for light ... But, to feel the strong necessity of fame, and to be conscious that without intellectual excellence life must be insupportable – to feel all of this with no simultaneous faith in your power – these are moments of despondency for which no immortality can compensate (I, xi).

During his illness, Disraeli lived with his family in Bloomsbury Square, kept to his room and saw no one.[41] 'I am so decided an invalid', he wrote in response to an invitation, 'that at present I am obliged to forgo altogether the *deliciae* of society.'[42] He made trips with his family to the countryside during the summers in search of health, and wrote a novel called *Popanilla*, which is very slight. But otherwise he did almost nothing. 'For I am one, though young', the narrator in *The Young Duke* exclaims, 'yet old enough to know, Ambition is a demon; and I fly from what I fear ... Let us once aspire, and madness follows'(II, vii). The situation was evidently grave, and Disraeli's family was concerned: there are hints that both his mind and life were feared for.[43] Toward the end of the third year of his convalescence, after his family had moved permanently to a country house in Buckinghamshire during the summer of that year, his condition apparently improved somewhat. He showed renewed interest in his career, settling first upon a scheme to set up as a country gentleman, which proved abortive, and then determined to take a long tour of the Mediterranean and Near East. To secure the funds for the latter, he wrote *The Young Duke*, which showed more vigour than his two preceding works. He embarked upon his tour in the spring of the fourth year of his illness, or at the age of twenty-five.

In his correspondence with his family during his travels, he describes somatic symptoms – headaches, heart palpitations and fatigue (frequent accompaniments of depression) – and seems to refer to his symptoms collectively as 'the great enemy'.[44] He told his mother that 'the moment I attempt to meditate or combine, to ascertain a question that is doubtful or in anyway to call the greater powers of intellect into play, that moment I feel I am a lost man. The palpitation in my heart and head increases in violence, an indescribable feeling of idiocy comes over me, and for hours I am plunged in a state of the darkest despair.'[45] Consumed with self, the narcissist becomes preoccupied with every symptom. Because he was anxious and depressed he had symptoms; and because he had symptoms he became more deeply depressed and anxious. Contarini Fleming is reduced to 'little better than an idiot' (IV, vi) by his illness, and is terrified by 'the idea that I might live ... in this helpless and unprofitable condition. When I contrasted my recent lust of fame ... and indomitable will, with my present woeful situation of mysterious imbecility, I was appalled by the marvellous contrast'(IV, vi).

Disraeli was only one of many casualties of the high-speed competitive chase after lucre, power and position in the nineteenth century; and the associated state of prostration, to which the middle classes were especially prone, came to be called 'neurasthenia'.[46] The latter was considered to stem from exhaustion of the nervous system – nervous collapse resulting from excessive expenditure of energy. Sufferers from this affliction experienced lassitude, irritability, lack of concentration, worry and hypochondria – all symptoms of depression.

The heart palpitations which Disraeli mentions were also signs of depression and fatigue. He was being treated for them while writing *The Young Duke*, by a fashionable doctor named Bolton, who prescribed digitalis to slow the heart muscle, in addition to cupping. But as Stanley Weintraub suggests, this was to prescribe depressants for depression.[47] Some of Disraeli's symptoms may have been due to digitalis toxicity. He told Benjamin Austen that he had passed a week 'nearly in a *trance* from the digitalis. I sleep literally sixteen out of twenty four hours, and am quite dozy now'.[48] Disraeli mentions two other depressive symptoms: loss of appetite,[49] which he shared with Contarini, and 'very troubled and broken sleep'(IV, iv).

Until his marriage at the age of thirty-four, he suffered mild and sporadic recurrences of his symptoms. Critical conjunctures in his affairs (as he liked to call them) gave him headaches. 'The dear head is it better?' his mistress and surrogate mother, Henrietta Sykes inquired. 'I would be such an affectionate old Nurse to my child and kiss and soothe every pain ... – your Mother.'[50] He fainted in front of the George Inn after travelling all night to a by-election at Aylesbury at the age of thirty-two.[51] But after his marriage, he settled into a rhythm of excitement and exertion during parliamentary sessions, succeeded in the autumns by nervous prostration and retirement amid books and trees at Hughenden. He wrote in middle age to Lady Londonderry, for example, from the latter place that, 'tho' I left town quite well, I had not been eight and forty hours before I found myself in a complete state of nervous prostration, and quite unable to write the shortest letter on the most ordinary business. I suppose it is the sudden cessation of excitement, too complete and abrupt for our mortal frames.'[52]

He was also sometimes subject to sharp swings of mood, according to the vicissitudes of his fortunes – Derby, at an early stage of their partnership, sneered (according to his son's diary) at Disraeli's 'tendency to extremes of alternate excitement and depression'.[53] The major depression described above was preceded by hypomania, which indeed indicates that the tendency to extremes resulted on at least one occasion in a distinct 'bipolar' swing, amounting to a manic-depressive episode. But there was no recurrence of that acute illness – he remained fairly stable after his marriage. The excited exertions during parliamentary sessions suggest the prodigious expenditure of energy by individuals of a hypomanic temperament – stimulated by being in the public eye – only to be followed by a letdown – a kind of depletion syndrome. The periods of nervous prostration at Hughenden were probably recurrent but limited depressions, as it is improbable that the collapses would have lasted as long as they did if they had been based only upon fatigue. But the sheer physical strain of the Commons – always watching in his place, often until the early hours of the morning, in the miasma created by the gas lamps and polluted London air which circulated in the chamber – took its toll upon a constitution which was far from strong. The change of season may also have fuelled his depression – the tendency for the latter to develop in the autumn is quite common in seasonal affective disorder. His spirits sank with 'the fall of the leaf' (as he put it); and being partial to sunshine, he was ultimately killed by the east wind.[54] The collocation of occasional excitement, recurrent but limited depression, often with a seasonal pattern and hypomanic temperament, may have been different aspects of the same underlying 'bipolar' tendency.[55]

But after the disastrous low ebb and illness of his twenties, the pattern of Disraeli's life was in essence that of the successful narcissist. In both his personal relations and political career his exaggerated needs for love, attention, admiration and support reflected a 'hunger for confirming and admiring responses to counteract [his] inner sense of worthlessness and lack of self-esteem'.[56] His intimate relationships seemed calculated to sustain these emotional needs, to compensate for the motherly adoration he never received and thirsted for. His mistresses were almost always older women, whom he cast in the role of adoring mothers. His wife, who was twelve years his senior, also played this part. 'No one attended the funeral [of her brother]', he told her, 'except your child.' 'How is his darling?', he wrote again, 'When will she come to see her child?'[57] Kernberg asserts that the narcissist is impelled by a 'hopeless yearning … for an ideal mother';[58] but Disraeli's wife was a fair approximation of the latter. She gave him the love, admiration and adulation that he required. In the Preface to *Sybil,* he called her 'a perfect wife', and might have added 'mother' – hence the success of the marriage. Indeed, her constant and devoted emotional support was of critical importance in stabilizing him. His female friends also tended to serve as 'mirrors', providing the reflected adulation the narcissistically wounded yearn for. An example is Mrs Brydges Willyams, an elderly Jewess who 'had worshipped him' as Buckle puts it, and was 'absolutely wrapped up in her "dear Dizzi"'.[59] The pattern even applies to his sister. In his letters to her during his rise to power, he invites her to admire him against a backdrop of 'brilliant ball[s]',[60] 'delightful *fête[s]*'[61] and political successes. Reminded in the year he became prime minister that she was not alive to witness his triumph, he declared, 'Ah, poor Sa, poor Sa! We've lost our audience.'[62]

Robert Blake has observed that Disraeli did not seem to enjoy the society of his equals: 'To say that Disraeli only gave his confidence to young men and old women would perhaps be an overstatement, but not an outrageous one.'[63] As a young man, he had patrons like Lord Lyndhurst, and as he grew older he had young admirers like George Smythe, Lord Stanley and Lord Henry Lennox. Disraeli did not enjoy male society much, and wrote in his 'Mutilated Diary' that he made it a rule 'never to throw myself open to men'.[64] It is difficult to think of many friendships with equals that were loyally sustained. In middle age Disraeli came to regard Bulwer-Lytton as a vanity case;[65] and his relationship with Count D'Orsay was somewhat parasitic.[66] It is perhaps a measure of his cynicism, that his friendship with James Clay – the debauched whist expert turned MP – is one of the few friendships to last until late in life. But for the consummate narcissist, after all, there is no equal. The primary function of his relationships is to sustain his self-esteem. He characteristically surrounds himself with admirers who are viewed as extensions of himself and from whom a stream of adulation is required. Because he has difficulty empathizing with other people, and apprehending that others have needs and feelings of their own, loyalty regularly suffers in his relationships.

Disraeli was a solitary figure in the higher echelons of British politics. As a Jewish *étranger* and man of genius, without a public school or Oxbridge background, this was perhaps natural. But it was also exacerbated by an underlying narcissistic incapacity for friendship. Extreme self-absorption and fear of dependence on others (the greatest fear of the narcissist),[67] made him ruthless and exploitative. Contarini Fleming feels 'disgustful mortification' at his 'boyish weakness' in allowing his schoolfriend Musaeus to exercise influence over him, and cuts him with a coldness by which he is astonished (I, viii). We know from the diaries Disraeli kept during the year after he left school, that he had a deeply cynical view of friendship[68] – a view which he seems to have turned into a kind of credo when he began his assault on the fashionable and political worlds. In *The Infernal Marriage*, published at the age of twenty-nine, he wrote that 'those who want to lead ... must never hesitate about sacrificing their friends'(III, ii). From his entry into politics until his marriage he can be seen wheedling for funds here, sponging there – a process delineated in detail by Jane Ridley, who says of his egregious relations with the Austens (whose loans he received but whom he dropped as he made his way in the *beau monde*), that he 'cut old friends with the ruthlessness of an *arriviste*'.[69]

The need for attention, not friendship, was the passion of his life: Disraeli was a dandified exhibitionist who lived for fame and glory. Several months before his departure for the East, he was described by William Meredith as coming up Regent Street 'when it was crowded, in his blue surtout, a pair of military light blue trousers, blue stockings with red stripes and shoes! "The people", he said, "quite made way for me as I passed. It was like the opening of the Red Sea, which I now perfectly believe from experience. Even well-dressed people stopped to look at me." '[70] Such an exhibitionistic posture comes naturally to the narcissist who sees himself as something for others to admire. In addition to simulating folly,[71] Disraeli was, according to Andrew Elfenbein, enacting an 'ersatz Byron', with a suggestion of homosexuality, to gain the attention of, and admission to, fashionable society.[72] When the political adventure landed him on the front bench, the nature of the exhibition changed, and he was obliged to enact the grave statesman. But the purpose of all this self-display was fame. In an early speech he exclaimed, 'I love fame; I love public reputation; I love to live in the eyes of the country.'[73] He told

Bright at Westminster that, 'We come here for fame!'[74] – the implication being that self-glorification takes precedence over the realization of principles or ideas.

Disraeli was possessed of the Machiavellian subtlety,[75] and flexible, self-interested conscience, often found in political narcissists. This was one of the reasons why he was loathed by 'stern' and 'unbending' Victorians like Gladstone, who wrote of him: 'it is a very unsatisfactory state of things to have to deal with a man whose objects appear to be those of personal ambition and who is not thought to have any strong convictions of any kind upon public matters'.[76] To Disraeli, politics was always the 'great game';[77] and if he possessed beliefs or principles, he tended to regard them ironically. When he first stood for parliament, for example, he changed political postures with dizzying alacrity. His attempt to play the Radical and Tory cards at the same election caused Greville to describe him as 'a mighty impartial personage'.[78] Yet when he was attacked as a chicaner, his response was invariably a moral one. The narcissist tends to see himself as scrupulous and principled; and Disraeli seems to have felt an intense compulsion to demonstrate and assert his consistency of political purpose. 'A great mind that thinks and feels', he wrote in his election pamphlet *What is He?*, 'is never inconsistent and never insincere.'[79] Beliefs are instrumental for the narcissist, and as circumstances change, so do his beliefs. The only central and stable belief for the political narcissist is his belief in himself.

The lack of fixed beliefs arose from an unstable and inconsistent sense of psychological identity. During his illness, Contarini Fleming says that he 'was not always assured of my identity, or even existence; for I sometimes found it necessary to shout aloud to be sure that I lived' (IV, v).[80] Disraeli may have got another dose of this because of problems with his Jewishness. As Todd Endelman has shown, the home life of boys with Jewish antecedents, who were baptized and had a foreign name, left them without a strong sense of identity and with an inability 'to cope with even low levels of contempt and exclusion'.[81] This sensation of identity confusion seems to have been conjoined to narcissistically derived feelings of inferiority, which may also have had a nexus with his Jewishness. He wrote in his 'Mutilated Diary' that, 'When I was considered very conceited *indeed*, I was nervous, and had self confidence only by fits.'[82] When Contarini Fleming is asked why he is unhappy, he responds: 'Because I have no one I love – because there is no one who loves me – because I hate this country – because I hate everything – because I hate myself'(I, xxi). After a period of self-discovery and self-invention while travelling in the East, both feelings tended to diminish in intensity.

In order for a nature hypersensitive to criticism to withstand the innumerable darts – racial and otherwise – that were directed at him throughout his career, he developed a mask of cold indifference, which is often seen in political narcissists. A journalist who watched one of Disraeli's early Budget speeches wrote that, 'During a whole week they had baited him; night after night they had derided and ridiculed him … [but] [h]e scarcely seemed to hear, and not at all to feel'; his face wore 'that cold changeless look which, in natures such as his, covers depths of smouldering emotion'.[83] Another observer likened him to 'one of those stone figures of ancient Egypt that embody the idea of motionless quiescence for ever'.[84] Behind this 'expressionless … antique mask'[85] – partly prepared during his travels in the East; part residue of his depressive experience of death, and partly a result of the supernatural self-command he began to cultivate during his illness – he saw himself as dwelling in splendid isolation, and leading a lonely but glorious existence – of which there is some sense, for example, in his life at Hughenden. 'I write this from my lonely Buckinghamshire château', he told Prince Metternich. 'It is sylvan and feudal.'[86]

Notwithstanding the appearance of indifference, vengefulness is fundamental to narcissism. When the narcissist, whose grandiosity rests upon a foundation of insecurity, suffers a narcissistic 'wound', it can cause self-righteous rage and an all-consuming thirst for revenge, based on a thwarted sense of entitlement. Of Disraeli's behaviour at a by-election at the age of twenty-seven, an observer wrote that, 'it would seem as if he thought that he had but to shew himself … in order to be at once the shining light of the day, to be courted as a leader … by political parties'.[87] When he lost, he was supposed to have lashed out: 'The Whigs have cast me off, and they shall repent it.'[88] He responded ferociously at the age of thirty to Daniel O'Connell's anti-Semitic attack, swearing to 'pursue his existence' with an 'unextinguishable hatred'.[89] But the most significant act of vengeance of his early career was exacted, with a *sang-froid* which had previously eluded him, at the expense of Sir Robert Peel, whom he attacked in a series of brilliant philippics, after being denied office in the latter's cabinet at the age of thirty-six. Disraeli's vision may have been obscured by a narcissistic sense of entitlement, and by power fantasies, if he supposed that a raffish literary dandy would be selected by a man like Peel to sit in a cabinet containing only one commoner. After Disraeli took his seat on the front bench, the vengefulness died away. But the mordant wit and sarcastic drawl; the mastery of all of the arts of irony, satire and ridicule remained, and made him a dangerous opponent – one who became perhaps the greatest leader of the opposition in English history.

The attacks on Peel occurred when Disraeli was forty; while he was in the midst of a mid-life transition – a time when he evaluated his achievements. Especially for the narcissist with dreams of glory, when the process of self-measurement indicates he will be unable to achieve his heroic destiny, it can lead to a feeling of profound imbalance and a sense of exaggerated urgency to achieve the place to which he feels entitled. Disraeli was old at that time for a politician who had not held office; and as an outlet for his frustrated energies he had turned to Young England 'to be hero-worshipped by patrician youths',[90] and had written fiction in order to form the national consciousness. He began his assault on Peel with time running out and when he no longer saw a chance of preferment by the latter. When Peel was ousted, and Disraeli found himself on the front bench, he began to experience serenity: 'for now what was out of joint [had] been placed into balance, and the role of greatness [could] be played out … He was at last where he was destined to be.'[91]

As leader, there was in much of what he did more appearance than substance. This is typical of narcissists. There is often a brilliant facade which can be impressive initially but does not tolerate searching examination. Disraeli's unconventional education left him with a taste for the mysterious and the emotional, and a preference for unscientific knowledge, so that, as Bagehot puts it, he did not have 'the gift of thinking out a subject, and when he tries to produce grave thought he only makes platitudes'.[92] He did not possess the legislative mind of his adversary Gladstone. He knew how to create a tone; to appeal to the imagination, to coin ideas for popular consumption. It is as a seer, prophet and man of ideas that he has left his mark on the Conservative party. But his personal legislative achievement is small. Although he was worn out by ill-health, old age and the effort of climbing when he attained power, he never had an inclination for legislative work or detail. His cabinet colleague, the earl of Carnarvon, said of him, 'He detests details … He does no work … M. Corry [Disraeli's private secretary] is in fact Prime Minister.'[93] This disdain for details and reluctance to set themselves systematically to a task is frequently found in narcissists. It is as if they are entitled to be recognized as brilliant by the very nature of their being without having to work at it. Viscount Cranborne noticed that, 'The suggestions for action which he would bring before his colleagues, though brilliantly original and often largely conceived, were discursive, inconsequent, constantly varying, at times self-contradictory.'[94] The prescriptions of the political trilogy – upon which his subsequent political conduct is supposed by some to have been based – are cloudy and vague. Viscount Morley lamented the fact that a man who understood his country's problems brought only the 'childish bathos of Young England'[95] to their solution. The novels reveal an author with a fondness for glittering surfaces; an inability to touch the deep emotions, and a limited capacity to project himself into the lives of others (except, perhaps, the aristocracy). And yet, although he had no university education and, like Lincoln and Churchill, was self-educated, he was almost always dogmatically sure. Walter Allen wrote of Disraeli's novel *Coningsby*: 'It admits of no hesitations, no half-lights; it is completely sure, completely dogmatic. It is the prose of a superb lawyer presenting a case, seemingly holding nothing back.'[96]

Another important manifestation of narcissism in Disraeli's personality upon which we wish to touch, is his belief that he had a special, divinely endowed role to play in history – a messianic strand frequently found in political narcissists. Evidence that Disraeli had messianic self-conceptions as a young man can be found in his novel *Alroy*, which he published at the age of twenty-eight, whose eponymous hero was a Jewish, messianic pretender in twelfth-century Persia. Disraeli wrote in his 'Mutilated Diary' that this work gave expression to his 'ideal ambition'[97] – a statement which has puzzled his biographers.[98] But *Alroy* can be seen as representing the ego ideal for Disraeli – that is the idealized self – because, *inter alia*, of the sense of divine election that it offered him, together with demigod-like status before adoring followers, instead of the hostile or indifferent population, which it was his 'active and real ambition'[99] to dominate. The 'ideal ambition' offered Disraeli a kind of finality in the healing of his 'wound'; and an apotheosis of his 'grandiose self'. It was a means of making himself a god. 'You worship no omnipotent and ineffable essence...', Mrs Felix Lorraine tells Vivian Grey, 'shrined in the secret chamber of your soul, there is an image, before which you bow down in adoration, and that image is – YOURSELF'(III, vi).

Disraeli may well have dreamt of restoring the Jews to Palestine, and seems to have been haunted by the idea later in life.[100] But a career in England rendered this impractical; and his actual political ideas, as articulated in his political trilogy of novels, are of what Vamik Volkan calls a 'reparative'[101] character. The narcissistic leader, according to

Volkan, 'may in fact attempt to uplift',[102] or to heal the 'wounds' of his followers, from whom he wants adoration. Thus, in *Sybil*, Disraeli purports to unify the 'two nations', by restoring the gentlemen of England, rallying around a real throne, to their rightful position as leaders of the people, while expelling the parasitic bourgeois. In *Coningsby*, the arid bourgeois liberalism of Sir Robert Peel is to be supplanted by recurrence to the Tory populism of Lord Bolingbroke. And in *Tancred*, the Victorian crisis of faith is to be resolved by the Hebrew prophetic revelation of the 'great Asian mystery'(II, xi).

By uplifting his followers, Volkan asserts, the narcissistic leader 'strengthens the cohesiveness and stability of his grandiose self by idealizing a group of others whom he then includes in an idealized extension of himself'.[103] This process of idealization began early in Disraeli, who told his father at the age of twenty-one that, 'I feel now that it is not prejudice, when I declare that England – is worth all the world together.'[104] In *The Young Duke*, he admires what is ideal in England, while urging the expulsion of his whipping boy, the bourgeois utilitarians:

> Oh, England! – Oh! My country ... I am proud to be thy child. Thy noble laws have fed with freedom a soul that ill can brook constraint ... In thy abounding tongue my thoughts find music; and with the haughty fortunes of thy realm my destiny would mingle!– What Rome and Carthage were, thou art conjoined my country! ... Earth has none like unto thee, thou Queen of universal waters! ... Oh! my countrymen ... Feel – feel, that wealth is but a means, and power an instrument. Away then, with the short-sighted views of harsh utility! (III, xviii).

Disraeli believed passionately in the greatness of England, as he believed in his own greatness. He admired the genius of its institutions, and desired to uphold the stability of its aristocratic settlement, while asserting its imperial influence in the world. As Salisbury said of him, 'Zeal for the greatness of England was the passion of his life.'[105] Isaiah Berlin noticed Disraeli's tendency as an outsider to over-idealize the community from which he was excluded;[106] but it is evident that it was also as a narcissist that he did so.

Narcissistic personalities often have a hysteroid tinge; and this was the case with Disraeli. His personality was self-dramatizing and flamboyant.[107] After the 'wounding' by his mother, Contarini Fleming is subject to visions and fantasies, which, at the age of eight, are supplanted by madness 'for the playhouse'(I, v).

I had now a pursuit, [Contarini declares] for when I was not a spectator at the theatre, at home I was an actor ... Books more real than fairy tales and feudal romances had already made me muse over a more real creation. The theatre at once fully introduced me to this new existence, and there arose accordingly in my mind new characters. Heroes succeeded to knights, tyrants to ogres, and boundless empire to enchanted castles (I, v).

Contarini's acting is succeeded by serious depressive fits (I, v).[108]

As a boy, Disraeli identified with various characters – Wolsey, Craut, d'Ilgen, Dorfling, Alberoni, Ripperda, Byron and Alroy[109] – and had a special affection for acting those which were powerful in both the spiritual and political worlds. These roles gave full expression to his own strangely divided personality. During his first efforts on the hustings, he acted Bolingbroke: using the same apocalyptic language; engaging in the same struggle for the nation against the factious Whigs, as that brilliant opportunist, who, in reality, only brought left and right against the centre. For the next twenty years the great Augustan's shadow can be seen moving through Disraeli's life. With Young England he is Bolingbroke and the Boy Patriots; at Hughenden, he is his master at Bucklebury; and with Lord George Bentinck he is his hero with Sir William Wyndham.[110] As a leader of his party, Disraeli became an 'impresario and an actor manager',[111] as Robert Blake puts it. This thespian quality has often been remarked, with obvious amusement or implied censure, by those who, with Plato, would rid the Republic of actors – of selfish men purporting to believe in something other than themselves.[112] But Disraeli, at least, was a great actor – one in whom '[p]ose and sincerity' were 'inextricably interwoven',[113] and who acted from the deep well-springs of his psychology.

Prior to taking his place on the front bench, role playing for Disraeli was a means of discovering and creating a coherent identity; of finding a place in the external world which conformed with his inner life and inclination. But it was also a vehicle for avoiding the painful sense of limitation which attended his status as a middle-class Jew, driven by boundless ambition, in a highly class-conscious society. His dreams were often preferable to the pain of reality. His propensity to act roles derived from an underlying incohesion[114] in his personality, as a consequence of which he was prone to feelings of depersonalization, or subjective feelings of the loss of personal identity – sensations which were probably exacerbated by depression. As a young man he lived dangerously through his fantasies and imagination, and came to regard the latter as his supreme gift, and worst enemy. His 'cure' had much to do with learning to control his imagination. But the impulse to avoid reality through dissociation came early to him, as is often seen in hysterical personalities. 'I reclined beneath a shady tree', the young Contarini Fleming says, 'and I covered my eyes with my little hand, and I tried to shut out the garish light that seemed to destroy the visions which were ever flitting before me.' When the visions disappear, he shivers 'under the cold horror of my reality' (I, iii).

Disraeli describes a group of symptoms that symbolize this desire to escape, or dissociate from, his perception of himself and the world. Symptoms of this kind, which occurred more frequently in the past, are sometimes part of a pattern of hysterical illness; but in Disraeli's case, in current differential diagnosis, they are seen as a part of his depression, or as an hysterical elaboration of it.[115] Depressive illness tends to be coloured by the basic personality of the sufferer, so that Disraeli's depression may have tended to show hysterical features accordingly. He 'fell down in a fit',[116] which may have been attended by seizures, and lost consciousness in public after travelling all night to a by-election at Aylesbury at the age of thirty-two. Several years earlier, something similar, though less severe, occurred, which was preceded by a 'determin[ati]on of blood' to the head.[117] Contarini Fleming also suffers from fits or fainting spells during his illness, which sometimes occur after 'a rushing of blood' into his brain, and after auditory disturbances, which are described in great detail (IV, v).

One evening in his 'chamber', Contarini hears a ticking noise, which he imagines emanates from his watch; but after satisfying himself that this is not the case, he rises from his chair to examine the room, and realizes that the noise is in his own ears. It then increases rapidly in volume. 'From the tick of a watch it assumed the loud confused moaning of a bell tolling in a storm ... It became louder and louder. It seemed to be absolutely deafening. I could compare it to nothing but the continuous roar of a cataract'(IV, iv–v). Finally, he suffers from a fit or fainting spell. Similar symptoms are attributed to the protagonist in *The Young Duke* (IV, ix).

Contarini also describes feelings of depersonalization, together with hypersensitivity of sensation, or hyperesthesias.

> I have sometimes half believed, although the suspicion is mortifying, that there is only a step between his state who deeply indulges in imaginative meditation, and insanity; for I well remember that at this period of my life, when I indulged in meditation to a degree which would now be impossible, and I hope unnecessary, my senses sometimes appeared to be wandering. I

cannot describe the peculiar feeling I then experienced ... but I think it was that I was not always assured of my identity, or even existence; for I sometimes found it necessary to shout aloud to be sure that I lived; and I was in the habit, very often at night, of taking down a volume and looking into it for my name, to be convinced that I had not been dreaming of myself. At these times there was an incredible acuteness, or intenseness, in my sensations; every object seemed animated, and, as it were, acting upon me (IV, v).

Disraeli needed to construct the persona with which he confronted the world because he had the frail sense of identity of a half-assimilated Jew who had missed the 'fearful rigidities'[118] of school, friendship, predestined occupation, religion, state – out of which most human beings are fashioned. The dissociative tendencies of depression and hystero-narcissism, were encouraged and developed by his subscription to post-Kantian idealism, whose essence was disdain for vulgar physical reality, together with what Jean Paul called *Sehnsucht* – or the 'longing for what is not there'.[119] The need to dissociate became acute during the illness, when the idea that he was a detested, Jewish bankrupt and failure, driven by limitless but thwarted ambition, became intolerable to him.

Disraeli seems to have regarded his dissociative symptoms as 'mortifying' portents of 'insanity'. His writings at this time are dotted with references to madness;[120] although Contarini Fleming says he never lost his 'mind or memory'(IV, vi). There is no mention of fainting in his correspondence with his family, only of more 'somatic' symptoms like headache and palpitations – probably because he wished to avoid the stigma of mental illness. 'I am determined to prove to all', he told his mother, 'that I am not suffering under hypochondria.'[121] The very denial, of course, betrays his focus on bodily manifestations. This is characteristic of the narcissist, who is over-invested in all aspects of the self, including the body, and can become quite preoccupied with the most minor of physical manifestations.

On the other hand, Disraeli seems to treat these symptoms as signs of superiority – of special election – and seems almost to revel in them. The philosophic stranger, Winter, tells Contarini Fleming that his symptoms are 'beneficent', and 'peculiar to men of your organisation'(IV, vii). To the European romantic confraternity, of which Disraeli aspired to be a leading light, the mad genius, endowed with an 'aura of "mania"', was the divinely inspired 'heir of the ancient Greek poet and seer',[122] and was set apart from the ugly bourgeois. 'People who have no madness in themselves',

Schelling wrote, 'are of empty, unfruitful understanding ... Therefore the divine madness of which Plato speaks, of which the poets speak.'[123] Moreover, in some of Disraeli's writings, particularly in the Byronic digressions in *The Young Duke*, the line between suffering and self-indulgence is difficult to discern. The narrator in that work speaks of 'a dark delight in being miserable' (V, iv) – a tendency which Nietzsche saw in Byron, and described less flatteringly as his being 'lost in the mud and almost in love with it'.[124] Macaulay wondered at the fact that Byron's theatrical despair had such mass appeal;[125] but clearly there was an audience for it, and for something more.

Disraeli was acting within a certain vogue of nervous sensibility. The eighteenth-century 'cult of sensibility', 'which encouraged so much fashionable indisposition in Georgian years',[126] once intensified and refracted by the prism of romanticism, created sympathy with men prone to nervousness and introspection; whose personal relations were distinguished by gentleness, empathy, susceptibility to tears, and 'open expression[s] of true emotion'.[127] 'In such an atmosphere', Janet Oppenheim concludes, 'a man who suffered nervous breakdown could expect to receive sympathy.'[128] Breakdown was a sign of good breeding and ethereal qualities, although this should not be overstated.[129] After 1850, when mid-Victorian ideas of manliness came to the fore, such behaviour was less well received. Perhaps this is why Disraeli's persona was in certain ways out of date after mid-century.[130]

But one symptom in particular established the sufferer's exquisiteness of sensation and refinement – and that was fainting. The latter was the most significant physical manifestation of hysteria at that time, according to the historian of the disease, and arose in response to 'social expectancy, tastes, [and] mores'.[131] Because women (the most frequently afflicted) were supposed to be frail and vapourish, fainting became the fashion. But men of sensibility, to whom womanish postures were not foreign, fainted too. It is a measure of the extent to which this behaviour obtained, and was even expected from 'higher men', that the fainting fits of the showman Franz Liszt appear to have created such titillation in his audience.[132]

Disraeli's illness and personality, far from being strange or aberrant, corresponded to much of what was around him – men like Byron, Poe and Shelley also manifested hysterical and narcissistic traits.[133] They struggled without success for a sense of political incorporation and community – Shelley in radical politics, Poe at West Point and Byron in the House of Lords – and as a consequence they lived, like the Creature in *Frankenstein* (that half-portrait of Shelley), in vengeful isolation – lacking as they did Disraeli's political acumen and knowledge of himself.[134] Disraeli was 'the outsider that got inside'[135] – he stood before the polity; they knelt before the pool.

The political arena is populated by narcissists aspiring to greatness, who suffer from recurrent disappointments and depressions when, because of their limited abilities, they do not achieve their grandiose dreams of glory. The goal of psychoanalysis for such troubled individuals is to help them to reduce the painful gap between exalted dreams and chastening reality and thus come to peace with themselves by giving up their unrealistic fantasies. But Disraeli was a rare phenomenon in the world of neurosis. As a consequence of his auto-analysis in *Contarini Fleming*, and his first efforts on the hustings, he realized that he was as great as he had imagined himself to be.[136] All that was required was greater self-knowledge, self-mastery and self-belief for him to soar to gigantic proportions, like the genie from the oriental lamp.

4

Disraeli and orientalism

PATRICK BRANTLINGER

'But the question is, what is the Eastern question?' (Consul-General Laurella in *Tancred*, V, ii)

'The East is a career' (*Tancred*, II, xiv). Quoting this epigram in the introduction to *Orientalism*, Edward Said adds: Disraeli 'meant that to be interested in the East was something bright young Westerners would find to be an all-consuming passion'.[1] Further, through such a career 'one could remake and restore not only the Orient but also oneself'.[2] As Said implies, Disraeli certainly 'remade and restored' his own career via the Orient, albeit in the complicated, paradoxical ways I explore in this chapter. In a sense, Disraeli was not just an orientalist; he was also a self-made oriental. The aspiring young writer and politician dreamed in at least two contrary ways about the Orient: in *Alroy*, *Contarini Fleming*, and *Tancred*, Disraeli fantasized about replacing Ottoman with British rule over the Near East; but even more significantly, he fantasized about himself as an oriental – a 'Semite' of aristocratic blood who was the equal of any Ottoman or, for that matter, British ruler. In short, while in a general way the young Disraeli chimed in with others' orientalist schemes for imperializing and perhaps westernizing Asia, he was simultaneously orientalizing himself.

From childhood, as his novels and letters attest, much of Disraeli's fantasy life revolved around the Orient. But for the future prime minister, fantasy had a way of becoming reality; far more than for other, less imaginative statesmen, what Disraeli thought and felt about 'the great Asian mystery' (*Tancred*, II, xi) influenced modern history both in Britain and abroad, in the Orient itself. With Disraeli as his key example, Said stresses that, for the imperializing British, fantasizing about the Orient and ruling it were closely connected:

> To write about Egypt, Syria, or Turkey, as much as traveling in them, was a matter of touring the realm of political will, political management, political definition. The territorial imperative was extremely compelling, even for so unrestrained a writer as Disraeli, whose *Tancred* is not merely an Oriental lark but an exercise in the astute political management of actual forces on actual territories.[3]

The qualifications I would make to Said's claims about Disraeli's orientalism are, first, that it was less a unified ideology than a mixture of hybrid, changing, often contradictory ideas, attitudes and poses; second, that it was mainly positive rather than negative (that is, that it celebrated rather than denigrated things eastern); and third, that Disraeli was himself (as he insisted throughout his career) a hybrid character – both British and Jewish, and perhaps as much oriental as orientalist. By oriental, moreover, I do not mean simply Jewish: Disraeli self-consciously 'remade' his own familial ties to Judaism into a more general oriental persona, invested with the world-conquering 'intellect of Arabia' (*Tancred*, IV, vii), which was just the more general form of the world-transcending 'Hebrew intellect' (*Coningsby*, IV, xv). That Disraeli's oriental self-fashioning was in part a bold, aggressive defence against the anti-Semitism that he had to combat throughout his career is an almost self-evident corollary.

I

In response to Said's influential analysis, various scholars have argued that orientalism was never so monolithic nor so uniformly negative as he suggests. Adding a psychoanalytic dimension to Said's Foucauldianism, Homi Bhabha insists upon the 'overdetermined' quality of orientalism (and 'colonial discourse' in general), such that 'mastery and pleasure' are as much at work as 'anxiety and defence'.[4] For a romantic orientalizer like the young Disraeli, the Orient evoked 'fetishistic' fantasies based more upon desire than on the 'phobic' responses that are more manifest in negative racist stereotyping. Even without psychoanalytic considerations it is apparent that what Said identifies as orientalism was highly heterogeneous, varying from occasion to occasion and even within single authors and texts. According to Nigel Leask, 'the anxieties of empire' expressed in 'oriental tales' from Samuel Johnson's *Rasselas* to John Keats'

Endymion and beyond were 'more various than Said's thesis will allow', and this observation applies also to Disraeli's eastern narratives. Similarly, in her reading of a number of British and French writers, Lisa Lowe stresses the heterogeneity of 'orientalizing formations' even for a single author; thus, in Flaubert's writing, eastern themes and motifs 'are divided and polyvocal, containing orientalist postures as well as critiques of those postures'.[5] Much the same can be said of eastern themes and motifs in Disraeli's writings and speeches throughout his career, with the added difference that Disraeli's orientalist but also oriental 'postures' were centred upon his own family history and personal experience in relation both to Judaism and to anti-Semitism.

Said recognizes but understates the fact that 'the nineteenth-century academic and imaginative demonology of "the mysterious Orient"'[6] was often matched by or mixed with a romantic fascination that, while also stereotypically reductive, was positively rather than negatively valenced. Despite Disraeli's general 'enthusiasm for the Orient', Said claims that *Tancred* (for example) 'is steeped in racial and geographical platitudes; everything is a matter of race, Sidonia states, so much so that salvation can only be found in the Orient and amongst its races'.[7] However, Said too quickly characterizes the curious notion of 'salvation' via 'the Orient' and its 'races' as just more of the same, basically negative, orientalism. Embedded in that notion of 'salvation' is Disraeli's linking of the concept of racial 'genius' or uniqueness to religion. For Disraeli, it was the specifically racial 'genius' of the 'Semites', 'Bedouins' or 'Arabians' (terms he uses interchangeably) that had created the world's great religions. And the 'Hebrew race' was the leading branch of the 'Semites', which made them also the superiors of their racial next of kin the Europeans, an opinion that Disraeli bravely – his opponents thought brazenly – voiced throughout his career, as in his chapter on 'The Jewish Question' in *Lord George Bentinck*. Further, Said does not explore Disraeli's quite different emphasis on the positive effects of the mingling of 'races' in imperial sites far removed from London such as Constantinople. Despite Disraeli's evident relish for what is nowadays glibly called 'otherness', Said suggests that Disraeli's racial 'platitudes' simply reproduce the negative stereo-typing they were intended, at least in part, to counteract. But both Disraeli's insistence upon the racial supremacy of the Hebrews and his youthful self-fashioning along oriental lines expressed a 'pro-Semitism' that was at once a form of romantic racism akin to nationalism and a direct response to anti-Semitism.[8]

One obvious ingredient in Disraeli's early self-fashioning was his family's Jewish roots reinforced by his reading about Judaism and Jewish history – reading that informed his historical romance *Alroy*, based on the life and legend of Menahem ben Solomon al-Ruhi, who in the 1100s led a revolt of the Jews in Azerbaijan against their Moslem overlords. While *Alroy* is Disraeli's most serious or least ironic early novel, it is also an oriental fantasy belonging to the genre of eastern tales that, from the early eighteenth century onwards, were partly inspired by the first European translation (into French) of the *Arabian Nights* (1704–12), but that were also in some sense reflections of Britain's (and Europe's) increasing commercial, military and imperial involvement in India and the rest of Asia. Disraeli was enamoured of the *Arabian Nights* and of other oriental tales like William Beckford's *Vathek* (1786). Shortly after his eastern tour in 1830–1, he apparently even proposed, to one or more publishers, translating them, no doubt from the French, as monthly part issues, to which he would add his own editorial comments and imitations.[9] But the most direct models for his own eastern narratives (especially *Alroy*, *Tancred* and those parts of his other major fictions that involve eastern travel, as in *Contarini Fleming* and *Lothair*) were undoubtedly furnished by Byron. Disraeli patterned his own travels on Byron's, and his fictional versions of those travels on Byron's oriental tales (*Don Juan*, *Lara*, *The Giaour* and so forth). In Byron's wake, oriental tourism like Disraeli's increasingly came into vogue. Both Judaism and Byronism were factors motivating Disraeli's own tour of Spain and the Near East in 1830–1. And both continued to inform Disraeli's later writings and political activities. As Robert Blake puts it, 'The experiences of the roué and dandy of 1830–31' on his travels through Spain, Malta, Albania, Greece, Turkey, Syria (or the 'Holy Land') and Egypt 'were to affect the attitude of the Prime Minister and statesman nearly half a century later at the Congress of Berlin.'[10]

That Disraeli interpreted much of what he encountered during his eastern travels in terms of literary, orientalist preconceptions – partly biblical, partly Byronic – is evident throughout his letters and novels. 'I longed to write an Eastern tale', Contarini Fleming declares in the midst of his own (and Disraeli's) eastern tale (*Contarini Fleming*, V, xii). Contarini travels through such colourfully exotic scenes that, despite the desolation of recent warfare, he is enchanted by 'the now almost obsolete magnificence of oriental life ... It seemed to me that my first day in a Turkish city [Yanina] brought before me *all the popular characteristics of which I had read*

... I gazed about me with a mingled feeling of delight and wonder' (V, xii; my italics). It is a 'delight and wonder' both in the 'infinite novelty' (V, xxiii) that Contarini discovers especially in Constantinople and in a thoroughly conventional, stereotypic sense of pastoral ahistoricity that fits neither the changing scenery nor the warfare in which Contarini partici-pates. In the following passage Disraeli does indeed resort to 'platitudes' of a sort that can be found in numerous eastern tales from *Don Juan* back to *Rasselas*:

> There is a charm in oriental life, and it is Repose. Upon me, who had been bred in the artificial circles of corrupt civilisation ... this character made a forcible impression. Wandering over those plains and deserts, and so-journing in those silent and beautiful cities, I experienced all the serenity of mind which I can conceive to be the enviable portion of the old age of a virtuous life. The memory of the wearing cares ... and vaunted excitement of European life, filled me with pain ... Truly may I say that on the plains of Syria I parted for ever with my ambition (*Contarini Fleming*, VI, ii).

Before dismissing such a passage as trite pastoral with an eastern flavour, however, it is worth comparing it to the similar but less conventional celebration of 'Arabian' life that Contarini offers when he sojourns among the 'Bedouins' of Syria: 'this singular people, who combined primitive simplicity of habits with the refined feelings of civilisation ... appeared to me to offer an evidence of that community of property and that equality of condition, which have hitherto proved the despair of European sages, and fed only the visions of their fanciful Utopias' (VI, iii).

In this and similar passages, Disraeli approximates the celebrations of 'primitive simplicity' that can be found in some other 'orientalists' who quite deliberately orientalized themselves by adopting, at least for ex-tended periods of their lives, oriental customs, habits and languages. From Edward Lane (author of *Manners and Customs of the Modern Egyptians*, 1836, and first translator of *The Arabian Nights* into English, 1838–41) through Sir Richard Burton down to T. E. Lawrence and beyond, a number of Britons strongly identified with and practised eastern ways.[11] That behaving like Turks or Arabs – one version of 'going native' – was not incompatible with the orientalist aim of the imperial domination of Asia is evident, however, in each of these cases and in Disraeli's career as well. Disraeli is an example of orientalist and oriental 'going native' to the extent that he constructed both his public and his private personas as oriental. Furthermore, that Disraeli's eastern tales themselves express a utopianism critical of aspects of European society and culture needs to be

borne in mind in analysing his romantic and Hebraic versions of orientalism.

Disraeli's grand tour, as had his earlier trip to the continent with the
Austens, followed in Byron's footsteps, and Disraeli, like many young
intellectuals and politicians after Byron's tragic-heroic death at Misso-
longhi in 1824, fancied himself a potential shaper of the political destinies
of the places he visited. However, though Disraeli adopted suitably
Byronic poses, the political opinions he already held were decidedly
different from Byron's. In his letters home during the tour, and in the
fictional account of his travels in *Contarini Fleming* (parts V and VI),
Disraeli expresses a quite clear sympathy for the Ottoman Empire versus
Greek nationalism. Yet in *The Rise of Iskander*, the hero-liberator is a
Greek fighting against Moslem domination, suggesting that Disraeli, like
Byron and Shelley, was more interested in heroism, rebellion and libera-
tion in general than in particular racial, cultural or national identities.
During his stay at Malta, however, Disraeli apparently decided to offer to
participate in the Ottoman campaign against the rebel Albanians, a desire
to see the military action in Greece at first hand that Contarini Fleming
fulfils.[12] But to side with the Turks against the Greeks was, for a young
British radical and Byronian, strangely unradical and un-Byronic. 'Disraeli, for whatever reason', writes Robert Blake, 'took the view that the
polyglot empire of the Sultan was a barrier against anarchy and barbarism.
He was [also], all his life, totally unsympathetic to the spirit of nationalism
which was the dominating force in his time.'[13]

Disraeli's attitudes toward nationalism were, however, more complicated than Blake suggests, for at least two reasons. First, the ideologies of
nationalism and imperialism are not antithetical (once they have broken
free from older dominations and established independent nation states,
nationalisms often spawn new empires and imperialisms). And, second,
Disraeli's pro-Semitism was also a proto-Zionism that can be construed as
a kind of higher nationalism in contrast to the narrow-minded nationalisms, racisms and religious prejudices that plagued him throughout his
career. Already in *Alroy*, the hero's attempt to liberate the Jews from their
Moslem overlords is couched in nationalistic terms that foreshadow
Zionism:

> Empires and dynasties flourish and pass away; the proud metropolis
> becomes a solitude, the conquering kingdom even a desert; but Israel still
> remains, still a descendant of the most ancient kings breathed amid these
> royal ruins, and still the eternal sun could never rise without gilding the

towers of living Jerusalem. A word, a deed, a single day, a single man, and we might be a nation (*Alroy*, IV, ii).[14]

The 'we' in this passage is inclusive: this is the narrator (or Disraeli) rather than Alroy meditating on the restoration of Israel. But for the modern narrator/author the chief obstacle to that restoration was apparently not the Ottoman Empire.

Certainly in regard to Greek nationalism versus Ottoman imperialism, the young Disraeli took the exact opposite position from that of his hero Byron (whose life he celebrated, along with Shelley's, in *Venetia* (1837)). Throughout his letters from Greece and Turkey Disraeli expresses much sympathy for the Turks, little for the Greeks. 'I confess ... that my Turkish prejudices', he wrote to Bulwer-Lytton, 'are very much confirmed by my residence in Turkey.'[15] Disraeli was fascinated by Moslem customs and costumes. I add 'costumes' because, as a young dandy, Disraeli saw the world, *pace* Carlyle's Teufelsdröckh, very much in terms of clothes. That 'the Turks indulge[d] in all combinations of costume' was not the least of their charms; 'the meanest merchant in the Bazaar looks like a Sultan in an Eastern fairy tale'.[16] Moreover, the effects of his own wardrobe on the Turks and their subjects was not lost upon Disraeli. About his experiences in Navarino in Greece, he wrote:

> I am quite a Turk, wear a turban, smoke a pipe six feet long, and squat on a Divan ... I find the habits of this calm and luxurious people [the Turks] entirely agree with my own preconceived opinions of propriety and enjoyment, and I detest the Greeks more than ever. I do not find mere Travelling on the whole very expensive, but I am ruined by my wardrobe ... When I was presented to the Grand Vizier I made up such a costume from my heterogeneous wardrobe, that the Turks, who are mad on the subject of dress, were utterly astounded ... Nothing wo[ul]d persuade the Greeks that we were not come about the new King and I really believe that if I had 25,000£ to throw away I might increase my headache by wearing a crown.[17]

While this sartorial fantasy is playful, and while it invites the very critiques of superficiality and inauthenticity that Carlyle, for one, would later make of Disraeli (the Jewish 'old clothes dealer', etc.), it nevertheless expresses a quite modern political pragmatism that recognizes the importance of image-making, symbolism and credit or belief in the forging of status and power, as well as in the always political process of self-forging or fashioning.

'There is only one way to travel in the East with ease, and that is with an appearance of pomp', Contarini Fleming declares. 'The Turks are much influenced by the exterior, and although they are not mercenary, a well-dressed and well-attended infidel will command respect' (VI, v). Similar statements about the political importance of image-making are frequent in western travelogues and exploration journals throughout the nineteenth century, according to which keeping up appearances is at least as important for pacifying restless natives as gunboats and artillery.[18] Disraeli's letter about his 'wardrobe' expresses a clear-sighted realism about politics that he would stress throughout his career: belief is the basis of power. At the same time, the letter contains a considerable dose of ironic egocentrism. If only, Disraeli speculates, he had been able to complement his exotic but elegant dress with a crown, the Greeks might have taken him for their new king. But 'Disraeli was no doubt joking.'[19]

II

That Disraeli's manifest early sympathies for the Ottoman Empire are somehow related to his later imperialistic policies is suggested by the theme of empire in his novels from *Alroy* to *Tancred*.[20] In the earliest of Disraeli's oriental romances, Alroy is an empire-builder on a grand scale, a Jewish Napoleon, attempting to transform the dispersed, invisible empire of the Jews into a real, 'restored' empire. Throughout his career, Disraeli thought of the Jews as forming an invisible empire, the spiritual power behind the earthly powers that governed the European nation states and much of the rest of the world. Thus Sidonia can tell Coningsby that 'at this moment, in spite of centuries, of tens of centuries, of degradation, the Jewish mind exercises a vast influence on the affairs of Europe. I speak not of their laws, which you still obey; of their literature, with which your minds are saturated; but of the living Hebrew intellect' (*Coningsby*, IV, xv). And in *Tancred*, Sidonia speaks of 'the spiritual hold which Asia has always had upon the North' (II, xi). Why, Disraeli/Sidonia wonders, do the 'Saxon and Celtic societies persecute an Arabian race' to whom they owe so much? 'Vast as the obligations of the whole human family are to the Hebrew race, there is no portion of the modern population so much indebted to them as the British people' (*Tancred*, IV, iv).

At the same time, *Tancred* appears to abandon the specifically Jewish identity of the fantasy of spiritual empire that is basic to *Alroy*. The last novel in Disraeli's Young England trilogy is a tale of the empire-building aspirations of its 'crusading' Christian hero and his oriental ally, the young Syrian emir Fakredeen. Yet it would be more accurate to say that *Tancred* enlarges Disraeli's personal identification with Jewish history to incorporate a more general 'Arabian' or 'Semitic' (that is, oriental) identity. While *Tancred* like *Alroy* is an 'Oriental fantasia' whose main theme 'is the essential aristocracy of the Jewish people',[21] Disraeli's racial and religious categories were flexible enough, or perhaps inconsistent enough, to involve some curious forms of imaginative miscegenation. In *Alroy*, the hero is inspired by a vision of the ghost of King Solomon, who comes to him in the Tombs of the Kings at Jerusalem. In *Tancred*, the hero is inspired by a vision (or is it just a dream?) of 'the Angel of Arabia', who comes to him on Mount Sinai and who, among other higher truths, informs him that Christianity, Judaism and Islam alike are only alternative versions of 'theocratic equality' provided to the world at large by 'the Most High' through 'the intellect of Arabia'. Tancred learns that Christendom itself is just 'the intellectual colony of Arabia' (*Tancred*, IV, vii).

Disraeli often insisted that God had chosen to reveal His truths in just one part of the world and to just one race – the Arabian race, to which the Hebrews belonged. Christianity is simply the consummation of Judaism, a fulfilment accomplished by Jews. 'The first preachers of the gospel were Jews, and none else; the historians of the gospel were Jews, and none else. No one has ever been permitted to write under the inspiration of the Holy Spirit, except a Jew.'[22] This is also part of what Sidonia tells Coningsby about 'Hebrew intellect', which continues to hold invisible sway over Europe because of its racial superiority and purity. It helped to know, moreover, that the Jews were the preservers of an ancient religious tradition that they had maintained through centuries of persecution and Diaspora: 'the Jews', Sidonia tells Coningsby, 'are essentially Tories' (*Coningsby*, IV, xv). But Sidonia enlarges his supposedly oriental or Semitic racial category even farther – beyond the 'Arabian' – by identifying it as 'Caucasian':

> The fact is, you cannot destroy a pure race of the *Caucasian* organisation. It is a physiological fact; a simple law of nature, which has baffled Egyptian and Assyrian Kings, Roman Emperors, and Christian Inquisitors. No penal laws, no physical tortures, can effect that a superior race should be absorbed in an inferior, or be destroyed by it. The mixed persecuting races disappear; the pure persecuted race remains (*Coningsby*, IV, xv; my italics).

Here and in similar passages Disraeli outflanks the Anglo-Saxonism or

Teutonism that was basic to British and, more specifically, English nationalism in the nineteenth century. Disraeli doesn't reject Anglo-Saxonism, but revises it by following Johann Friedrich Blumenbach's racial classification, which included both European and Semitic groups under the Caucasian rubric. Beyond the Anglo-Saxons' seemingly ancient racial roots lies an even older, more inclusive and influential, racial configuration. Disraeli 'looks beyond not only the Norman invasion but the celebrated Saxon institutions themselves to find in Hebrew culture the most profound basis of English national life'.[23] In short, Disraeli accepted Anglo-Saxonist racial and nationalist categories only to supplement them through the claims of his pro-Semitism. But these claims, involving a positive version of orientalism, were no more bizarre, arbitrary or illogical than those of the Anglo-Saxonism that they sought to contest by way of a paradoxical supplementarity. A superb *bricoleur* of the conventional ideas of his era, Disraeli constructed a paradoxical intellectual arsenal that, while according his Jewish origins both racial and religious dignity, suited him well as a politician climbing 'the greasy pole'.

Disraeli/Sidonia insists upon the religious basis of all principled politics. Economic self-interest or narrow utilitarian aims are completely inadequate to explain collective behaviour. World history is in the first instance the history of its great religions, and of the empires founded and destroyed by faith. The point of origin of all visionary empires as of all religions, moreover, has been the Orient (or, more specifically, the Near East) Sidonia himself, scion of the 'pure' race of the Sephardic Jews of Spain (*Tancred*, II, xi), exemplifies the spiritual genius of the Hebrews, which is also the world-conquering genius *par excellence*. As the narrator of *Coningsby* says of Sidonia:

> Such a temperament, though rare, is peculiar to the East. It inspired the founders of the great monarchies of antiquity, the prophets that the Desert has sent forth, the Tartar chiefs who have overrun the world: it might be observed in the great Corsican, who, like most of the inhabitants of the Mediterranean isles, had probably Arab blood in his veins. It is a temperament that befits conquerors and legislators, but, in ordinary times and ordinary situations, entails on its possessor only eccentric aberrations or profound melancholy (IV, x).

On this account, Napoleon is as much an 'Arab' as a 'Corsican' – like Disraeli/Sidonia, both oriental and European. Napoleon's 'Arab blood' explains his world-conquering talent, but the racial explanation is simultaneously a spiritual explanation – again, a sort of pro-Semitism that is also a form of positive orientalism.

'Man is only truly great when he acts from the passions', Sidonia tells Coningsby, 'never irresistible but when he appeals to the imagination. Even Mormon counts more votaries than Bentham' (*Coningsby*, IV, xiii). In *Tancred*, the Angel of Arabia delivers the same message to the 'crusading' hero: empires (indeed, all successful politics) are based on 'the passions', on 'imagination', and ultimately on faith. It does not seem to matter what that faith is; a great religion, faithfully adhered to by leaders and masses alike, will translate into the conquest and rule of great empires. The Ottoman Empire, though in decline, is one example; the British Empire is another, albeit also threatened by decline because its rulers are neglecting its 'visionary' or religious basis for mere material, utilitarian, profit and loss concerns.

The lessons that he learns from the Angel of Arabia Tancred teaches to Fakredeen, who aspires to be a Syrian Napoleon and to conquer the world. Even before his encounter with the Angel, Tancred teaches Fakredeen that 'The world was never conquered by intrigue: it was conquered by faith' (IV, iii). Once Fakredeen accepts this apparently 'Arabian principle' (IV, vii) that Tancred knows better than he does, the two young aristocrats join forces, more visionary than actual, in a scheme to overthrow the Ottoman Empire and to conquer most of Asia for the British Empire. 'We wish to conquer [the] world, with angels at our head', Tancred tells the queen of the Ansaray (VI, iii). Such heroic idealism is appealing: even if he and Fakredeen do not conquer Asia, Tancred conquers the queen's heart. Disraeli, no doubt, was as much amused by as serious about Tancred's quixotic escapades; the political machinations that he and Fakredeen become embroiled in continue to seem more like 'intrigue' than like religious inspiration. Nevertheless, Disraeli clearly believed that world conquest depended at least as much on 'faith' as on 'intrigue'. Further, he also believed that nationalisms tend to become imperialisms: as Napoleon demonstrated, nationalisms can lead to attempts at world conquest. And Disraeli maintained, both in *Tancred* and in his other writings and speeches, that the Near East (more specifically, the 'Semitic' race or races including the Hebrews) was the source of the 'visionary' principles necessary for the forging and rule of all great empires, including the British Empire.

'All is race; there is no other truth', Sidonia declares (*Tancred*, II, xiv), a theory that Disraeli often reiterated in later texts and contexts. Insofar as orientalism is a variety of racism supportive of the western imperialization of Asia, there is no doubt that Disraeli was an orientalist. Disraeli's insistence that race was the central category of politics and history led a few of his earliest critics to consider his views outlandish.[24] But more often than not the critics themselves also viewed race as the central category of politics and history; they objected only to Disraeli's pro-Semitism or positive orientalism (and to his Jewish origins). The numerous intellectuals and politicians (and, no doubt, ordinary British citizens) who believed that the Anglo-Saxon or, at least, Germanic or Aryan race was supreme and destined to rule the rest of the world had perforce to believe Jews and all other non-Germanic peoples inferior. Anglo-Saxon supremacy was the positive side of a coin whose reverse included anti-Semitism, orientalism and other forms of the stereotypic denigration of the other races of the world. Anglo-Saxon supremacists such as Dr Thomas Arnold, E. A. Freeman and Charles Kingsley, in common with 'Aryanists' like the artist Mr Phoebus in *Lothair*, were perforce to some degree or in some manner anti-Semitic (though, as with all ideologies, there were shades and degrees of anti-Semitism then as now).[25]

III

In *Lothair* Disraeli's early orientalism and oriental self-fashioning come full circle. Once again, Disraeli sends a youthful protagonist with both a political and a religious vocation on an eastern pilgrimage culminating in Jerusalem. Once again, the young hero learns of the intellectual and spiritual supremacy of orientals and, more specifically, of the Jews. More clearly than in the earlier novels, however, the opinions of Mr Phoebus help to contextualize Disraeli's pro-Semitism in relation to its virulent opposites. According to Phoebus:

> The fate of a nation will ultimately depend upon the strength and health of the population ... As for our mighty engines of war in the hands of a puny race, it will be the old story of the lower empire and the Greek fire. Laws should be passed to secure all this, and some day they will be. But nothing can be done until the Aryan races are extricated from Semitism (*Lothair*, xxix).

'Welcome, my friend!' says Phoebus to Lothair as they disembark on the former's Aegean island; 'Welcome to an Aryan clime, an Aryan landscape, and an Aryan race. It will do you good after your Semitic hallucinations' (*Lothair*, lxxii). From Disraeli's perspective, however, it is Phoebus who hallucinates, along with Aryanism in general, which has lost sight of the true racial basis of both civilization and religion. Later, near Jerusalem, Lothair learns the truth about these matters from Paraclete, the Syrian who, in Disraeli's penultimate novel, plays Sidonia's role of speaking racial wisdom to the protagonist:

> 'In My Father's house are many mansions,' and by the various families of nations the designs of the Creator are accomplished. God works by races, and one was appointed in due season ... to reveal and expound in this land the spiritual nature of man. The Aryan and the Semite are of the same blood and origin, but when they quitted their central land they were ordained to follow opposite courses. Each division of the great race has developed one portion of the double nature of humanity, till after all their wanderings they met again, and, represented by their two choicest families, the Hellenes and the Hebrews, brought together the treasures of their accumulated wisdom and secured the civilisation of man (*Lothair*, lxxvii).

Here Disraeli is responding especially to Matthew Arnold's argument in *Culture and Anarchy* that Victorian society has become overly 'Hebraic' – that it needs to correct the imbalance by 'Hellenizing'. Arnold himself may have been partly responding to Disraeli's frequent reiterations of the debts that modern British and European civilization owed to the ancient (and modern) Hebrews. Both Arnold and Disraeli found the racist discourse of their age inescapable, though both tried to remodel that discourse in anti-stereotypic directions. In both cases, moreover, it is not always clear how seriously, or with what degree of biologistic determinism, their racial categories are to be understood. Both were master ironists, capable simultaneously of self-mockery and mockery of the foibles, contradictions and irrationalities of their age.[26]

Just how seriously did Disraeli take his positive orientalism or pro-Semitism? It is certainly one of the most consistent, clearly articulated features of his ideas from start to finish of his career. Through his positive orientalism, Disraeli cannily positioned himself to criticize his political adversaries on religious grounds which were simultaneously racial grounds (the neglect of religious ideals by worldly politicians is a neglect of what the 'Hebrew intellect' taught wiser politicians in the past). Disraeli clearly agreed with probably the great majority of his contemporaries that race was the most important causal force in history and culture, though he also inverted conventional ideas about race and employed these inversions as elements of his self-fashioning and of his continual struggle against anti-Semitism.

Yet the question of irony remains. While Disraeli seems to put some of his most serious, consistent ideas about race into Sidonia's words, how is the reader to react to the Angel of Arabia in *Tancred*? Disraeli's amusement over Tancred's quixotic excesses verges at times on satire, though such satire would necessarily entail self-mockery. One way that Disraeli as a writer mirrors Byron is through his frequent combinations of romantic flights of fancy or imagination with irony and satire: stories of idealistic young adventurers and lovers as recounted by presumably mature, disillusioned narrators. Especially in the early novels (with the exception of the comparatively solemn and certainly overwritten *Alroy*), the clashes between romance and ironic deflations of romance produce a sort of undecidability that was also an aspect of Disraeli's intellectual and emotional armour.

This undecidability is, perhaps, at work in Disraeli's treatments of what he clearly perceives as racial and cultural stereotypes or oversimplifications. In common with other orientalists, Disraeli also, according to Said, thinks that 'an Oriental lives in the Orient, he lives a life of Oriental ease, in a state of Oriental despotism and sensuality, imbued with a feeling of Oriental fatalism'.[27] But while all of these traits fit some of the oriental characters whom Disraeli portrays in his novels and letters, they do not fit the heroic protagonist of *Alroy*, and in *Tancred* they do not fit Fakredeen, the beautiful Jewess Eva (with whom Tancred falls in love), or for that matter the half-orientalized Tancred himself who matures into a hybrid figure in some ways like Disraeli (or like Disraeli wanted to be). On the other hand, the racial traits that Disraeli ascribes to Fakredeen are 'all the qualities of the genuine Syrian character in excess' (*Tancred*, III, vi). But these traits read like a critical self-portrait of the artist as a young man (a more realistic self-portrait, at least, than the obviously idealized ones of Sidonia and Tancred). Disraeli may be reproducing orientalist stereotyping, but he is surely also half-mocking himself when he writes that 'the genuine Syrian character in excess' is 'vain, susceptible, endowed with a brilliant though frothy imagination, and a love of action so unrestrained that restlessness deprived it of energy, with so fine a taste that he [Fakredeen] was always capricious, and so ingenious that he seemed ever inconsistent' (*Tancred*, III, vi). Perhaps here the 'ingenious' Disraeli, both ironically and in a somewhat self-indulgent mode, beats his anti-Semitic critics to the punch by caricaturing himself. Shorn of their 'excess', however, these same racial traits (sensitivity, imaginative brilliance, love of action, taste, ingenuity) also fit Sidonia, the idealized Jewish mentor of both Tancred and Coningsby, who by praising the 'Hebrew intellect' to Coningsby and by encouraging Tancred to explore 'the great Asian mystery' mediates between West and East for two out of three of Disraeli's Young England heroes. Sidonia, in other words, is also a figure of hybridity – a partly oriental figure such as Disraeli wished or willed himself to become.

'Orientalism was ultimately a political vision of reality whose structure promoted the difference between the familiar (Europe, the West, "us") and the strange (the Orient, the East, "them").'[28] This 'vision' involved racial and cultural stereotyping of the sort evident in James Mill's *History of British India* (1819), with its claims of European superiority and of the inability of Indians to achieve civilization without British intervention. Disraeli contested negative orientalism with the weapons of his positive version, his pro-Semitism, from the beginning to the end of his career. In the case of the Jews, their very survival in the face of centuries-long hostility from other races was a sign of their racial purity and superiority: 'the degradation of the Jewish race is alone a striking evidence of its excellence, for none but one of the great races could have survived the trials which it has endured'.[29] That Disraeli's positive orientalism was in large measure a pro-Semitism aimed at countering anti-Semitism is evident in this and many similar passages throughout his writings. To quote his chapter on 'The Jewish Question' in his life of Bentinck once more:

> The Saxon, the Sclave, and the Celt, have adopted most of the laws and many of the customs of these Arabian tribes, all their literature and all their religion. They are therefore indebted to them for much that regulates, much that charms, and much that solaces existence. The toiling multitude rest every seventh day by virtue of a Jewish law; they are perpetually reading, 'for their example,' the records of Jewish history, and singing the odes and elegies of Jewish poets; and they daily acknowledge on their knees, with reverent gratitude, that the only medium of communication between the Creator and themselves is the Jewish race. Yet they treat that race as the vilest of generations; and instead of logically looking upon them as the human family that has contributed most to human happiness, they extend to them every term of obloquy and every form of persecution.[30]

Disraeli's early self-fashioning, involving his Byronism and his eastern travels, also involved his celebrations of Turkish, Syrian, Jewish and more

generally oriental customs and cultures. While, with the exception of
Judaism, his knowledge of any of the cultures, religions and societies of
the Orient may never have been much more than touristic, in *Alroy*,
Contarini Fleming and elsewhere he was already situating the 'Hebrew race'
in the context of the larger categories of the 'Semitic', 'Arabian' and
ultimately 'Caucasian' races. These oriental – and European – races
formed a hierarchy of empires, religions and cultures at the apex of which
(could good British Christians, no matter how anti-Semitic, deny it?) were
the Jews, the one race (again, from a Christian perspective) through which
God had chosen to reveal His everlasting truths to mankind. Such a thesis
allowed Disraeli not just to agree with both his friends and his enemies
that, despite his conversion to Christianity, he remained Jewish and to
some degree oriental, but to assert his Jewish and oriental affiliations with
pride. As Robert Blake puts it in his account of the young Disraeli's
eastern travels in 1830–1: 'The identity which Disraeli sought was found
on his tour of the Near East. He was a member of a great race'[31] –
Caucasian, Semitic, Arabian, but, above all, Jewish.

5

‎——

'A Hebrew to the end': the emergence of Disraeli's Jewishness

TODD M. ENDELMAN

Benjamin Disraeli's character consistently provoked strong reactions, often at violent odds with each other. For some, he was a vulgar, cynical careerist; for others, a visionary, patriotic statesman. Few were indifferent. Amid the welter of conflicting assessments, however, there was one point on which both admirers and detractors agreed: Disraeli was a Jew and being Jewish was central to his self-understanding – despite the fact that he had been baptized at the age of twelve. As one of his earliest biographers, James Anthony Froude, concluded, 'At heart he was a Hebrew to the end.'[1] But to conclude that being Jewish mattered to Disraeli does not speak to the question of how it mattered or in what sense 'he was a Hebrew'. It does not explain the meaning or content of Disraeli's Jewishness and its function in his emotional and political life.

In accounts of Disraeli's Jewishness, there has been little consensus. Historians and biographers have labelled him, variously, a proto-Zionist, a marrano, a racist, a proud Jew and a self-hating Jew. The truth is that none of these labels captures the complex, ambivalent character of what being Jewish meant to Disraeli at different times in his life. Indeed, it is this last point – the timebound rather than timeless character of his Jewishness – that needs to be stressed. For Disraeli, consciousness of being a Jew changed over time. It was not a fixed cultural or biological inheritance but, rather, an awareness and understanding that emerged and evolved over several decades, in response to external changes in his life, and stabilized only when he was in his forties. It drew on enlightenment deism, romanticism, racial ideas, Christian doctrine, Sephardi pride, family traditions and even normative Jewish belief, mixing notions from these diverse sources into an odd, eccentric *mélange*.

Disraeli's views about Judaism owed much to his father, as was also the case with his political views. London-born Isaac D'Israeli (as he spelled the family name) was a successful but minor man of letters, who moved comfortably in bookish, non-Jewish circles.[2] Like many of his kinsmen, he was not an observant Jew. Although he married within the fold, had his four sons circumcised and maintained membership in the Spanish and Portuguese synagogue in Bevis Marks (near the eastern edge of the City of London), his allegiance to Judaism was more a matter of familial and ethnic sentiment than belief and practice. He did not observe its domestic rituals nor attend worship services. In 1817, he quit the synagogue over a dispute that had been brewing since 1813, when he was elected *parnas*, or warden, and had refused either to serve or to pay the usual fine for declining to do so. (This was, it should be added, a standard procedure for raising revenue for the congregation.) But, as he explained to the synagogue authorities when he first declined the office, he was willing to continue his membership if they withdrew the fine since he felt bound to them by friendship and 'something like the domestic affections'.[3]

Isaac D'Israeli's secession from the Bevis Marks congregation was in no sense remarkable. In well-to-do Sephardi families that had become rooted in English social and cultural life, indifference or even hostility to the Jewish religion was becoming common in the late-Georgian period.[4] As these families drew closer to non-Jewish circles, the number of secessions, intermarriages and conversions rose – to the extent that the Sephardi population grew little, if at all, between 1750 and 1830, despite immigration from North Africa.[5] When the Sephardim who participated in the establishment of the Reform synagogue in 1841 offered a rationale for the introduction of religious reforms, they cited defections from the community. They were convinced that improvements in worship would 'arrest and prevent secession from Judaism', which was 'widely spread' among 'the most respectable families' in the community.[6]

Where Isaac D'Israeli differed from other Sephardim who cut their ties to Bevis Marks was in his long-standing espousal of a Voltaire-like, deistic critique of traditional Judaism. Early in life Isaac fell under the influence of the *philosophes*, whose views on religion in general and Judaism in particular he embraced. For him, Judaism had become a repository of the prejudices of earlier, barbarous eras. The Talmud was a mass of superstitions, contradictory opinions, rambling oriental fancies and casuistical glosses. The rabbis of old were dictators of the human intellect who tricked the Jews into accepting their decisions as divine law, thereby casting the people into the bondage of ridiculous customs. The system of dietary laws was the cruellest curse of all, for it estranged the Jews from sympathetic fellowship with other members of the human race, and, along with other particularistic customs, contributed to Christian prejudice against them. Isaac expressed these views in print on more than one occasion: in entries on the Talmud and rabbinical stories in his *Curiosities of Literature* (1791 and numerous editions thereafter), in his anti-revolutionary novel *Vaurien* (1797), in an article on Moses Mendelssohn in *The Monthly Magazine* (July 1798), in his discussion of Mendelssohn's self-education in his *History of Men of Genius* (1818) and in his *Genius of Judaism* (1833).

Although influenced by enlightenment views, Isaac D'Israeli was not a disciple or follower of Moses Mendelssohn, leader of the conservative wing of the Jewish enlightenment, as is often claimed.[7] Close examination of what Isaac wrote about Mendelssohn suggests that he had not read his work, most of which was inaccessible to him at the time, having appeared in German and Hebrew and remained untranslated. Instead, D'Israeli formed his view of Mendelssohn at secondhand on the basis of none-too-reliable sources.[8] However much Mendelssohn championed the broadening of Jewish cultural horizons and the inclusion of secular studies in the Jewish curriculum, he was no radical reformer but, rather, an observant Jew who believed that the Jewish people were to continue keeping all the commandments until God told them to do otherwise.

But it is also wrong to see Isaac D'Israeli as indifferent to or unconcerned with Jewish issues, again as is often claimed.[9] In fact, as we have seen, he held passionate, though critical, views about Judaism. Some of this is attributable to the influence of Voltaire and other enlightenment writers, some to the influence of Isaac's own mother, Sarah, whom Benjamin described in terms similar to those used to characterize self-hating Jews. In a biographical sketch of his father, written as an introduction to a new edition of *The Curiosities of Literature* (1849), Benjamin reported:

> My grandmother ... had imbibed that dislike for her race which the vain are too apt to adopt when they find that they are born to public contempt. The indignant feeling that should be reserved for the persecutor, in the mortification of their disturbed sensibility, is too often visited on the victim; and the cause of annoyance is recognised not in the ignorant malevolence of the powerful, but in the conscientious conviction of the innocent sufferer.

Proud, beautiful and ambitious, Sarah 'never pardoned [her husband] for his name' and 'resented upon her unfortunate race the slights and disappointments to which it exposed her'. She was 'so mortified by her social position that she lived until eighty without indulging in a tender expression'.[10] It is most unlikely that Isaac remained untouched by his mother's contempt for her own Jewish origins.

Isaac, in turn, communicated his negative views about Judaism to his children. Benjamin wrote to his benefactor Sarah Brydges Willyams, the childless widow of Sephardi ancestry whose fortune he inherited, 'I, like you, was not bred among my race, and was nurtured in great prejudice against them.'[11] This recollection, however, cannot be taken at face value without qualification. Isaac's attitude to Judaism was not unrelentingly hostile. It should be recalled that he maintained his membership in the Spanish and Portuguese synagogue until he was in his fifties and repeatedly took up Jewish themes in his writing. In addition, he arranged for his son Benjamin to receive weekly Hebrew instruction when he was at boarding school at Blackheath.[12] Moreover, if the Judaica in his library is indicative, it seems that Isaac had a more than casual interest in Jewish history and literature, whatever his antagonism to rabbinic tradition.[13] An avid book collector, he acquired at least fifty to sixty Judaica titles – histories, apologetics and polemical works in the main, with a smattering of books on philosophical and theological themes. Because he did not read Hebrew, his own Jewish education having been rudimentary, his acquisitions were limited to Romance-language and English-language works and did not include modern or classical Hebraica. On his shelves were several works of Menasseh Ben Israel and the learned Anglo-Jewish shoemaker/hat dresser David Levi, the Latin translation of David Ganz's history *Tsemah David*, the Abbé Grégoire's book on the regeneration of the Jews, Leon Modena's account of Jewish customs, Moses Samuel's biography of Moses Mendelssohn and the English translation of Diogene Tama's transactions of the so-called Parisian or Napoleonic Sanhedrin.

Benjamin, thus, did not grow to manhood in a household in which Jewish concerns and interests were treated with either complete indifference or contempt. It would be more accurate to say that his family was neither fully in the Jewish fold nor fully without, but occupied an intermediate or indeterminate place somewhere between these two poles. While this seems not to have disturbed Isaac or to have thrown up obstacles to his career, it was a problem for his eldest son, as it was so often with talented, ambitious sons from well-acculturated families. At school, because his social status and identity were open to question, Benjamin was especially sensitive to being seen as different or marginal. He and another Jewish boy were compelled to stand at the back of the classroom during school prayers, for example, a well-intentioned practice that troubled, nonetheless, Jewish children with an ambiguous sense of their own Jewishness (as we know from autobiographical evidence from later periods).[14]

The confused nature of his Jewishness also made Disraeli vulnerable to anti-Jewish taunts from his schoolmates. Although the legal and social status of English Jews was better than that of most European Jews, slurs and slights, rooted in age-old myths about Jewish difference and malevolence, were a well-entrenched feature of cultural and social life.[15] While Disraeli left no direct mention of having endured anti-Semitism while at school, either before or after his baptism at age twelve, he would have been exceptional to have escaped it, given the cruel intolerance of children in general, and the prevalence of popular prejudices against Jews in particular. The best evidence we have that he suffered from his Jewishness while at school is indirect but nonetheless compelling. As Charles Richmond shows in chapter 1 of this volume, unpublished diaries and memoranda that Disraeli wrote in 1821 (he had left school in late 1819 or early 1820) reveal that he was concerned with religious persecution. In one passage, he denounced the exclusion of 'the follower of ano[the]r faith' from 'the benefits of the constitution' because of fears that he might change it and the legislature.[16] In addition, in two early novels, *Vivian Grey* (1826) and *Contarini Fleming* (1832), both of which are now recognized as rooted in personal experience, the eponymous heroes experience rebuffs at school. Self-conscious about his 'Venetian countenance', Contarini Fleming, whose very name proclaims his mixed background, feels he is an outsider. 'Wherever I moved I looked around me, and beheld a race different from myself.' In adulthood, he recalls his youth not with fondness but bitterness: 'I was a most miserable child; and school I detested more than ever I abhorred the world in the darkest moments of my experienced manhood' (I, ii). Both protagonists, it should be added, fight and thrash boys who insult them.

As these autobiographical fragments suggest, Disraeli's baptism – at St Andrew's Holborn, in July 1817 – did not have an immediate, positive impact on relations with his schoolmates. In the long run, of course, it made possible his political career, since professing Jews were not allowed to sit in parliament until 1858. But since it failed to alter his un-English looks and name or erase knowledge of his Jewish origins, he was still regarded as a Jew, whatever his civil and religious status. In fact, in the short run, his baptism might have made his situation at school even more intolerable. Newly minted Christians, especially those with marked Jewish features, often fared worse than unconverted Jews whose Jewishness was unambiguous.[17] In general, the hybrid character of acculturated, 'non-Jewish' Jews troubled contemporaries, since it blurred differences seen as essential. In an essay written in the early 1820s, Charles Lamb vented his unease about 'the approximation of Jew and Christian which has become so fashionable'. Exasperated, he confessed: 'I do not understand these half-convertites. Jews christianising – Christians judaising – puzzle me. I like fish or flesh.'[18]

We know nothing about how the twelve-year-old Disraeli himself viewed his baptism. In any case, the decision to become a Christian was not his, but that of his father, who remained a deist and unconverted Jew. Although Isaac left no record of why he decided to have Benjamin and his other children converted – a decision made easier by the death of his own father in November 1816 – his motives are not difficult to infer. That religious conviction was no consideration is clear from Isaac's own repudiation of revealed religion and lack of interest in becoming a Christian himself. His close friend the historian Sharon Turner, author of the multi-volume, best-selling *History of the Anglo-Saxons*, apparently urged him to take the step, but it is doubtful that Isaac needed to be convinced of its wisdom. Dozens of Sephardim, similar to Isaac in background and outlook, including his brother-in-law George Basevi, were doing the same thing, hoping to advance their own or their children's worldly happiness. Not content to remain within commercial and financial spheres, in which Jews faced no barriers to success, they saw baptism as a means to escape the popular stigma attached to Jewishness and gain unimpeded access to professional, bureaucratic, artistic and social circles that had not included Jews earlier. In the words of the pioneer Anglo-Jewish historian James Picciotto, who wrote from firsthand knowledge of the period: 'The mart, the exchange, the Synagogue, the domestic circle, did not suffice for their aspirations.'[19]

In his earliest efforts to make his way in the world, whether as fop, man about town, lover, speculator, journalist or novelist, the young Disraeli paid little or no attention to his Jewish origins. His conversion, on the face of it, appeared to be a strategic success, even if his career at the time was not. (His repeated failures to launch himself, to fulfil his ambition, were not due to his origins but rather his ineptitude.) He seemed to be indifferent to his Jewish background, at least before the winter of 1829–30, when he started work on his novel about David Alroy, a twelfth-century false messiah. If it did concern him in the 1820s, it remained a private, unarticulated concern. Perhaps he was unaware, at a conscious level, that it was or could be a source of discomfort. Whatever the case (and we can never know for sure), his Jewishness was not something to which he called attention or upon which he reflected in conversation or writing. It was not an obsession, as it would later become. There are few references to Jews in his letters or novels before the publication of *The Wondrous Tale of Alroy* in 1833.

Moreover, even after he started to read Jewish history in earnest in preparation for writing *Alroy*, he exhibited few public signs of a reawakened sense of Jewishness. The most telling evidence of this can be seen in the letters he wrote during the sixteen-month tour of the Mediterranean and the Near East that he made in 1830–1.[20] What is striking about these letters, in the light of his later racial chauvinism, is how little interest he showed in Jews and Jewish sites he encountered in Jerusalem and other Ottoman cities. When he wrote to his sister in March 1831 from Alexandria about his visit to Jerusalem, he made no mention of the Jewish population or the Western Wall, even then an object of veneration and pilgrimage. On the few occasions when he did mention Jews, it was in a formulaic way, as one of several 'exotic' peoples that made Levantine cities colourful in the eyes of western travellers. For example, he wrote to his father from Gibraltar in July 1830: 'This rock is a wonderful place with a population infinitely diversified – Moors with costume radiant as a rainbow or an Easter melodrame, Jews with gabardines and scull [*sic*] caps, Genoese, Highlanders, and Spaniards, whose dress is as picturesque as that of the sons of Ivor.' (In fact, it would have been surprising if the Jews he saw on Gibraltar were wearing 'gabardines', the stereotypical costume of Polish Jewish immigrants in western Europe; in all likelihood, they wore North African garb.) Similarly, during his earlier tour of Italy in 1826, which included visits to Venice, with its famous ghetto, and Cento, birthplace of his paternal grandfather, he mentioned Jews only once in his letters home. He told his father that the only ghetto he visited was that of Ferrara. Without affect, in a manner best described as matter of fact, he wrote that it was 'a tolerably long street enclosed with red wooden gates and holding about 3,000 Jews'.[21]

Although Jews and Judaism were not then central to Disraeli's sense of identity, his visit to the Near East, especially Jerusalem, was critical. In tandem with his work on *Alroy*, it initiated a period, lasting some ten to twelve years, during which Jewish themes came to occupy an increasingly prominent place in his thinking. Although his stay there did not transform him at once into a champion of the Jews, it made an immediate impression, nonetheless. When he first saw the city from the Mount of Olives, he wrote home that he was 'thunderstruck'. But his reaction, significantly, was that of a European romantic rather than a Jew: his words make no reference to Jerusalem's Jewish significance as the site of the Temple and the Davidic monarchy.

> I saw before me apparently a gorgeous city. Nothing can be conceived more wild and terrible and barren than the surrounding scenery, dark, stony and severe, but the ground is thrown about in such picturesque undulations, that the mind is full of the sublime, not the beautiful, and rich and waving woods and sparkling cultivation would be misplaced.[22]

One year after his return to England, Disraeli stood for parliament for the first time, driven by the desire, in Robert Blake's words, 'to create a sensation, to occupy the limelight, to act a part on the greatest stage in the world'.[23] He lost the contest, a by-election at Wycombe in June 1832, and three subsequent elections, before winning a seat at Maidstone in July 1837. It was this experience, his plunge into electoral politics, more than his visit to Jerusalem, that forced his Jewishness to the fore and led him to rethink its relevance. Standing for election gave a public dimension to his origins that he had not encountered earlier. He had met with slights and slurs before this, as he worked to cut a dash in fashionable London circles, but electioneering – and, later, the rough and tumble of national politics – exposed him to a level of anti-Semitic abuse that was (for him) unprecedented. As he entered Taunton in April 1835, boys called out 'Old clothes!' and offered to sell him slippers and sealing wax, references to low-status street trades with strong Jewish associations.[24] In a speech at Dublin several days later, Daniel O'Connell attacked Disraeli for remarks he made at Taunton, describing him as a Jew of 'the lowest and most disgusting grade of moral turpitude' with 'the qualities of the impenitent thief on the Cross' from whom, he claimed, Disraeli was descended.[25] Speaking to the people of Maidstone at the general election of July 1837, Disraeli was interrupted repeatedly with cries of 'Shylock!' and 'Old clothes!' and offers of ham and bacon, while his opponent mocked his foreign-sounding family name.[26] At Shrewsbury in June 1841, hostile members of the crowd waved pieces of roast pork on sticks, taunting him with the cry, 'Bring a bit of pork for the Jew', while one heckler drove up to the hustings in a cart announcing, 'I come here to take you back to Jerusalem.'[27] When Disraeli became a national figure in the 1840s, on his way up 'the greasy pole', his Jewish origins attracted even more attention. Cartoonists in *Punch* and other illustrated magazines regularly depicted him as a Jewish old clothes man, his head crowned with a stack of top hats, or as an importuning secondhand clothing dealer.[28]

Disraeli's initial response to the Jew-baiting that greeted his entry into electoral politics was to ignore it. His letters, speeches and novels from the 1830s do not dwell on Jewish matters, with the one curious exception of *The Wondrous Tale of Alroy* (1833), an 'oriental' adventure inspired by the leader of a messianic movement in twelfth-century Kurdistan. For a converted Jew like Disraeli, whose Jewish education was minimal, this was an unusual choice of subject, to say the least. David Alroy was an obscure figure, little known, if at all, to even professing Jews in Victorian England.[29] In Disraeli's hands, he became a larger-than-life conqueror, wielding both kabbalistic lore and a mighty sword, who in the end is distracted from his mission to reclaim Jerusalem by his love for and eventual marriage to a daughter of the caliph of Baghdad. As in much of his writing, Disraeli's own passions and needs are close to the surface: in this case, his desire to be a powerful leader in an alien land and his urge to validate the primacy of imaginative experience, as opposed to worldly, rational calculation, in human affairs. That he chose a Jewish military leader (and lover) to make these points is no coincidence. It reflected his own sense of being an outsider, as well as the impact of his visit to Jerusalem. In the preface to a new edition of *Alroy* in 1845, he claimed: 'Being at Jerusalem in the year 1831, and visiting the traditional tombs of the Kings of Israel, my thoughts recurred to a personage whose marvellous career had, even in boyhood, attracted my attention, as one fraught with the richest materials of poetic fiction.' While this may not be the literal truth, it has to it the ring of emotional truth.

Still, it is possible to read too much into the oriental fantasies in *Alroy*. In the early 1830s, Disraeli was no champion of the Jews, exulting in their antiquity, nobility, racial purity and creative genius – nor had he yet stood for election and had his Jewishness thrown in his face. Whatever the impact of his visit to the Land of Israel, the claim that it stimulated 'fantasies of revived Jewish hegemony'[30] exceeds the evidence. It makes Disraeli a proto-nationalist or Zionist *avant la lettre*, which does not fit with what else is known about his thinking in the 1830s. In fact, there are passages in *Alroy* that are hostile to the Jewish religion, if not the Jewish people, passages that echo his father's deistic critique of rabbinic tradition. A 'learned' exchange between rabbis Zimri and Maimon early in the tale mocks talmudic discourse and the rabbinic penchant for aggadic (non-legal) hyperbole. Later Alroy explodes in anger when he learns that zealous soldiers have plundered a mosque, in fulfilment of the biblical commandment to destroy utterly 'all the places where the nations ... served their gods' (Deut. 12: 2). 'Come I to a council of valiant statesmen or dreaming Rabbis?', he demands to know. His meaning is clear: the laws of Moses are no 'school for empire'; they will not 'establish the throne of Israel'; their time has passed (VI, iii; VIII, v).

Disraeli's obsession with Jewish themes took hold only in the 1840s, that is, after he entered politics. Early in his parliamentary career, he kept quiet when bills to remove Jewish disabilities came before the House of Commons. In 1837, soon after taking his seat, he voted with the majority against emancipation. He wrote to his sister after the division, 'Nobody looked at me and I was not at all uncomfortable, but voted in the majority (only of 12) with the utmost sangfroid.'[31] During the 1841 debate on a bill to enable Jews to hold municipal office, he was silent. He also remained silent in 1845 when his own party sponsored and successfully guided through the Commons another emancipation bill, despite having voiced Jewish concerns, as well as eccentric views on emancipation, in *Coningsby*, which had been published the previous year. (His first speech in parliament in favour of Jewish emancipation came in 1847; it was not well received and provoked angry responses from both Tories and Liberals.)[32]

In *Coningsby*, which he began writing in September 1843, Disraeli articulated for the first time in public the sentiments that henceforth formed the core of his Jewish identity, sentiments to which he returned repeatedly in subsequent publications, speeches, conversation and letters. In this novel, the first of his celebrated political trilogy, he introduced the mysterious Jewish banker Sidonia, his *alter ego*, the embodiment of his desires and fantasies and spokesman for his most cherished beliefs. Sidonia is cultivated, cosmopolitan, wise in the ways of the world and able to influence world events with a word or two to princes and ministers.[33] He informs the aspiring politician Coningsby that the Jews are a powerful race, masters of the world's money markets, arbiters of European thought and sensibility, lords of secret diplomacy and explosive revolution. Their pre-eminence, he explains, derives from their racial purity, their refusal to intermarry with other nations. In his words, 'the Hebrew is an unmixed race' and 'an unmixed race of a firstrate organisation are the aristocracy of Nature' (*Coningsby*, IV, x). Wherever Sidonia looks, he sees Jewish power and influence. For example, he tells Coningsby:

> There is not a company of singers, not an orchestra in a single capital, that is not crowded with our children under the feigned names which they adopt to conciliate the dark aversion which your posterity will some day disclaim with shame and disgust. Almost every great composer, skilled musician, almost every voice that ravishes you with its transporting strains, springs from our tribes (IV, xv).

Sidonia also sets forth an unorthodox case for emancipation. Eschewing what he calls 'political sentimentalism' (that is, the liberal argument for religious toleration), he reasons that as the Jews are allowed to accumulate property – the basis of power – they have become a force and should be incorporated into the political nation rather than forced into permanent opposition to its establishment. (Thomas Babington Macaulay, who shared little else with Disraeli, made the same argument.)[34] The Tory refusal to grant them emancipation has pushed them temporarily into the ranks of levellers and latitudinarians. 'The Tories lose an important election at a critical moment; 'tis the Jews come forward to vote against them.' With each generation, they will acquire more power, thanks to their racial purity and accumulation of property, and thus become increasingly dangerous to the establishment. 'It is a physiological fact; a simple law of nature ... No penal laws, no physical tortures, can effect that a superior race should be absorbed in an inferior, or destroyed by it. The mixed persecuting races disappear; the pure persecuted race remains.' But, Sidonia adds, the English have little to fear, for the Jews are at heart Tories, essentially monarchical, deeply religious and thus, if allowed to enter political life, will strengthen the ranks of conservatism, where by nature they belong (*Coningsby*, IV, xv).

Sidonia adds one further reason for England to remove the Jews' political disabilities: gratitude for their fundamental contributions to western, Christian culture. He tells Coningsby that Europe owes to them 'the best part of its laws, a fine portion of its literature, all its religion'. He asks him, 'What are all the schoolmen, Acquinas [*sic*] himself, to Maimonides? And as for modern philosophy, all springs from Spinoza' (*Coningsby*, IV, xv).

Three years later, in *Tancred*, the romantic tale of a young English lord's spiritual quest in the Holy Land, Disraeli carried this racial boastfulness even further. He first stressed Europe's cultural indebtedness to the Jews and its spiritual roots in the Near East. On a pilgrimage to Mount Sinai, Tancred asks himself why he, 'the child of a northern isle', has come to this 'great and terrible wilderness' and what his connection to it is. He concludes that there is an indissoluble, profound link: 'words had been uttered and things done, more than thirty centuries ago, in this stony wilderness, which influenced his opinions and regulated his conduct every day of his life, in that distant and seagirt home'. The sublime laws of Sinai protect the life and property of Englishmen and guarantee working people a day of rest in every seven. The most popular poet in England is not Wordsworth or Byron, he realizes, but 'the sweet singer of Israel'. The heroic history of ancient Israel animates and inspires the English in their pursuit of liberty. Above all, his countrymen owe a debt to the Jews for knowledge of the true God and for the means (Jesus) through which they find salvation (*Tancred*, IV, iv). In regard to this last point, Disraeli gave a novel twist to Jewish apologetics about the crucifixion. Instead of denying eternal, collective Jewish responsibility, he affirmed their role, for which he believed Christians should be forever grateful, since Jesus' death gave them the means to be redeemed. The Creator having preordained the crucifixion since the start of time, the Jews were simply carrying out one more divinely appointed task. 'Where then was the inexpiable crime of those who fulfilled the beneficent intention? The holy race supplied the victim and the immolators. What other race could have been entrusted with such a consummation?' (*Tancred*, III, iv).

However muddled his views, Disraeli's intentions were serious. His message was twofold: first, England's civilization, with its worship of progress, 'its false excitement, its bustling invention, and its endless toil' was tired and superficial; its politics meaningless and futile; second, to save itself, to find inspiration, imagination and faith, it had to look Asia-ward, to the Near East, to the sources of its religion and values. 'A great thought', such as had gone forth before 'from Mount Sinai, from the villages of Galilee, from the deserts of Arabia', could revive England and its people; it could 'remodel all their institutions, change their principles of action, and breathe a new spirit into the whole scope of their existence' (*Tancred*, IV, ix). In Disraeli's imaginative universe, civilization came from Mediterranean nations, to which, of course, he traced his own roots.

All the great things have been done by the little nations. It is the Jordan and

Ilyssus that have civilised the modern races. An Arabian tribe [the Jews], a clan of the Aegean, have been the promulgators of all our knowledge; and we should never have heard of the Pharaohs, of Babylon the great and Nineveh the superb, of Cyrus and of Xerxes, had it not been for Athens and Jerusalem (*Tancred*, III, vii).

Jerusalem, moreover, ranked higher than Athens, for it was in the Land of Israel alone, and nowhere else, that God revealed himself, which is the reason that Tancred journeys there. As he tells Eva, 'I know well, though born in a distant and northern isle, that the Creator of the world speaks with man only in this land.' But after pouring forth his prayers at all its holy places and receiving no heavenly sign, Tancred realizes another 'desolating' truth: God does not speak to Europeans. Much to his regret, he discovers 'that there is a qualification of blood as well as of locality necessary for this communion, and that the featured votary must not only kneel in the Holy Land but be of the Holy Race' (*Tancred*, IV, iii). God, it seems, speaks only to Jews.

Disraeli's embrace of Jewish chauvinism in the 1840s seems at first to make little sense. Born an outsider, he had had some success by the mid-1840s in overcoming the obstacles his non-aristocratic, alien origins posed. He had become a well-known figure in national politics, having played a central role in the breakup of the Conservative party and the fall of Sir Robert Peel in June 1846. With Lord George Bentinck, he was leader of the protectionist faction in the House of Commons and sat with Bentinck on the opposition front bench when parliament convened in January 1847. But he was still consumed by ambition, driven to shine ever more brightly, eager to take the lead, to hold national office. To trumpet his origins and spout racial claptrap about Jewish superiority were unusual steps for someone in his position. Did he believe that this was the best method to win the affections of the well-born Christian landowners whose leader he wished to become? A more obvious strategy would have been to muffle his Jewishness, avoiding constant mention of it, minimizing its relevance, perhaps even expressing contempt for it in order to prove that he had transcended it. This is what other converted or deracinated Jews in similar circumstances did, figures as diverse as Ferdinand Lassalle, Edwin Montagu, Walther Rathenau, Victor Adler, Leon Trotsky and Bruno Kreisky. When reminded of their Jewish origins or confronted with anti-Semitism, they became even more discrete and reticent about their Jewishness or even more contemptuous of Jews and their behaviour and concerns. Rosa Luxemburg's response to her friend Mathilde Wurm from her cell in the Wronke fortress in 1917 was typical: 'What do you want with your special Jewish sorrows? The wretched victims of the rubber plantations in Putamayo, the Negroes in Africa, with whose bodies Europeans play catch, are just as close to me ... I have no special corner in my heart for the ghetto.'[35] Why, then, did Disraeli? How can we understand his extraordinary, seemingly self-destructive behaviour?

The answer, which Hannah Arendt first suggested and Isaiah Berlin later developed at length, is that Disraeli's racial chauvinism was a compensatory countermyth, forged to combat his feelings of social inferiority through assertions of an ancient racial lineage more noble than that of the English aristocracy.[36] He countered the caste pride of the great landowners whose acceptance he craved and whose leader he wanted to be with his own imagined racial pride. He was led to inflate his Jewish birth into a claim of noble birth, Berlin noted, 'in order to feel that he was dealing on equal terms with the leaders of his family's adopted country, which he so profoundly venerated'.[37] In Disraeli's racial construction of history, the English aristocracy came from less noble stock than his own. They were, he wrote in *Tancred*, 'sprung from a horde of Baltic pirates, who were never heard of during the greater annals of the world'. His people, the Jews, on the other hand, were God's chosen, with whom alone He communicated, the creators of an advanced civilization 'at a time when the inhabitants of England were going half-naked and eating acorns in the forest'[38] and its bishops were 'tattooed savages' (I, xi; VI, iv).

Arendt suggested that Disraeli's espousal of these ideas represented a calculated strategic move. In her eyes, he was 'the potent wizard' who 'never took himself quite seriously and always played a role to win society and find popularity', a playful charlatan who manipulated his Jewishness to his social and political advantage. What her interpretation ignores, however, is that Disraeli took these ideas seriously, however theatrical their presentation. These ideas spoke to his deepest feelings; their adoption represented a profound psychological response to his status as an outsider, an alien in both Jewish and Christian society. He came to them through unconscious as much as conscious calculations and in the end could not leave them alone. When he wrote about Jews, he always went too far, harping on their power, exaggerating their importance, introducing them into contexts in which they did not otherwise belong (witness the chapter on Jews and Judaism in his biography of Lord George Bentinck[39]), 'trying to force his Jewish jackasseries on the world', as Thomas Carlyle saw it.[40] In this sense, he was obsessed with Jews, and, as is the case with obsessions in general, was unable to take up the subject and put it down at will. The emergence of his Jewishness was a psychological transformation, the coalescing of a new self-understanding, what Berlin called 'an inner image of himself with which he could establish for himself a place in the world, and play a part in history and society'.[41]

Expressions of racial pride also allowed Disraeli to assert his independence at a time when, in fact, his advancement was becoming more tied to aristocratic patronage.[42] In 1848, Lord George Bentinck's two brothers lent Disraeli £25,000 to purchase Hughenden Manor, the estate that he needed to occupy a county seat in parliament and that was a social prerequisite for leading the Tory party. Although the Bentincks had no intention of calling in their loan, viewing it as an investment in the political future of the Tories rather than a business venture, as 'a contribution from one of the great landowning families of England to enable their class to be represented by one of the most brilliant men of the day',[43] Disraeli was in their debt nonetheless. He also remained subordinate to Edward Stanley (earl of Derby from 1851), one of the grand seigneurs of landed England, who headed the Tory protectionists in the 1850s and 1860s. Not until 1868, when Derby became too ill to continue and resigned his post, was the way clear for Disraeli to become undisputed leader of the party and prime minister.

The outrageous racial ideas that Disraeli embraced in the 1840s constituted the core of his Jewishness. Aside from them, it had little or no other content. In Sidonia's pithy formula in *Tancred*, 'All is race; there is no other truth' (II, xiv). He and the other Jewish characters in Disraeli's novels, for example, do not lead Jewish lives – that is, they do not observe Jewish customs, read or expound Jewish texts, take a role in Jewish communal organizations, socialize in the main with other Jews or act in ways recognizably different from other characters, except by giving vent to their racial pride. Sidonia is unwilling to marry a non-Jew, Disraeli tells us in *Coningsby*, because he is as devoted to his race as other persons are to their religion: 'No earthly consideration would ever induce him to impair that purity of race on which he prides himself' (VII, i). Judaism as a body of beliefs, customs and ethics is usually absent in his fiction and other writing. Like his father, it seems, he believed that the Jewish religion had ceased to be a vital source of inspiration and meaning for modern societies. Lady Battersea (*née* Constance de Rothschild), who knew Disraeli well, captured the essence of his Jewishness when she wrote to her husband just after Disraeli's death in 1881: 'His racial instincts were his religion and he was true to that religion until he drew his last breath.'[44]

In constructing his Jewishness on racial lines, Disraeli had recourse to the long-lived myth of Sephardi superiority, a myth that originated in medieval Spain and later migrated to western and northern Europe with the expansion of the Sephardi diaspora.[45] The core of the myth was the belief that Jews from the Iberian peninsula were different in kind from other Jews, that they were superior by virtue of their culture, learning, wealth, descent, manners or, indeed, even blood. Although Disraeli himself was not, in a strict sense, a Spanish or Portuguese Jew – his grandparents and their parents were all Italian born – family ties to the Spanish and Portuguese congregation gave him licence to claim Iberian descent.[46] In his romanticized version of his family history, as much fiction as fact, his ancestors fled from Spain at the end of the fifteenth century and settled in Venice. There they flourished as merchants for two centuries, before his great-grandfather Disraeli sent his youngest son to London in the mid-eighteenth century.[47]

In conversation and correspondence as well, Disraeli identified himself with Spanish and Portuguese Jews and emphasized their superiority. He told Lord Stanley in 1851 that there were 'two races among the Hebrews' and that the Sephardim were 'the superior race'. Earlier, in 1844, he had written to his fellow Tory MP Richard Monckton Milnes, then visiting Berlin, that although German Jews were 'now the most intelligent of the tribes' they did not 'rank high in blood', not being Sephardim. In letters to Sarah Brydges Willyams, the childless widow of Sephardi ancestry whose fortune he inherited, he wrote often of their shared background, of their common descent from the aristocratic Laras, of 'the mysterious sympathy' that bound them together.[48] At the same time he described Ashkenazim, Jews of central and east European background, in unflattering, stereotypical terms, as objects of 'prejudice, dislike, disgust, perhaps hatred'. Imagine, he asked readers of *Tancred*,

> a being … born to hereditary insult, without any education, apparently without a circumstance that can develop the slightest taste, or cherish the least sentiment for the beautiful, living amid fogs and filth, never treated with kindness, seldom with justice, occupied with the meanest, if not the vilest, toil, bargaining for frippery, speculating in usury, existing for ever under the concurrent influence of degrading causes (V, vi).

In private, the young Disraeli used condescending, derogatory terms in referring to Ashkenazim. In a letter to his father in December 1835, for example, he described the merchant banker Isaac Lyon Goldsmid as 'a sharp Tedesco'. (The word 'tudesco' (the more usual Sephardi ortho-graphy) is an iberianized form of the Italian word 'tedesco' (German). By the mid-seventeenth century, it had become almost an epithet in western Sephardi usage.) In a similar vein, after meeting James de Rothschild for the first time, at a dinner in Paris in 1842, he described him to his sister as 'a happy mixture of the French Dandy & the orange boy' – a description that linked the elegant Frankfurt-born banker to the ragged Ashkenazim who hawked oranges (a Jewish speciality) in London's streets.[49]

The claim that Spanish and Portuguese Jews were superior to German and Polish Jews was a stock feature of Sephardi apologetics in the eighteenth and nineteenth centuries. Spokesmen for ex-converso commu-nities in western and northern Europe used it regularly to distance themselves from more recent, less westernized Jewish immigrants, hoping thereby to convince statesmen and civil servants of their worth and fitness for citizenship. In Disraeli's case it is clear that his father was the conduit through which the myth reached him. In his *Genius of Judaism*, Isaac borrowed, without attribution, Isaac de Pinto's formulation of the myth in his *Apologie pour la nation juive*, published in Amsterdam in 1762 in response to Voltaire's defamation of Jews. He restated Pinto's claim that the Jews were not one but several nations, each, like the chameleon, reflecting the colour of the spot on which it rested. He then explained that the first Jews to settle in England were 'noblemen, officers, learned physicians, and opulent merchants' from Spain and Portugal who brought with them 'their national characteristic ... their haughtiness, their high sense of honour, and their stately manners'. Later arrivals from Germany and Poland, on the other hand, were 'a race in every respect of an inferior rank'.[50]

The Sephardi myth reinforced Disraeli's penchant to think in terms of racial difference, a trait he shared with novelists and historians of the period who used the discourse of Anglo-Saxonism.[51] At the same time it gave his racial thinking an extra dimension. It allowed him to root his claim to noble status both in the soil of ancient Israel, with its spiritual and ethical legacy, and in the 'golden age' of Spanish Jewry, with its heritage of *convivencia*, courtiers and cultural distinction. Under its sway, Disraeli was able to imagine himself a descendant of haughty, honour-conscious, opulent hidalgos with polished manners, like his fictional *alter ego* Sidonia. Of course, at one level these two claims were in conflict with each other.

Did Jewish nobility derive from biblical Israel, in which case it was the inheritance of all Jews? Or did it derive from the Iberian experience, in which case it was a scarcer commodity, limited to families like his own? In any case, he seems not to have been troubled by the tension between the two claims and repeatedly advanced both of them.

Although ethnic rather than religious ties were the core of Disraeli's Jewishness, he was not insensitive in middle age to the attractions of religious rituals. In *Alroy*, written when he was in his twenties, in his father's house, at the same time that Isaac was writing *The Genius of Judaism*, he had mocked rabbinic tradition. But fourteen years later, in *Tancred*, he was more sympathetic. In an extended passage describing the celebration of Sukkot, or the Festival of Tabernacles, in northern Europe, Disraeli remarked that there was 'something profoundly interesting in this devoted observance of Oriental customs in the heart of our Saxon and Sclavonian cities'. He went on to describe how celebration of the holiday transformed the down-trodden Houndsditch Jew.

> The season arrives, and the mind and heart of that being are filled with images and passions that have been ranked in all ages among the most beautiful and the most genial of human experience; filled with a subject the most vivid, the most graceful, the most joyous, and the most exuberant; a subject which has inspired poets, and which has made gods; the harvest of the grape in the native regions of the Vine (V, vi).

With genuine warmth, Disraeli then described how this humble Jew built his *sukkah* and how, after returning from synagogue, 'he sups late with his wife and his children in the open air, as if he were in the pleasant villages of Galilee, beneath its sweet and starry sky'.

In his tribute to Sukkot and its ancient customs, however, Disraeli ignored the historical, redemptive dimension of the holiday, its commemoration of the period after the exodus from Egypt during which the Israelites dwelled in temporary booths, and instead concentrated on its agricultural aspect, especially the harvesting of grapes and making of wine, a theme that is absent in Jewish tradition. What attracted him were not the religious ideas associated with the holiday but its potential for being given a national or racial twist. Eva, daughter of a wealthy Jewish merchant in Jerusalem, refers to Sukkot as 'one of our great national festivals'. Even though the vineyards of Israel had ceased to exist and the Jews had no fruits to gather, Disraeli observed, they still persisted in 'celebrating their vintage'. Such a race would 'regain their vineyards', he prophesied. 'What sublime inexorability in the law! *But* [my emphasis] what indomitable spirit in the people.' To reinforce the racial lesson he drew from Jewish ritual perseverance, Disraeli contrasted the 'noble' behaviour of his Houndsditch Jew with the boorish, drunken behaviour of a passing party of 'Anglo-Saxons', who sneer at the 'horrible feasts' of the 'cursed Jews' (*Tancred*, V, vi).

Disraeli's frequent references in *Alroy*, *Tancred* and elsewhere to the return to Zion suggest that his sense of Jewishness included a nationalist as well as ethnic dimension. His most unambiguous declaration of interest in the restoration of the Jews came in a conversation with Stanley in January 1851. While walking outdoors in the country, Disraeli talked to him 'with great earnestness on the subject of restoring the Jews to their own land'. (Was Disraeli to be the messianic figure who would effect their return?) Ignoring the cold, to which he was usually sensitive, and speaking with 'great apparent earnestness', Disraeli set forth a detailed plan. Rothschild and other Jewish bankers would purchase land from the Turks, whose empire was in ruins and would do anything for money. Agricultural colonies would be established, with their security guaranteed (Disraeli did not say how). The 'question of nationality' – the eventual political status of the reclaimed Jewish homeland – would be postponed until the colonies had taken firm root.[52]

If in the 1840s and 1850s Disraeli entertained fantasies about the territorial restoration of the Jews, he did nothing to advance their realization. Even his purchase of the Khedive's Suez Canal shares much later, in 1875, seems to have been unconnected to these earlier fantasies. But as we are concerned more with his state of mind – his feelings, sentiments and desires – than his policies, his failure to take action is irrelevant. That he dreamt such dreams and then spoke of them is what is critical. In my view, these fantasies reflected his need to possess a heroic, noble heritage and to see this heritage restored to its former glory. In this sense, he was a Jewish nationalist. However, his thoughts on the future of the Jewish people defy neat categorization. He was no proto-Zionist pure and simple for when he thought about the restoration of the Jews he tended to associate it with Christian myths and motifs. In the same passage in *Tancred* in which he described Sukkot in nationalist terms, he also referred to the *kiddush*, the blessing over wine recited at the start of festival and sabbath meals, as 'the very ceremony which the Divine Prince of Israel, nearly two thousand years ago, adopted at the most memorable of all repasts [the Last Supper], and eternally invested with eucharistic grace' (*Tancred*, V, vi). In the same diary entry in which Stanley recorded the above mentioned conversation, he also noted that Disraeli once said to him 'with earnestness' that 'if he retired from politics in time enough, he should resume literature, and write the *Life of Christ* from a national point of view, intending it for a posthumous work'. And during the Commons debate on Jewish emancipation in 1847 he identified his own views with those of the evangelical Lord Ashley (earl of Shaftesbury from 1851), a millenarian philo-Semite who looked forward to the restoration of the Jews to the Holy Land and their subsequent conversion.[53]

To assert, then, that Disraeli became a proud Jewish nationalist, while true, is not the whole truth. He also remained a believing, if somewhat unorthodox, Protestant. In some fundamental religious matters, to be sure, his thinking was quite conventional. He believed (or said he believed) that Jesus was the Christ, 'blending in his inexplicable nature the divine essence with the human elements, a sacrificial mediator' whose 'atoning blood' purified 'the myriads that had preceded and the myriads that will follow him'. In order to be completed, Judaism had to assimilate Christianity. It was deplorable that 'several millions of the Jewish race should persist in believing in only a part of their religion', but understandable, since it had been made known to them largely in a debased form (Roman Catholicism) by peoples who persecuted and tormented them. Now, however, with the Christian nations having grown more humane and tolerant and with the Jews having better opportunities to know pure, reformed Christianity, different results could be expected.[54]

While Disraeli's belief that Christianity completed, or superseded, Judaism was conventional, his other views about the relationship between Judaism and Christianity were not.[55] In the late 1840s and early 1850s, as Paul Smith has observed, Disraeli was working to reconcile his Jewish background and his Christian religion. He was then becoming leader of the party that championed the established Church and needed to develop a balance (however awkward) between Judaism and Christianity – to explain how a Jew could head both a Christian party and a Christian state.[56] Although his pronouncements on this matter will not stand up to rigorous theological scrutiny, there is a consistent theme or impulse that runs through them: the overwhelming urge to blur distinctions, bridge gaps and break down barriers between the two religious traditions. For example, in the Commons debate on Jewish emancipation in 1847, he argued for the removal of Jewish disabilities on the basis of the affinity between Judaism and Christianity and the latter's spiritual and ethical indebtedness to the former. 'Where is your Christianity', he asked his fellow legislators, 'if you do not believe in their Judaism?'[57] In *Tancred*, this blurring of theological and historical differences was even more pronounced. In one passage, Tancred asks Eva whether she worships Jesus. She replies, 'It sometimes seems to me that I ought, for I am of his race, and you should sympathise with your race.' He then asks her whether she has read the Gospels, which, of course, she has, the Anglican bishop of Jerusalem having given her a copy. And she has found it a good book, 'written ... entirely by Jews'. 'I find in it many things with which I agree; and if there be some from which I dissent, it may be that I do not comprehend them.' Excitedly Tancred tells her that she is already 'half a Christian!' (III, iv). Later in the novel, in explaining revelation to a Muslim emir, Tancred tells him that through Jesus, the last and greatest of Israel's princes, the Hebrew mind came to mould and govern the world. He concludes his explanation with the arresting but simple-minded formula 'Christianity is Judaism for the multitude, but it is still Judaism' (VI, iv). Disraeli was able to collapse distinctions between Judaism and Christianity in this way because his sense of being Jewish was rooted in race, or descent, rather than religion and thus lacked a distinctive theology, ethics or ritual. If 'all is race', the Jewish racial background of Christianity was more significant than the daughter religion's later theological and institutional development.

Disraeli's Christianity was as muddled as his Judaism and for much the same reason: neither the doctrinal nor experiential side of religion was important to him.[58] He himself did not find spiritual meaning or consolation in religion. Indeed, in his diary Stanley noted that Disraeli mocked all religions in private. Some of this irreverence comes through in his correspondence. For example, in a letter to his sister in 1851, he related how the duke of Portland had sent him half a buck as a present and how he had sent it on to the Lionel de Rothschilds 'as we [he and his wife] have dined there so often, & they never with us'. Afterwards, realizing that the meat was not kosher (the Rothschilds observed the dietary laws), he joked that 'as I mentioned the donor [Portland], & they love Lords, notwith[standin]g that they throw out their [emancipation] bill, I think they will swallow it'.[59] When defining his personal connection to the Church of England, he did so in racial terms. He wrote that he looked upon the Anglican Church as 'the only Jewish institution that remains' and, thus, 'irrespective of its being the depository of divine truth' he 'must ever cling to it as the visible means which embalms the memory of my race, their deeds and thoughts, and connects their blood with the origin of things'.[60] Hardly a stirring confession of faith! Even on his death bed, he remained religiously indifferent, refusing clerical ministration or any talk of religion.[61]

In public, of course, Disraeli was a faithful communicant of the Church of England, or at least as faithful as other Tory notables.[62] But, then, to have absented himself from church would have been unthinkable. He went because that was what was done and, equally, because he saw the Anglican Church as a bastion of tradition and a pillar of the established order. Before he became leader of the Tories, in fact, he had found Catholicism attractive for similar reasons: its antiquity, traditionalism, changelessness, pageantry – and the fact that it stood for everything opposed to whiggery. In his early novels and his Young England trilogy, he invariably treated Catholic characters with great sympathy. Witness the model well-born landowner, the old Catholic Eustace Lyle in *Coningsby* (III, iii–v). However, if his opposition to whiggish and Radical views made him a High Church enthusiast in his Young England phase, he did not remain one afterwards. He became increasingly Protestant with time and, in 1874, while prime minister, supported a bill to suppress High Church ritualistic practices – without much enthusiasm. He would have preferred to leave the issue alone and took it up largely to please Queen Victoria. In general, he showed little interest in religious issues when he was in office, despite what he had written in *Tancred* and elsewhere. When he had to make Church appointments, for example, he was ignorant of the names and qualifications of candidates for promotion. The dean of Windsor remarked in November 1868 that he 'showed an ignorance about all Church matters, men, opinions, that was astonishing'.[63]

Once Disraeli succeeded in climbing to the top, he ceased to harp on Jewish themes in the way he had in the first two decades of his political career. This was due, in part, to his having less time (or need) to write fiction. From the late 1840s, politics absorbed most of his creative energies. But this was also due to a change in his personal fortunes: having gained the Tory leadership, he no longer needed to restate his claims to noble origins with the urgency that drove him earlier. Having made it to the top and won the reluctant admiration of the Tory magnates, who could not produce a leader of equal calibre from their own ranks, he no longer experienced the same pressure to counter their myth with one of his own. He did not, to be sure, abandon or repudiate his earlier views. Rather, he was less insistent in airing them. Having served their purpose, they took a back seat to more immediate political concerns. Tellingly, when once again his Jewishness was used as a club with which to beat him – during the Eastern crisis of 1876–8 – he did not respond, as before, with assertions of Jewish racial pride. In fact, he did not respond at all to the blatant anti-Semitism of his Liberal and Radical critics, who targeted both him personally and English Jews generally. Instead, he took the high road of defending Britain's geopolitical interests as he saw them.[64] As prime minister and, from August 1876, a hereditary lord, his ambition had been satisfied; his credentials as an Englishman and a patriot were secure.

Appendix: Judaica from the Disraeli library sold in October 1881

Annunciaçao Justiniano, Diogo da. *Sermãs do Auto da Fé*. Lisbon, 1705.

Bail, Charles Joseph. *Etat des juifs en France, en Espagne, et en Italie depuis le commencement du cinquième siècle de l'ère vulgaire jusqu'à la fin du seizième*. Paris, 1823.

    Des juifs au dix-neuvième siècle. Paris, 1816.

Barbequière, J. B. *La maçonnerie mesmérienne*. Amsterdam, 1784.

Bauer, Georg Lorenz. *The Theology of the Old Testament, or A Biblical Sketch of the Religious Opinions of the Ancient Hebrews*. London, 1838.

Benjamin of Tudela. *Travels of Rabbi Benjamin*. Edited by R. Gerrons. London, 1783.

Beugnot, Auguste Arthur. *Les juifs d'occident, ou recherches sur l'état civil, le commerce, et la littérature des juifs en France, en Espagne, et en Italie pendant la durée du moyen âge*. Paris, 1824.

Bible. *The Song of Songs*. 1867.

Castro y Rossi, Adolfo. *The History of the Jews in Spain*. Translated by Edward D. G. M. Kirwan. Cambridge and London, 1851.

D'Israeli, Isaac. *The Genius of Judaism*. London, 1833.

    Narrative Poems. London, 1803.

    Romances, third rev. edn. London, 1807.

Dulaure, Jacques Antoine. *Des cultes qui ont précédé et amené l'idolatrie, ou l'adoration des figures humaines*. Paris, 1805.

Fleury, Claude. *Essais historiques et critiques sur les juifs anciens et modems, ou supplément aux moeurs des Israélites*. Lyons, 1771.

    Les moeurs des israélites et des chrétiens. Paris, 1720.

Ganz, David. *Chronologia sacra-profana*. Leiden, 1644.

Gaulmin, Gilbert. *De vita et morte Mosis*. Hamburg, 1714.

Gawler, George. *Observations and Practical Suggestions in Furtherance of Jewish Colonies in Palestine*. London, 1845.

Grégoire, Henri. *An Essay on the Physical, Moral, and Political Reformation of the Jews.* London, 1791.

Le Clerc, Jean. *Twelve Dissertations out of Monsieur Le Clerk's Genesis.* Translated by Mr Brown. London, 1696.

Lettres juives du célèbre Mendelssohn, philosophe de Berlin, avec les remarques et réponses de monsieur le docteur Kölble et autres savants hommes. N.p., 1771.

Leon Templo, Jacob Judah Aryeh. *Tratado de los cherubim.* Amsterdam, 1654.

Levi, David. *A Defence of the Old Testament, in a Series of Letters Addressed to Thomas Paine.* London, 1797.

Letters to Dr Priestley in Answer to Those He Addressed to the Jews. London, 1787.

A Succinct Account of the Rites and Ceremonies of the Jews. London, 1783.

Lewis, Thomas. *Origines Hebraeae: The Antiquities of the Hebrew Republick.* 4 vols. London, 1724–5.

Lopes, Isaac. *Sermão pregado no K.K. de T.T. em Sabath Emor.* Amsterdam, 1719.

Margoliouth, Moses. *The Jews in Great Britain.* London, 1846.

Meier, Johannes. *Tractatus de temporibus s. et festis diebus Hebraeorum.* Amsterdam, 1724.

Menasseh, Ben Israel. *The Conciliator.* Translated by Elias Haim Lindo. London, 1842.

Of the Term of Life. Translated by Thomas Pocock. London, 1699.

Del Conciliador. Parts 3 and 4. Amsterdam, 1650–1.

De resurrectione mortuorum. Amsterdam, 1636.

Thesouro dos dinim. Amsterdam, 1710.

Modena, Leon. *The History of the Present Jews throughout the World.* Translated by John Gwen. London, 1707.

The History of the Rites, Customes and Manner of Life of the Present Jews throughout the World. Translated by Edmund Chilmead. London, 1650.

Mocatta, Moses, trans. *The Inquisition and Judaism.* London, 1845.

Nieto, David. *Esh dat.* London, 1715.

Pimentel, Abraham Cohen. *Questoes e discursos academicos.* Hamburg, 1688.

Priaulx, Osmond de Beauvoir. *Quaestiones Mosaicae, or The Book of Genesis Compared with the Remains of Ancient Religions.* London, 1842.

Proteus. *A Dissertation on the Celestial Sign of the Rainbow, in Connection with the Sacred 'Oath of the Seventh'.* Dublin, 1879.

Rittangel, Johann Stephan, trans. and ed. *Liber Iezirah.* Amsterdam, 1642.

Rossi, Giovanni Bernardo de. *Bibliotheca judaica antichristiana.* Parma, 1800.

Rowley, Adam Clarke, trans. *Joel. A Translation in Metrical Parallelisms according to the Hebrew Method of Punctuation.* London, 1867.

Sabatier de Castres, Antoine. *Apologie de Spinosa et du Spinosisme.* Paris, 1810.

Samuel, Moses. *Memoirs of Moses Mendelssohn,* second edn. London, 1827.

Stehelin, John Peter. *The Traditions of the Jews, or The Doctrines and Expositions Contain'd in the Talmud and Other Rabbinical Writings.* 2 vols. London, 1742–3.

Taylor, Francis, trans. *Targum prius et posterius in Esteram.* London, 1655.
Tama, Diogene. *Transactions of the Parisian Sanhedrim.* Translated by F. D. Kirwan.
    London, 1807.
Yossipon. *A Compendious and Most Marvellous Historie of the Latter Times of the Iewes
    Common Weale.* Translated by Peter Merwyn. London, 1596.

In addition to the above, the list includes one Hebrew book, whose title is not
indicated, since the clerk who recorded the books was, presumably, unable to read
Hebrew, and two volumes of miscellaneous tracts on Jewish matters, the first
covering the period 1747 to 1753, the second the period 1753 to 1794. There is
also one book whose author and title I have been unable to decipher.

Source: list of books sold, October 1881, DFam/E/1/9A, Rothschild Archive,
London. I have corrected spelling and other errors and listed the books in a
manner consistent with current bibliographical conventions.

6

Disraeli's interpretation of English history

PETER JUPP

I

One of the principal ways in which Disraeli fashioned an identity and a role for himself in public life was by constructing a particular interpretation of the past and giving it repeated publicity through a steady stream of writings. He began the enterprise with the publication in 1826 of his socio-political novel *Vivian Grey* and, following additions in correspondence and other publications, gave it fullest expression in a political tract, *Vindication of the English Constitution*, published in complete and abbreviated forms in 1835–6. Later, in the 1840s, he enlarged on his interpretation in his trilogy of novels, particularly on those aspects related to race, but from a reading of all Disraeli's works – his publications, his correspondence and his speeches – one of the most remarkable features of his thesis was the consistency with which he adhered to it over more than fifty years. The views that he formed in the late 1820s and early 1830s remained substantially the same until his death.

Although his interpretation is well known to Disraeli scholars, most praise its imaginative qualities but find it lacking in substance. W. F. Monypenny, for example, in a more optimistic judgement than many, wrote in 1912 of its containing an element of paradox but also large measures of truth, originality and insight that would be well received by those who were being emancipated from the 'tyranny of the Whig writers'. Since then, however, judgements have been less favourable. Richard Faber in *Beaconsfield and Bolingbroke* (1961) draws out some useful similarities between Bolingbroke's and Disraeli's views of the past but suggests that overall Disraeli's are romantic and shallow. Robert Blake, while setting out clearly the views Disraeli expresses in the *Vindication*, later caricatures them and concludes that they are of questionable validity. John Vincent suggests that he borrowed his ideas from his father and that his overall interpretation is 'palpable, crass, unblushing, philistine, optimistic, evolutionary Whig history; and having written it, he ingeniously turned it to Tory ends'. Jane Ridley, the most recent contributor, although being specific about borrowings from Burke in the *Vindication*, suggests that its opening sections are a re-hash of Whig views and that the later revisions in *Sybil* are based on little or no research. Overall the conclusion to be drawn from the historiography is that Disraeli's interpretation is not to be taken too seriously, either as history or as a means by which Disraeli established a purpose for himself and a role in the eyes of the public.[1]

The objective of this chapter is to examine his interpretation afresh and, in particular, the political and historiographical contexts in which the substance of it was devised – that is, in the period *c.* 1820–35. This should enable us to assess how far and in what ways Disraeli's history was constructed to meet the needs of his political career; and to what extent it was in tune with contemporary historiography. We will then be in a position to judge what part his history played in a serious fashioning of the self.

II

In the last thirty years or so our understanding of British politics in the period when Disraeli constructed his interpretation has altered significantly. The period used to be regarded as a crucial stage in an era of 'reform' or 'improvement', exemplified by the giving way of the narrowly based toryism of Lord Liverpool to the more popular whiggism of Lord Grey. The Whigs' Reform acts of 1832 provided the foundation for the evolution of a more 'modern' system of government, part of which was the development of a two-party 'system' in which each party had a different set of principles and appealed to an ever-expanding electorate.

Recent research, however, suggests a much more complex and, in some respects, a very different picture. Thus much more emphasis is placed now on the central role of the monarchy in the governing process and its popularity with the general public. George IV's and William IV's reluctant acquiescence to Catholic relief in 1829 and the Whigs' Reform bills in 1832 were therefore far from being minor irritants to what contemporary utilitarians referred to as 'the march of intellect'. At the time they were key issues in high politics and a matter of great debate. The power of the monarchy certainly suffered a reverse in 1829 and 1832 but, as the controversy surrounding William IV's dismissal of Lord Melbourne in 1834 demonstrates, the future role of the monarchy was an important political issue when the *Vindication* was written at both the parliamentary and popular levels.[2] Indeed it remained important until Queen Victoria adjusted to a non-partisan role in the early 1840s.

A similar point can be made about the House of Lords. Until comparatively recently the Lords was thought to be of little account in contemporary politics. Today, however, it is recognized that it mattered in three particular respects. One was the fact that it was in the Lords that the leadership of the campaigns against Catholic relief and parliamentary reform was based. Although the first of these was much more popular with the English public than the latter, they made the role of the House a prominent issue in post-Reform politics. The second concerns the composition of the House. In the course of the previous half century the number of peers had doubled to around 400, many of the newcomers being ennobled for service to the state rather than in recognition of their landed wealth. Moreover it was also thought that many of the established peerage families were now drawing more income from trade and manufacture than they did from the land. This created fears that the role of the House as the ultimate defender of the landed interest was under threat and that its submission to Catholic relief and parliamentary reform was a portent of worse concessions to come.[3] Finally, there was the question, after 1832, of the relationship between a predominantly conservative Lords and a largely liberal Commons. How far should the Upper House bend to the will of the Lower? This was the issue to which the *Vindication* was specifically directed.

Parliamentary politics are regarded as much more fluid in this period than was previously thought. The principal cause was the breakup of the traditional party of government in 1828–9. Labelled Tories by their opponents, the party under Lord Liverpool was a loose confederation consisting of the following elements: the ministers and their acolytes, most of whom were pragmatic, professional politicians who did not refer to themselves as Tories and had a semi-detached attitude to the concept of party; a growing number of active backbenchers who were ready to describe themselves as Tories because they felt that the Protestant constitution and the landed interest were under threat; and a large number of members who only attended in emergencies and even then more in hope of favours from the executive than from any attachment to party. On the Catholic question and other issues between 1828 and 1830, this confederation split into three: the pragmatists and dependants who were prepared to concede Catholic relief; a substantial number of Tories, now named Ultra-Tories, who refused to make the concession and went into opposition; and the Canningites who supported relief but disliked the government's pragmatism on other matters and did likewise. This sparked a lively debate amongst all three factions on the role of principles in politics.[4]

The dislocation of party politics continued after the fall of the Wellington government. The Whig party, which was the traditional party of opposition but had virtually ceased to exist between 1827 and July 1830, formed a junction with some ex-Canningites and some Ultra-Tories on taking office in November 1830. In 1832 a large number of Radicals entered parliament and by 1835 O'Connell's Irish party had come into existence. Further, recent research suggests that even after the Reform acts, the new Conservative party under Wellington and Peel was still disposed to think of itself principally as a traditional party of opposition rather than a new type of national political organization.[5] In short, what is particularly notable about parliamentary politics during the period when Disraeli was devising his interpretation was the proliferation and permutations of parties after nearly fifty years of comparative stability.

There is also a growing body of evidence that popular participation in parliamentary as well as other forms of politics in the pre-Reform period was much higher than used to be thought. Recent studies demonstrate that elections in most counties and many towns in England were open tests of opinion amongst electorates that consisted predominantly of the lower ranks of society and on average involved 30 per cent or more of the adult male population.[6] In addition, studies of individual counties and towns have revealed a rich popular political culture in which there were high levels of political partisanship that increasingly reflected the party battle at Westminster. This culture was sustained by a plethora of popular organizations and means of association: friendly clubs, trades unions, co-operative societies, mechanics institutes, churches and chapels, pubs, coffee houses and reading rooms. Further, the 1820s saw a huge growth in petitioning parliament for the redress of grievances on the part of a large number of pressure groups, many of them of a popular character. Overall, what is striking about pre-Reform popular politics is not only its richness but also its increasing focus on parliament as the institution to which local communities should turn for remedies to problems. It is also significant that, with the exception of the Catholic question, the pre-Reform parliaments were remarkably open to such pressures.[7] From this perspective, the Reform acts and the £10 franchise did not necessarily guarantee a more open system.

As far as the state of political opinion is concerned, the traditional picture of an elite toryism confronting various strands of popular liberalism has now been discarded. Liberalism, in the sense of free trade, the removal of civil disabilities on non-Anglicans and a utilitarian approach to institutions, was certainly the majority opinion of the substantial newspaper press and its predominantly middle-class readers. On the other hand, the evidence suggests that it was very much a minority creed as far as the wider pre-Reform public was concerned. Far more popular was what one historian has referred to as 'popular constitutionalism', a hybrid consisting of the following components: a love of monarchy and of country; anti-Catholicism; hostility to over-rewarded and oligarchic officialdom in central and local government; support for reduced government expenditure and for lower taxes on consumption; and a belief that it was the constitutional duty of parliament to support the rights of 'free-born Englishmen' when pressed by constitutional means to do so. In 1829 many who subscribed to such views supported the campaign against Catholic relief but in 1830–2 popular constitutionalism made common cause with middle-class liberalism and the relatively small number of Paineite radicals and Hodgskinsonian socialists in support of parliamentary reform – principally to produce a parliament that would be more responsive to pressure to reduce taxation and relieve agricultural distress. After 1832 a key issue was whether the 'new' parliamentary conservatism of Peel would be able to reach an accommodation with the mixture of traditional radicalism and toryism that made up popular constitutionalist opinion.[8]

Thus the period when Disraeli devised his interpretation was one of exceptional fluidity and complexity. Some of the pillars of the constitution had been torn down leaving others such as the monarchy and the House of Lords with an uncertain future. The traditional parties of government and opposition had disintegrated and were in the process of reformation. Public opinion, fashioned now by a vigorous and expanding newspaper press as well as by an extraordinary number of clubs and societies, was divided between the minority creeds of liberalism and Paineite radicalism and a more popular form of constitutionalism containing elements of historic radicalism and toryism.

III

It was against this background that Disraeli developed his interpretation. The questions at issue are how far it was influenced by the features of contemporary politics adumbrated above; and how far by his own political objectives. These are the questions that are pursued in the following section.

The interpretation, as reconstructed from all his publications, takes the form of an analytical narrative stretching from ancient to modern times. The reason for such a long time span was his assumption, which is set out in the first part of the *Vindication*, that prescription was the guiding force in English history. Each generation, he argues, was born with 'filial duties' to the state. It gradually acquired a reverence for antiquity and through that reverence, which it 'placed above law, and held superior to reason', it acquired a respect for the 'binding force' of historic contracts. This was one explanation for the sequence of building blocks of liberty: the laws of Edward the Confessor, Magna Carta, the Petition of Right and the Declaration of Right – a sequence he described as 'a pedigree of six centuries'.[9]

The narrative traces the main contributors to the evolution of liberty from Anglo-Saxon to later medieval times, drawing the conclusion in the *Vindication* that, by the end of the reign of Henry VI, a virtual balance of power had come into existence and 'the present Constitution of England was amply, if not perfectly, developed'. This was due to the fact that the Lancastrian kings owed their throne to parliament; that the aristocracy 'headed the nation'; and that it became customary for the House of Commons to ally with the 'discontented party among the Peers'. As a result the Crown acknowledged several of parliament's existing 'rights' and conceded to the Commons the important new right of formulating bills.[10]

From the Tudor period onwards Disraeli's interpretation is increasingly influenced by contemporary politics. As we shall see, the emphasis he places on the role of the monarchy and the House of Lords, and his insistence on the strength of Tory opinion amongst the public, all reflect contemporary realities. In addition, he clearly shaped the interpretation to suit his own political requirements. This can be seen in his indictment of the Whigs and the exhortation in the *Vindication* that the Tory-dominated Lords should resist the Whig–O'Connell majority in the Commons in 1835–6 and, more generally, in the attempts to persuade the Tories in the

1830s and 1840s that they needed leadership of genius and principle, to link them once again with popular Tory sentiment in the English localities.

The attack on the Whigs began with his analysis of the political changes that had taken place under the Tudors. It was under their rule, he believed, that the supposed Plantagenet 'balance' had disappeared to the Crown's advantage. Henry VIII and Elizabeth, he argued in the *Vindication*, had been obliged to deal with a new phenomenon in politics – 'religious dissension' – and this they did in two ways: first, by balancing 'the great parties' of Catholics and Protestants; and, second, by commanding majorities in the Commons through the creation of new borough constituencies which they could easily control. This had enabled Elizabeth to pass on to her successor 'the sceptre of a despot'.

But Disraeli also believed that the aristocracy played a part. In the *Vindication* he argued that 'the great peers and chivalric Commons' had been so weakened by the Wars of the Roses that they had ceased to provide a lead to the 'nation'. Later, however, principally in *Coningsby*, he took the thesis a stage further and argued that the fortunes of some aristocrats had been restored by spoils from the dissolution of the monasteries. These aristocrats became a faction which, fearful that it might lose its ill-gotten gains at a Catholic restoration, abandoned its responsibility for the balance of power and encouraged instead 'political religionism' – the development of the Protestant sects. An unholy alliance had been formed – at least in Disraeli's mind – between aristocratic proto-Whigs and popular dissent.[11]

This was the thesis that he developed for the Stuart period. James I and Charles I had inherited arbitrary power from the Tudors: they did not seek to create it. On the other hand the aristocracy as a whole, having abandoned the sword for the pen during years of unprecedented prosperity, was within its rights to try and re-establish the balance that had existed under the later Plantagenets. The tragedy was that an accommodation could have been achieved. Charles I was willing to settle for a 'limited monarchy' and to make the following concessions to the Long Parliament in 1641 that would have gone far to achieve it: the establishment of triennial parliaments; the outlawing of ship money; and the abolition of the Star Chamber and the Court of High Commission. Moreover the majority of the public, nearly the whole of the peerage and all but eleven of the Commons would have accepted this settlement. It was only a narrow majority in the Commons and a minority of the

peerage and the public – the Whigs and the dissenters – who would not:
the Whigs being determined on an oligarchy and the dissenters on a
republic. An unnecessary civil war had therefore ensued. In addition,
Disraeli argued that much the same would have happened in James II's
reign had not the King's Catholicism united the aristocracy – both the
Tories and the Whigs – in placing William of Orange on the throne. The
Revolution of 1688 was not, therefore, Whig property. Further, 1688 and
the subsequent legislation that constituted the Revolution Settlement
added little of substance to the balance that Charles I's concessions of
1640 would have established had civil war not intervened. Indeed, in
Disraeli's view, the Revolution Settlement secured no more power to
parliament than it had possessed in the reign of Henry IV.[12]

This onslaught, as set out in the *Vindication* and later publications, was
continued for the post-Revolution period. The Whigs, he argued, as men
of great wealth who represented about two-thirds of the peerage, maintained their connection with the dissenters but allied themselves to a new
phenomenon in the state – the city financiers who grew rich by dealing in
the national debt that William III created to fund his foreign wars. Initially
they were kept in check by the King's 'adroit balance of parties', but
having 'disfranchised' Scotland with the Union of 1707, they established
the Hanoverians on the throne by a *coup d'état* in which the dukes of
Somerset and Argyll 'forced' a dying Queen to appoint the duke of
Shrewsbury as lord treasurer and thereby have George I proclaimed the
moment she expired and before any challenge to his succession could be
made. With the Hanoverians established, the Whigs promptly reduced the
monarchy to a cypher by gaining a monopoly of power in the executive
and legislature. This they achieved by banning the Tories from holding
offices in the state; by electoral malpractice; and by such means as the
Septennial act which prolonged the life of parliaments in which they had
secure majorities. Indeed they would have gone further, and established a
permanent majority in the Lords with the Peerage bill of 1719, had not the
Tories mustered in the Commons to defeat it. The King, to use Disraeli's
famous metaphor, had been reduced to the position of a doge in the
oligarchic state of Venice – a position with which those sympathetic to the
plight of George IV and William IV in 1829 and 1831–2 would have had
instant empathy.[13]

This state of affairs lasted until 1760 when George III restored the
balance and consigned the Whigs to opposition, a position in which they
largely remained until 1830. Attempts were made, Disraeli argued,

principally by Edmund Burke, to convert the Whigs to non-oligarchic politics and restore their 'moral existence', but these had failed. They toyed with jacobinism in the wake of the French Revolution, but in the new century took up liberalism (including what Disraeli referred to as the cause of the Irish Catholic middle class), in order to resume their station as the hereditary guardians of the Hanoverian dynasty. This was the objective that lay behind their Reform acts of 1832. Since then they had re-established an oligarchy by means of a renewed alliance with dissent and fresh allies in Daniel O'Connell's Irish party, the political expression of the Catholic middle class. Disraeli's overall argument against the Whigs was now complete: in the 1540s and 1640s they made an alliance with dissent to achieve their objectives; in the early eighteenth century they added the new power in the land, the London financiers; and in the 1830s they were prepared to ally with Irish nationalism to keep the Tories of England in the cold.[14]

In the case of the Tories, Disraeli's central belief was that they had always formed the majority in England. Initially – principally in Anne's reign – their natural leaders had been forced into excessive royalism in order to resist Whig oligarchy. Subsequently, however, their need was for new leadership that could devise fresh principles and policies. These had been supplied by three key figures: Lord Bolingbroke, the political philosopher, in the 1730s; Lord Shelburne, the short-lived prime minister in the early 1780s, whom Disraeli referred to as one of the 'suppressed characters' of English history; and Pitt the Younger, whom Disraeli described as Shelburne's disciple in matters of policy. It was these three who weaned the Tories from Whig-induced royalism and provided them with national as opposed to factional policies. These were a sinking fund with which to pay off the national debt and curb the growing influence of the 'monied interest'; freer trade based upon reciprocal treaties with other powers; friendship with France; parliamentary reform to accommodate the middle classes; and a re-invigorated peerage which would reward merit as well as wealth.[15]

Unfortunately, however, the French wars frustrated the fulfilment of these policies. Pitt lacked 'that passionate and creative genius required by an age of revolution' and consequently 'revived the old policy of oligarchy he had extinguished and plunged into all the numerous excesses of French wars and Dutch finance'. Even more unfortunately, his successors 'inherited all his errors without the latent genius'. In passages which clearly drew upon his own observations in the 1820s, Disraeli referred to them as 'pseudo-Tories' on account of their pragmatic as opposed to 'imaginative' responses to the great problems thrown up by the war and the Industrial Revolution. Prospects for a revival of true toryism had brightened when Canning and Huskisson joined the cabinet of the 'Arch-Mediocrity', Lord Liverpool, in 1822–3. Under their influence there was 'a partial recurrence' to the principles of Bolingbroke, Shelburne and the Younger Pitt. In the *Vindication* Disraeli eulogized the results, taking the story beyond Liverpool's ministry to include that of Wellington, the leader of the Tories in the Lords in 1835–6. During that time the Tories had pruned government expenditure, reformed the criminal code, revised the currency, remodelled the commercial system, relieved the dissenters and emancipated the Catholics. Later, however, principally in *Coningsby*, he revised this verdict in order to attack Peel and the now evergreen Wellington. Thus, although the presence of Canning and Huskisson in Liverpool's government had resulted in a period 'of happy and enlightened practice', it did not lead to a serious examination of the principles upon which this practice was based. If this had been the case, the Tories under Wellington (and, by implication, Peel) would have been able to cultivate the strong Tory sentiment in the localities and therefore give themselves the means to organize the party on 'a broad, a permanent, and national basis'. Such imaginative foresight would have enabled them to tackle the great questions of religious toleration and parliamentary reform in ways that would have prevented the growth of that new force in the state – powerful extra-parliamentary pressure groups. This, however, had not been the case. As a consequence, Disraeli found the Tories in the early 1830s not only confronted by a re-established Whig oligarchy but in a state of 'ignorant stupefaction' and in need of a new messiah. Initially he advocated the creation of a new national party that would unite Radicals and Tories in pursuit of true Tory ideals. In the late 1830s he saw prospects of achieving his objectives within Peel's Conservative party. By the 1840s, however, Peel was revealed to be a pragmatist in the tradition of Liverpool and therefore deserved to be replaced by a politician who had a special empathy with popular English toryism.[16]

A comparison between this interpretation and the state of contemporary politics reveals a number of obvious connections. The reduction of the first two Hanoverians to the position of a Venetian doge was not too distant from the forcing of both George IV and William IV to accept measures they did not approve. The repeated references to the aristocracy and the House of Lords as guardians of the constitution reflect contemporary concern over their respective roles. The labelling of the ministers in the party of government in the 1820s as 'pseudo Tories' touches on a contemporary debate about pragmatism and principles, as does Disraeli's argument of the 1840s that in his capacity as prime minister Wellington failed to harness popular toryism to his loosely knit parliamentary confederation and so reform the institutions of the state in the interests of the majority rather than the minority. Most significantly of all, the contention that toryism was the majority opinion in England has some basis in the light of events surrounding the Catholic question when anti-Catholic opinion in England was more numerous than pro-Catholic.[17]

As for the links between his interpretation and his own objectives, they are seen, most famously, in his attacks on the Whigs in the mid-1830s and on Peel in the first half of the 1840s. In the case of the former, Disraeli wished to convince the Tory peers to resist Whig oligarchy in the name of popular English toryism – a creed which he believed to be respectful of English liberties and which he subscribed to himself. In the case of the latter there was more opportunism at work, with the result that he altered his earlier judgement on the Tories in the 1820s in order to attack Peel.

But which came first? Did Disraeli's researches convince him that the Whigs and Peel deserved the criticism he heaped upon them? Or did Disraeli's political objectives lead him to find justification in the past for such attacks? A clue to the answer might lie in the qualities of Disraeli's interpretation in the light of the scholarship available to him. It is to that subject that we now turn.

IV

If Disraeli devised his interpretation at a time of exceptional fluidity in politics, the same could be said of the state of contemporary historical writing. As far as the intellectual status of the subject is concerned, the fashion for philosophical history as practised in the eighteenth century by David Hume and others had faded, but the days of history being regarded as a respectable, independent discipline were still well in the future. Within scholarly circles, history was still regarded as a branch of literature. On the other hand, important developments took place in the writing of history in the later eighteenth and early nineteenth centuries. There was, for example, a significant increase in the number of books published on various aspects of English and British history, particularly on the Anglo-Saxon and post-Conquest periods. Further, there was an overall increase in professionalism with more attention being paid to the citation and analysis of sources.[18] This led to the familiar growing pains of professionalization: complaints of a lack of official recognition and public support; acerbic criticisms of the work of other practitioners; and expressions of outrage at inadequate materials – in this case poor access to the public records unless historians had, in the words of one critic, 'the purse of Croesus and patience which rivals that of Job'.[19] There are also signs that interpretations of the past were beginning to play a more prominent part in parliamentary debate. One possible explanation may be that as classical models of rhetoric became outmoded, the increasing number of historical publications provided new materials with which to make a point. History, suggests a recent scholar, came to serve a function later occupied by political science.[20]

These developments increased the currency of history and had an important impact on the answers to the most prominent question asked by most historians: namely, who or what had been responsible for the growth in English liberties, best exemplified by the balance of power between King, Lords and Commons as established following the Glorious Revolution in 1688; and how had that balance fared since then? At the beginning of the nineteenth century there were three dominant theories. A traditional radical argument was that these liberties were founded in the Anglo-Saxon period but had been suppressed by the Normans in 1066 and had never been re-established. Another school argued that a collective consciousness of these Anglo-Saxon liberties had been transmitted over time from one generation to another and that this had led to their augmentation, principally in the thirteenth and seventeenth centuries. The key additions were alleged to be Magna Carta, the summoning of parliament in the thirteenth century, the Petition of Right, the Bill of Rights and the post-1688 settlement. This is best referred to as the prescriptive argument. A third school was more partisan and suggested that the heroes were the forebears of the Whigs who in the seventeenth century had formed an alliance with the dissenters and townsfolk to check the arbitrary designs of the Stuarts. By the early 1830s, however, increasingly professional research had cast doubt on all these propositions. Overarching interpretations of the kinds described above had fallen out of fashion and there was much debate about 'fortuitousness' – the possibility that events were the result of specific contemporary circumstances as opposed to being borne on a prescriptive tide. In other words, opportunities beckoned in history as well as in politics.

Disraeli certainly appears to have taken more trouble to seize the opportunity and make his mark as a historian than the established historiography suggests. As is well known, he had access as a boy to his father's substantial library of 25,000 volumes, much of which appears to have contained works of history. From the age of fourteen he was taking notes from Holinshed, Bacon and several other historians and this suggests that Vivian Grey's 'immense series of historical reading' with which his education began was probably based on Disraeli's own experience.[21] Jane Ridley argues convincingly that he was a voracious reader in his father's library when he was sixteen or seventeen, particularly of the classics but also of more modern authors such as Voltaire and Gibbon.[22] It was also at this time that he met Sharon Turner, the distinguished Anglo-Saxonist, and Henry Hallam, who was about to make his name as a constitutional historian, both of whom were friends of his father. In fact Turner became his godfather and was apparently responsible for his baptism. Later, following his father's move from London to Bradenham in Buckinghamshire, Disraeli continued to consult his father's library during the summer months, but it is likely that he also built up a library of his own at his wife's house in London. An inventory of the contents drawn up for the purposes of a mortgage in 1842 records a small library containing a number of historical works: Froissart's *Chronicle*; McCue's *History of the Reformation*; Hume's *History of England*; *The Ormonde Papers*; Burke's works; Gibbon's *Decline and Fall*; Henry Hallam's *Introduction to the Literature of Europe*; and his father's life of Charles I.[23]

The references in his writings also suggest a broad range of reading. In the sections on medieval history he pays tribute on more than one occasion to the scholarship of the seventeenth-century jurists, Sir Edward Coke and John Selden, ascribing to them his belief in prescription and drawing on their interpretations of baronial tenure and Magna Carta.[24] In the case of later historians, the list is more extensive and includes Harrington, Locke, Algernon Sidney, Clarendon, Burnet, Rapin-Thoyras (whose multi-volume *History of England* was the standard text until Hume's), de Lolme, 'the authoritative volumes' of Archdeacon Coxe and Thomas Madox; and of contemporary writers, Sharon Turner, John Lingard, Henry Hallam, Lord John Russell and Sir Francis Palgrave.[25] It is also worth noting that in his excursions into European history in *The Revolutionary Epick* he drew on Johannes von Müller's *An Universal History*, Capelle's *L'Origine et progrès de l'esprit révolutionnaire par un ancien ministre du roi de France* and Mignet's *Histoire de la révolution française depuis 1789 jusqu'en 1814.*[26] French scholars felt sufficiently confident about his historical knowledge to approve his election to the Société de l'Histoire de France in 1842–3.

However, the purpose of Disraeli's references is something of a puzzle. In view of his father's historical works and his own acquaintance with Turner and Hallam, Disraeli could not have been unaware of the growing professionalism in historical writing. Indeed he praised his father as a pioneer of source-based history; and complained on more than one occasion of the partisan histories of the eighteenth century and of the need for more impartial and scholarly accounts.[27] On the other hand his references to authorities are presented more as asides than as an indication of sources. Indeed there is not a single footnote in his historical writing despite the fact that footnotes were becoming the obligatory trademarks of the serious scholar. It is almost as if his purpose was to provide a veneer of learning that obscured its real depth and range. It is perhaps significant that this was also the impression he tried to create as an imaginative writer. When a serious enquirer asked him once who his favourite novelists were he replied, 'When I want to read a novel, I write one.'[28]

Yet despite an apparent indifference to scholarly standards, a comparison between Disraeli's interpretation and those of the major histories of Britain published before the 1830s confirms the view that his work was far from being a re-hash of the ideas of a handful of selected authors. The comparison may begin with Disraeli's argument that prescription was the most important dynamic in English history. As Ridley has pointed out, the words used to make the case bear a very close resemblance to those used by Burke in his *Reflections on the Revolution in France.* There are two points, however, that should be set against the view that Disraeli was indulging in mere plagiarism. The first is that prescription was by no means unique to Burke: it was common belief in the later eighteenth century. The second is that Disraeli's narrative recognizes that events could have other, equally powerful, causes. Indeed the clear paraphrasing of Burke on prescription almost takes the form of a respectful acknowledgement rather than an unqualified and well-thought-through endorsement.[29]

With regard to his narrative, Disraeli's choice of principal contributors to the development of English liberties in the medieval period had strong historiographical support. In the case of the long-standing controversy over the impact of the Norman Conquest, for example, Disraeli blended the theories of prescription and fortuitousness to conclude that key post-Conquest building blocks such as Magna Carta and the summoning of parliament had grown out of established Saxon rights and customs but were fashioned by particular contemporary circumstances. It was these developments, he argued, that led ultimately to the establishment of a balance of power between King, Lords and Commons in the reign of Henry VI.

His emphasis on the importance of the post-Conquest (as opposed to the Anglo-Saxon) period and the role of fortuitous contemporary events was in close accord with a growing number of contemporary historians. In the case of fortuitousness, for example, some, such as John Miller, went further than Disraeli did in the case of Magna Carta, arguing that self-interest rather than the public good was in the forefront of the baronial mind.[30] As for the origins of parliament, there is a very close resemblance between Disraeli's version and those of Lingard, Hallam and Sir James Mackintosh, the only oddity being his dating of the separation of the Lords and the Commons to the reign of Edward I.[31] Although it was generally agreed that the event was extremely difficult to date, Mackintosh favoured Henry III's reign and John Miller, Edward III's.[32] Apart from Disraeli, only the Record Commission, possibly under the direction of Palgrave, favoured Edward I and was scorned for its pains by at least one historian.[33] Moreover his argument that a balance of power had emerged in the reign of Henry VI was by no means novel. Most scholars preferred an earlier reign (and Disraeli himself later plumped for Henry IV's) but Lingard had made a special case for Henry VI in the first volumes of his *History* published in 1819.[34]

Disraeli's thesis on the collapse of the 'balance of power' under Henry VII and the emergence of a Tudor despotism that worked to the advantage of proto-Whigs also had support from contemporary scholarship. The argument that the collapse of the balance of power under Henry VII was due to the aristocracy being deprived of its leading role and the breakup of the alliance between discontented peers and the Commons was a modernized version of the views of a succession of scholars which can be traced back to Harrington.[35] The detail he provides on the creation of new constituencies by the Tudors is very similar to that found in Hallam.[36] Further, there was nothing novel in Disraeli's view that a link could be established between the Whigs and those who benefited most from the dissolution of the monasteries. The thesis that the dissolution enhanced the wealth of the gentry and yeomanry and thereby fuelled the political demands of the Commons against the Stuarts can be traced to the seventeenth century and the works of Harrington, and it resurfaced later in Bolingbroke and, indeed, Mackintosh and Lingard.[37] However, the thesis was given a more overtly political twist by two other early nine-teenth-century writers. One was Hallam who in his *Constitutional History*, which was first published in 1827, makes an oblique reference to the possibility of a direct connection by suggesting that the dissolution produced the families regarded as the most considerable in the 1820s, which would certainly have included the Whigs.[38] The other, William Cobbett, went further. In his *History of the Reformation* published between 1824 and 1827, he writes of the main beneficiaries of the dissolution being the real if not the literal ancestors of those who became the main opponents of James II, that is the Whigs.[39] Disraeli was simply stretching the thesis to its limit.

His interpretation of events leading to the Civil War and the Glorious Revolution was also in line with that of other historians. The characteriza-tion of James I and Charles I as having made foolish displays of arbitrary power that they had inherited from the Tudors, as opposed to having sought new powers, can be traced from Bolingbroke and Hume to De Lolme and Isaac D'Israeli.[40] It was by no means the universal view – Miller and George Brodie argue the case for arbitrary power being their conscious objective – but even Disraeli's Whig contemporary, Lord John Russell, described Charles I as foolish and with merely absolutist tenden-cies.[41]

There was also a growing consensus about Disraeli's judgements on the immediate prelude to civil war. Hallam agreed with him that the aristocracy was within its rights to seek a restoration of the balance of power and in the company of Lingard concurred in his view that Charles I made sufficient concessions at the end of the Long Parliament to achieve that end. In fact Hallam anticipated Disraeli's point that these concessions would restore the balance that had existed under the later Plantagenets.[42] Further, those who were well read in the literature would have found nothing surprising in Disraeli's argument that the Civil War was precipi-tated by a self-interested alliance between Whigs and dissenters in the teeth of majority opinion in the country; and that it was a combination of Whigs and Tories which brought about the Glorious Revolution. Boling-broke, Hume, Lingard and Hallam all make these points. Moreover Hallam added a point about the 1680s that Disraeli somewhat surprisingly fails to make: that the Tories then represented majority opinion.[43]

In fact the most novel part of Disraeli's interpretation is that dealing with the years after 1688. Its novelty, however, should not be exaggerated.

His central thesis for the period 1688–1760 of a restoration of a balance of power that led to the establishment of a Whig oligarchy sustained by a mixture of corruption and an alliance with the monied interest is one that can be traced from the neo-Harringtons of that period to Bolingbroke, Smollett (who continued Hume's history after 1688) and eventually to Hallam.[44] Even a reading of early nineteenth-century Whigs such as Archdeacon Coxe on Walpole and Pelham, or Lord John Russell on the constitution, does not seriously undermine the argument. Both admitted the unsavoury aspects of Whig government under the first two Hanoverians.[45] It is also worth noting that Disraeli's famous metaphor of the Hanoverians being reduced by the Whigs to the position of a doge in the Venetian oligarchy was far from original. Of his contemporaries, Byron had popularized the plight of a Venetian doge confronted by a corrupt aristocracy in his dramatic tragedy, *Marino Faliero, Doge of Venice,* and Hallam used the metaphor when describing the likely position of the monarchy if the Exclusionists had won the argument in the 1680s.[46] It is possible, however, that Disraeli was drawn to the metaphor for other reasons. In the Jewish memory oligarchy had been the fate of the Jews in exilic times and Jewish historians used the word 'presbyterianism' to describe that form of polity. As for the Venetian oligarchy, it had been a subject of fascination to seventeenth-century English political theorists because Venice was the only surviving example of ancient prudence. By using the term 'Venetian oligarchy', Disraeli was suggesting that the seventeenth-century Whigs had been dazzled by the example of Venice and that their eighteenth-century descendants had replicated it. It may well be, however, that Disraeli also had the earlier Jewish example in mind – indeed it may have been that example which engendered his venom against oligarchy in general and the Whigs in particular.[47]

Moreover a number of Disraeli's subsidiary points were anticipated by others, particularly Hallam. The favourable comparison between the balance of power after the Revolution Settlement and that under the later Plantagenets, the suggestion that Bolingbroke's career needed a reappraisal in view of his probable conversion of Tories from extreme royalism and the proposition that the Tories represented majority opinion during the oligarchy were all made by Hallam.[48]

With regard to the period after 1760, the historiography was comparatively thin, although Robert Bisset and John Adolphus had published histories of George III's reign by the time Disraeli began his work. He therefore had even more opportunity to be original. Even so some of his theories can be found in diluted form elsewhere. A number of commentators held the view that toryism and whiggism had been transformed since 1760. John Miller, for example, argued in 1803 that the two parties had forsaken their original ideas and had both espoused the principle of utility. Such a proposition is not too far away from Disraeli's view that the Tories had taken up pragmatism.[49] Moreover it is surely no coincidence that in *England and the English* which he published in 1833, Edward Lytton Bulwer, who was a close friend of Disraeli, castigated his compatriots for preferring 'practical men' to theorists as their politicians; and like Disraeli called for the formation of an independent and national parliamentary party to hold the balance between the Whigs and remnants of the Tory party. He did after all dedicate the second volume to Disraeli's father.[50]

V

But how was Disraeli's interpretation received; and how well has it survived the scrutiny of modern research? In the case of the contemporary response, there was none of any significance. The *Vindication* was reviewed in only one of the leading periodicals and although his novels received extensive notices, there was remarkably little comment on the accuracy of their historical content.[51] Moreover any impact his interpretation might have had was put into the shadow by the publication of the first volumes of Macaulay's *History* in 1848. By merging the prescriptive and Whig partisan schools, Macaulay established the famous 'Whig interpretation' which exercised a powerful influence on the writing of British political history until Sir Lewis Namier destroyed it in the 1920s.

With regard to the verdict of modern research, we may restrict our assessment to the period after 1714. As outlined above, Disraeli characterized the Hanoverian era as one when a battle between parties replaced the traditional battle between King and parliament. The Whigs secured the Hanoverian succession by a *coup d'état*. They then established an oligarchy by putting the Crown into commission, even holding cabinets without the King being present, and by such devices as the Septennial act, electoral corruption and the proscription of the Tories. They would have gone further and established a permanent stranglehold over the House of Lords by means of the 1719 Peerage bill had they not been thwarted by a Tory-led opposition in the Commons. As for the Tories, they represented the majority of the nation and being overawed by the Whig minority initially adopted extreme royalist views such as the divine right of kings, nonresistance and passive obedience. It was Lord Bolingbroke who weaned them from these misguided notions by 'the complete re-organization of the public mind' and laid the foundation for the future accession of a Tory party to power in a mixed constitution.[52]

As might be expected, some elements of this thesis have not survived the scrutiny of modern scholarship. A *coup d'état* is a simplistic interpretation of the Hanoverian succession and the Tories' supposed leadership of the campaign against the Peerage bill (which Disraeli mis-dated to 1718) has to be qualified. Thus, although 129 of their number did vote against it, five gave it their support and forty-two were absent. Further, for tactical reasons, none of those who voted against the bill actually spoke in that cause in the debate.[53] But the main body of the thesis has survived remarkably well. Modern research supports the argument that party politics became crucial and that the Whigs, at least a majority of them, established a supremacy, of which the Septennial act was seen as a cornerstone. More significantly, there is now authoritative support for Disraeli's contention that the Tories formed the majority of the state. Thus, in her study of the Tory party between 1714–60, *In Defiance of Oligarchy*, Professor Colley argues that throughout this period 'one-party whig government had been superimposed on a two-party, predominantly tory state' and that in most things the Tory party was 'in tune with the opinion of the majority of Englishmen outside Parliament'.[54] Further, there is some credibility in Disraeli's judgement of Bolingbroke. Thus a leading authority on eighteenth-century political ideas, Professor Dickinson, makes the point that it was chiefly Bolingbroke who was responsible for popularizing the idea that a country or national party could legitimately challenge the oligarchy and that clinging to extreme royalism was not the only path open to the Tories.[55]

Disraeli's view of Lord Shelburne provides another example of acute perception. In *Coningsby, Sybil*, and his letters and speeches of the 1840s, he praised Shelburne repeatedly as 'the ablest and most accomplished minister of the eighteenth century'. Shelburne, he said, was an intellectual with extensive connections with the international intelligentsia and a politician who relied on the force of ideas rather than the discipline of party to frustrate the re-establishment of a Whig oligarchy. It was therefore Shelburne who had revived the 'Bolingbroke system' of policy: permanent alliance with France and freer international trade based on reciprocal arrangements with other powers. In addition, Shelburne was the first major statesman to realize the importance of harnessing the rising middle class to the constitution by parliamentary reform and so prevent a future attempt at aristocratic oligarchy. Finally, Shelburne was the Younger Pitt's mentor and therefore a key member of the Tory apostolic succession.[56]

Disraeli was certainly correct to write that Shelburne's claim to fame was suppressed. Although his name was mentioned in debates on free trade in the late 1820s (usually on the assumption that few would know of his importance), nothing had been written about him by the 1840s; and Disraeli was unable to study his private papers despite his request to do so.[57] Only his parliamentary speeches were in print. In addition, it took some courage to praise him as he had been widely distrusted in his own day – so much so that he had been commonly referred to as the 'Jesuit in Berkeley Square'. His judgements have nevertheless stood the test of time remarkably well. His most recent biographer, John Norris, praises him for his prescience in recognizing that politics and administration would in future have to rest on public approval rather than private interest. In addition, John Erhman, the leading authority on the Younger Pitt and government and politics in the later eighteenth century, writes of Shelburne as 'one of the most impressive British prime ministers in his intellectual range'; that he did indeed abhor the ideas of party and developed policies, including that of reciprocal trade treaties, that bear a remarkable resemblance to those of the Younger Pitt. Where he differs with Disraeli is over the question of how far Pitt was Shelburne's disciple. He is cautious about making too close a connection, noting after an examination of the evidence that although Pitt arrived at similar conclusions to Shelburne on a range of matters, including all those mentioned by Disraeli, his methods of doing so were different.[58]

Disraeli's diagnosis of politics in Pitt's time and later is equally perceptive. His interpretation of Pitt remains sound and his argument that Pitt's successors in the early nineteenth century were too pragmatic to be labelled Tories, as the Whigs were prone to do, is in accord with modern scholarship. Moreover his argument that the entry of Canning and Huskisson into the cabinet in 1822 and 1823 opened up the possibility of a new style of governing more suited to the 'abstruse' and largely economic problems of the day – a style he described as 'happy and enlightened practice' – bears a close resemblance to a recent thesis by a leading authority on government then.[59] Finally, as we have seen earlier, Disraeli's insights into contemporary politics are in line with the conclusions of research conducted in the last three decades.

Disraeli's interpretation was therefore very much more than a work of imagination or casual plagiarism. The evidence suggests that his thesis on the development of English liberties from the Anglo-Saxons to the first two Hanoverians was based on extensive reading of the available literature and a clever synthesis of all but one of the conceptual approaches of his day, the exception being that of the Whig partisans. In the case of the period after 1760, his interpretation is more original and is strongly influenced by the events of his own day and his own political objectives. It is nevertheless the case that many of his more original arguments for that period have been endorsed by recent research.

VI

Disraeli undoubtedly took history and politics extremely seriously during the formative 1820s and early 1830s. For a young man as gifted and as ambitious as he clearly was, he evidently decided – no doubt with the help of his father and the latter's friends – that history was the principal means by which he could place contemporary politics in context and establish a justifiable cause for himself. His strength of purpose on this score has hitherto been underestimated. Thus the evidence shows that his interpretation highlighted issues which were of great concern to his contemporaries even though they were neglected or overlooked by subsequent historians – issues such as the roles of the monarchy and the House of Lords; the pragmatism of Wellington and Peel in conceding Catholic relief in the face of considerable English public opinion; and the strength of popular constitutionalism. In addition, there can be little doubt that he put very considerable effort into mastering English history. His interpretation is therefore based on very extensive reading and a careful synthesis of contemporary conceptual approaches to the past. The fact that he kept faith with the main thrust of his interpretation until his death is surely a measure of the seriousness with which he regarded it.

History was therefore an important part of the fashioning of the self. Serious reflections on contemporary politics and extensive study of English history convinced him that Whig oligarchy had often triumphed over the popular constitutionalism of the English majority as a result of opportunistic Whig alliances on the one hand and weak Tory leadership of the majority on the other. This discovery not only gave him historic connections with the suppressed opinion of the English majority; it also gave him a cause.

7

—

Disraeli's politics

PAUL SMITH

'Madam, Mr Di has had to make his position, & men who make their positions will
say & do things, wh: are not necessary to be said or done by those for whom
positions are provided.'[1]

Lord Stanley's words in overcoming the Queen's reluctance to accept
Disraeli, during his abortive attempt to form a ministry in February 1851,
may stand in their urbane cynicism for the prevalent view of his
subordinate's political character, then and since. The opinions Disraeli
professed and the courses of action he pursued have most often been
viewed, with greater or lesser reprobation – from John Bright's clucking at
his inability to 'comprehend the morality of our political course' to
Benjamin Jowett's only half-reluctant appreciation of 'a rascal whom I
rather like for his pluck & his cleverness'[2] – as functional purely to the
purpose of advancement in political life.

It is not an interpretation that ruffled Disraeli overmuch. He did not see
politics, any more than life in general, as a moral gymnasium, in which the
egoism of the individual could be sublimated simply by the strenuous
assertion of principle or disinterested exertion for the public good. The
political arena, like other arenas, was a proving ground of the self, and the
Disraelian self carried its own morality in its knapsack, along with its
marshal's baton. The words ascribed to Stanley above are Disraeli's own,
his recollection of what Stanley told him after seeing the Queen. Set down
probably in the early 1860s, in a series of reminiscences which may have
been designed to assist future biographers or memoirs to be written in
retirement,[3] they evidently represent a view of the nature and necessities
of Disraeli's earlier political career which he was not unhappy to lay
before posterity. He had seldom troubled to conceal the driving force of

his desire for a great public position, not even when deceiving his Shrewsbury constituents, in August 1844, into believing that he had never asked Peel for office in the latter's ministry. 'There is no doubt, gentlemen', he told them, 'that all men who offer themselves as candidates for public favor have motives of some sort. I candidly acknowledge that I have, and I will tell you what they are: I love fame; I love public reputation; I love to live in the eyes of the country; and it is a glorious thing for a man to do who has had my difficulties to contend against.'[4]

Yet, if Disraeli seems to have been content to acknowledge in his reporting of Stanley's words an inevitable servitude to some of the greasier arts of pole-climbing, it does not follow that climbing provides a sufficient definition of what his politics were about. If they were a politics of position and place, it was not simply the position coveted by worldly ambition or the place conferred by political success. Disraeli's political exertions, like his other endeavours in the world, were designed not merely to lift him but to locate him: to negotiate the terms on which the marginal figure he found himself to be in English society and politics could achieve a settlement and engineer a role corresponding to his sense of his genius. Nor was the making of a position conceived purely in an English frame. Disraeli was being characteristically self-complacent but he was not indulging in mere intellectual swagger when, in 1833, in the so-called 'Mutilated Diary', he wrote: 'My mind is a continental mind. It is a revolutionary mind.'[5] He saw himself always as caught up in the exciting maelstrom of world-historical processes and events. His self-fashioning had to operate on three levels. It had to situate his genius, first, in the spectrum of the cataclysmic developments in Europe which stemmed from the French and Industrial Revolutions; then, in relation to the special circumstances of the country which he inhabited; finally, because of the need to transcend his local position through the invocation of his place in a greater scheme of things, in the context of world civilization as animated most vitally by the special genius of his 'race'.

In moving between and across these planes of self-location and self-projection, Disraeli was commuting constantly between insider and outsider positions. An insider, at least in his own reading, in terms of the racially determined evolution of the human spirit and its expression in the intellectual and political development of contemporary Europe, he was an outsider when it came to finding the means of fulfilling his genius in an island on the edge of Europe, where, as he noted in 1833, the 'fixed character of our English society, the consequence of our aristocratic institutions, renders a *career* difficult'.[6] In his early years, he was conspicuously wrenched between the exhilarating sense of soaring above the native and local prejudices of his accidental place on the map, and the urgent ambition and need to achieve settlement and success in precisely that cold and unpromising clime. It is not surprising that, rather as the young Marx first saw the realization of his genius to lie in the life of a poet,[7] the young Disraeli channelled much of his initial effort to stamp his impression on the mind and fashion of his age into literature. Yet literary aspiration ran always in tandem with political. The assault on power of the hero of his first novel, *Vivian Grey*, represented, he later wrote, his 'active and real ambition',[8] and, indeed, the publication of the work in 1826 followed immediately upon his first essay in acquiring political influence, through his part in the setting up of the *Representative* newspaper. When the news of the Reform bill reached him on his eastern tour in 1831, he responded with alacrity to the sense that 'all was stirring', as he would put it in *Hartlebury*,[9] the novel written jointly with his sister, in which he recorded his first election contest.

It is the Reform bill crisis which prompts the hero of *Hartlebury*, Bohun, to return from his foreign travels. 'At the prospect of insurrection, he turned with more affection towards a country he had hitherto condemned as too uneventful for a man of genius' (I, xiv). Parliamentary reform held out the prospect of an era of change in British politics which might open new avenues for the advancement of talented young men without fortune or connection. Even 'insurrection' seemed a real possibility in the autumn of 1831. Disraeli reached England on 23 October. A fortnight earlier, the Lords had rejected the Reform bill; a week later, a mob sacked Bristol's Mansion House, in one of many violent responses; a visitation of the cholera all the while heightening the apocalyptic atmosphere of the moment. Yet, however much the continental and revolutionary mind might be excited by the prospect of an insular convulsion paralleling the European dramas of the Napoleonic era which it had come to consciousness agonizingly too late to share, it was in the mind that revolution would remain. In *Hartlebury* (II, i), the aristocratic Bohun has 'too great a stake in the existing order of society to precipitate a revolution, though he intended to ride the storm, if the hurricane did occur', and this seems close enough to Disraeli's position. He was already, since his family's move from Bloomsbury to the 1,300-acre estate of Bradenham in 1829, picking up a little gentry colouring, and beginning his rooting, however incongruous, in the landed property on which he always held the social and political stability of his country to depend. Bradenham gave him a settlement that Bloomsbury had not. 'Write to me about Bradenham, about dogs and horses, orchards, gardens, – who calls, where you go', he had begged his sister from Gibraltar in August 1830.[10] If Bloomsbury might have rushed to the barricades (though perhaps only to look), Bradenham would not. 'The times are damnable', Disraeli wrote to Benjamin Austen in November 1831. 'I take the gloomiest views of affairs, but we must not lose our property without a struggle.'[11]

Though Disraeli had just taken lodgings in the heart of fashionable London, it was the family property at Bradenham (albeit only leased) that allowed him to launch his successive attempts to get into parliament for the nearby borough of High Wycombe as 'an independent neighbour'.[12] His letters in the first half of 1832, as he courted the constituency while scribbling *England and France: A Cure for the Ministerial Gallomania*, an anonymous attack on the foreign policy of the Grey government, can be read as indicating a certain Tory penchant, as befitted the son of a father whose volumes on Charles I had been Tory enough in tone to earn him an honorary DCL from the University of Oxford.[13] But in the flux and confusion of parties which Peter Jupp has described,[14] commitment to the old shibboleths exercised no compulsion. 'Toryism is worn out', Disraeli told Austen in June 1832, 'and I cannot condescend to be a Whig.'[15] He might have condescended to the Whigs had they done so to him, but both his 1832 contests were against Whigs, and in any case he was an unlikely candidate for transfusion into the tight consanguinity of aristocratic whiggery. Disraeli was a reformer: the passage of the Whig government's bill was vital if politics were to become more open to aspirants like him. But faced with a son of the prime minister, Earl Grey, as an opponent at Wycombe, he quickly took the line that the government's version of Reform was too blatantly tailored to the interests of the Whigs, whose hostility to him, he alleged, rested on his lack of noble birth.[16] 'Grey and Reform', proclaimed his slogan, 'Disraeli and the People.'

In these circumstances, it was natural for Disraeli to adopt the holding position of an independent Radical, and natural for him also to seek to enrol against exclusive whiggery the resentment of the Wycombe Tories. By November 1832, he was invoking the Tory shades of Sir William Wyndham and Lord Bolingbroke in support of such Radical devices as triennial parliaments and the ballot deemed necessary to counter Whig designs.[17] This was a less cheeky and paradoxical operation than it has sometimes seemed. Radicalism in the 1830s allowed for all kinds of eccentricities. Disraeli's experimentation with it was another of his theatre workshops of the personality, neither naive witness of political conviction nor merely cynical vehicle of political manoeuvre, but rather the opening bid in a process of political self-materialization. His radicalism was not of the philosophic kind, nor that of the Birmingham men, about whom he was scathing when he met Attwood and his colleagues in May 1832.[18] His *entrée* to Radical circles was through his friend and fellow-novelist, Edward Lytton Bulwer, and his penchant was for the high-toned style of Sir Francis Burdett, whom Byron had thought the only reformer in whose company a gentleman would be seen.[19] Burdett, a supporter of equal electoral districts, annual parliaments and a direct taxation franchise, adopted a 'patriot' stance which linked him to the 'country' ideology of the late seventeenth and the eighteenth centuries, described his political creed as that of a Tory of the reign of Queen Anne, and owed a substantial debt to Bolingbroke. Disraeli, who failed to secure his endorsement at Wycombe but later came to be friendly with him, compared his views to those of Wyndham and Sir John Hynde Cotton and called him a Jacobite who had been mistaken for a Jacobin.[20] A figure like Burdett conferred living reality on Disraeli's linking of Radical with Tory traditions. Disraeli was already in his Wycombe contests testing the possibilities of creating a suitable intellectual and political vehicle for himself by reviving the 'country' opposition politics of Bolingbroke's day as a counter to what he regarded as the emergence of a new Whig oligarchy comparable to that under the early Hanoverians.

In so doing, he was also exploring the adaptability to his needs of the powerful current of popular constitutionalism outlined by Peter Jupp,[21] patriotic and monarchist, hostile to bureaucratic centralization and high government expenditure, and conservative of the rights of 'free-born Englishmen', which mingled elements of traditional radicalism with toryism. His address of 27 June 1832 employed the most basic rhetoric of that current in its direction to 'the free and independent electors of Wycombe', and the invocation of nation and empire was prominent in his campaigns.[22] Popular constitutionalism became vital in the effort of location which his entry into politics obliged him to accelerate. His political imagination thrilled to the titanic struggle between two principles of government contending for the mastery of the world, the aristocratic on the one hand, the revolutionary and democratic on the other, which it would dramatize poetically (though not poetically enough) in 1834 in the *Revolutionary Epick*, his last, bathetic bid to take world literature by storm by giving sublime expression to the spirit of the age. But it was hard to fix world-historical drama in Wycombe, or, once the proto-revolutionary moment had passed, to see the Reform bill crisis in England as more than a little local difficulty. Wycombe nonetheless was where Disraeli was, and locality was what he had to come to terms with. If in the spheres of literature and dandyism, and within the conventions of the romantic mode, the young Disraeli had been able to feel and function in a European rather than a merely national frame, finding the point of insertion into the political life of England, with its settled institutions, its aristocratic elite and its historic allegiances imposed a narrower focus. The limitless expansion of the romantic self, subversive in principle of all established forms, had now to be reconciled to the limits of time, place and tradition. Genius must compound with the *genius loci*.

'He conceives it right [Bright noted of Disraeli in 1852] to strive for a great career with such principles as are in vogue in his age and country – says the politics and principles to suit England must be of the "English type".'[23] Englishness was made central to Disraeli's fashioning of a political persona, both by his consciousness of not being accepted as fully or unconstrainedly English and by his sense of the superior understanding of England that the detachment of one not bred in native traditions and prejudices conferred. The status of outsider was at once his handicap and the means of overcoming it, the chief obstacle to his acceptance and the source of his title to lead and guide in England by virtue of the objective vision that only an outsider could possess. The urgency of his ambition drove him at once to escape from it and to exploit it the more in proportion as he was made to recognize that it could not be escaped. In his first political forays, his position rested on an unqualified identification with his country, betraying, perhaps, in its stridency an underlying sense that his credentials were not likely to pass unchallenged. Dismissing in the *Gallomania*, in April 1832, the outworn appellations of Whig and Tory, he wrote: 'My politics are described by one word and that word is ENGLAND.'[24] This 'very John Bull book', as he described it to his sister,[25] was published anonymously, but the tone was maintained in his October address at Wycombe, in which he conjured Englishmen to save from the 'rapacious, tyrannical, and incapable faction' of the Whigs 'the unparalleled empire, raised by the heroic energies of your fathers', to rid themselves of 'all that political jargon and factious slang of Whig and Tory', and to unite in forming 'a great national party which alone can save the country from impending destruction'.[26] The idea of a national party quickly reappeared in his pamphlet of April 1833, *What is He?*, as in his friend Bulwer's *England and the English*, a work which Disraeli said contained 'many a hint from our colloquies'.[27] For two Radical sparks in the hour of Reform, looking to a revitalized force of public opinion and popular energy to bring into being a new political world, it was tempting to envisage their talents shaping and directing the movement through the medium of a new national coalition, bringing together, Disraeli advocated in *What is He?*, Tories and Radicals to guide the transition from the aristocratic principle of government to the democratic which must now replace it. 'Great spirits may yet arise, spirits whose proud destiny it may still be, at the same time to maintain the glory of the Empire, and to secure the happiness of the People!'[28]

The politics of identification with England, Disraeli made clear in the *Gallomania*, involved confiding in the 'genius of the people' and governing in accordance with the national character, formed by 'particular modes of religious belief, ancient institutions, peculiar manners, venerable customs, and intelligible interests'.[29] The radicalism and democracy of his approach lay thus not in any desire to overturn established institutions or hand power to the masses, but in the conviction derived from his experience at Wycombe that political advancement for men like him depended on mobilizing a popular coalition to defeat the attempt of the Whigs to base a permanent oligarchical supremacy on a franchise carefully rigged and restricted for partisan ends. In *Hartlebury* (II, i) Bohun concludes that, under pretence of making changes required by the spirit of the age, the Whigs had set out to destroy the balance of parties, creating a situation in which the only way to get rid of them was to 'expand the Whig constituency into a national constituency' by the further prosecution of Reform. This version of the popular constitutionalist mix was an essentially conservative one, and adaptable from the first as much to a Tory as to a Radical platform, as Disraeli veered about in the attempt to enter parliament, from an abortive start for a Buckinghamshire county seat in December 1832, as a supporter of the agricultural interest, 'the only solid basis of the social fabric',[30] to a flourish as a Radical and anti-ministerialist candidate at Marylebone in the succeeding months. With the realization in 1834–5 that Reform was not going to produce the expected Radical surge, that, as parties regained their cohesion, 'He who aspires to be a practical politician must in this country be a party man',[31] and that Tory strength was forcibly reviving under Peel, its conservative colouring could be emphasized to support Disraeli's final candidature for Wycombe (with help from Conservative party funds) and his appearance as the official Conservative candidate at Taunton in April 1835. The internal logic which was plain to Disraeli was, however, less obvious to his critics, and at Taunton he had to exercise some ingenuity in rebutting charges that he was ratting on a Radical past, explaining, for example, that measures such as triennial parliaments and secret ballot, which it had been necessary to advocate as means of defence against the Whigs, were no longer required now that the true national party he had been endeavouring to promote had emerged with the renaissance of toryism under Peel.[32] It was time for more elaborate codification of his ideas. The politics of Englishness and of popular constitutionalism required some definition of England and its constitution, and formal commitment to the Tories some definition of their history and character. Politics obliged Disraeli to shift the focus of his moral imagining from the self to the environment in which the self must operate, the accommodation of each to the other dictating the terms for the fashioning of both. He moved thus in the mid-1830s and the 1840s from the individual mode of introspection, which had reached its apogee with him in *Contarini Fleming*, to the collective, to history, through which the special faculty of the seer could claim to discern the true character and destiny of organisms such as nations and parties, and, by peeling away excrescences and errors, could restore to them the knowledge of their identity and mission.

It was this reconceptualization of country and party, necessary to establish himself and his claim to lead in both, on which Disraeli embarked in the *Vindication of the English Constitution in a Letter to a Noble and Learned Lord*, published in December 1835. Though produced for the immediate polemical purpose of justifying resistance by Tory peers to the Municipal Corporations bill, and defending the House of Lords against Radical attacks, the *Vindication* contained an exposition of broad historical and political views from which Disraeli never in essence retreated, couched in the didactic tones of one confident that his father's library had added to superior intellectual gifts the benefits of unusual learning. It was, and in parts reads like, a long lecture to the English, designed to relieve them of 'confusion of ideas' by showing them what was 'essential', what 'adventitious', in the character of their institutions and their political parties. As yet, Disraeli's confidence did not extend to asserting the external standpoint which endowed the lecturer with special insight. His use of words like 'we' and 'our' in relation to periods centuries before his ancestors had set foot in England demonstrated a determination to belong: he was appropriating English history in writing about it.

The preceding chapter has examined the content and foundations of Disraeli's historical narrative, and his use of that narrative to achieve the strategic goal of reversing the stereotypes of contemporary Whig propaganda, by characterizing the Whigs as the oligarchic, the Tories as the national and popular party. Disraeli had not entered politics to languish on the unpopular side. Toryism, in his reading, became 'the proposed or practised embodification, as the case may be, of the national will and character', to the extent that it must sometimes 'represent and reflect the passions and prejudices of the nation as well as its purer energies and its more enlarged and philosophic views'.[33] Disraeli's Tory politics were literally England, his country, right or wrong. Government which deferred to the genius of the people must lead by following. 'A statesman', he had told the Wycombe electors in December 1834, 'is the creature of his age ... The people have their passions, and it is even the duty of public men occasionally to adopt sentiments with which they do not sympathize, because the people must have leaders.'[34]

Commitment to a politics of English essentialism, however, required Disraeli to conceive an essential England in which he could belong. Grafting himself on to an 'ancient people'[35] was a delicate operation. To define the nation in terms of origins and descent would place outside the circle a family which had yet to complete its first century in England. It was necessary to look to genius rather than genes: for all his embracing of 'our ancestors', Disraeli needed to describe the nation by its possession of a political prudence and a set of institutions and conventions, the benefits of which were entailed on every successive generation of loyal subjects and not simply on the successors by blood of the original family. His approach in the *Vindication* was to conceive the nation in terms of its embodiment in state, constitution and law, and the rights and liberties which they guaranteed. Perhaps this came naturally to one conscious of the dependence of the Jewish people across Europe, especially in their emergence from the ghettos of the continent, on the securing of civil liberties by the strength of a state in principle indifferent to ancestry and creed.

Disraeli contended in Burkean vein that the constitution embodied the wisdom of preceding generations that 'society is neither more nor less than a compact', that 'the foundation of civil polity is Convention', and that 'no right can be long relied on that cannot boast a conventional origin'.[36] The state, 'a complicated creation of refined art',[37] was not merely the guardian but the source of rights, and as such beyond challenge in the name of the abstract principles dear to the utilitarian theorists whose doctrines the *Vindication* energetically disputed.

> Had not the State been created, the subject would not have existed. Man ... was the child of the State, and born with filial duties ... Our ancestors could not comprehend how this high spirit of loyalty could be more efficiently maintained, than by providing that the rights, privileges, and possessions, of all should rest on no better foundation than the State itself. They would permit no antagonist principle in their body politic. They would not tolerate nature struggling with art, or theory with habit. Hence their reverence for prescription, which they placed above law, and held superior to reason.[38]

English liberty consisted in the enjoyment of equality of civil rights, as established by Magna Carta, 'without which, whatever may be its name, no government can be free, and based upon which principle, every government, however it may be styled, is, in fact, a Democracy'.[39] So far as Disraeli had a definition of the democratic principle of government, this was it. His glossing of it was impeccably conservative. The equality which he represented as the 'basis of English society', he distinguished, in Hegelian terminology, from the levelling French variety, which destroyed social and political cohesion, reducing 'the subject into a mere individual' and degrading 'the state into a mere society'.[40] It was 'the equality that elevates and creates', and its principle was that 'every one should be privileged ... an Englishman, however humble may be his birth, whether he be doomed to the plough or destined to the loom, is born to the noblest of all inheritances, the equality of civil rights; he is born to freedom, he is born to justice, and he is born to property'.[41]

Equality in this sense was entirely compatible with a hierarchical social structure – what Disraeli called 'gradation' – comprising 'classes' but not 'castes', and allowing for social mobility.

> Hence that admirable order, which is the characteristic of our society; for in England every man knows or finds his place; the law has supplied every man with a position, and nature has a liberal charter to amend the arrangement of the law. Our equality is the safety-valve of tumultuous spirits; our gradation the security of the humble and the meek. The latter take refuge in their order; the former seek relief in emancipating themselves from its rank.[42]

Civil equality was enjoyed and social stratification exemplified within a framework of local and national institutions which articulated the life and protected the liberties of the people. It was those institutions which made 'us' a nation. 'Without our Crown, our Church, our Universities, our great municipal and commercial Corporations, our Magistracy, and its dependent scheme of provincial polity, the inhabitants, instead of being a nation, would present only a mass of individuals governed by a metropolis.'[43] The political institutions of the country were recognized by the former solicitor's clerk and postulant country gentleman as having entirely 'emanated from the legal economy of the land'.[44] Landed property was still the base of political authority. Disraeli's essential argument for the representative character of the House of Lords was that it derived from the nature of the peers' property and their hereditary leadership 'especially of the cultivators of the land, the genuine and permanent population of England, its peasantry'.[45]

It was the obstacle the country's institutions posed to the arbitrary power of a would-be centralizing despotism that, in Disraeli's reading, caused the Whigs and their allies to attack them; and it was the historic function of the Tory party in defending them, as the only security for the people's privileges, that constituted its title to be 'the really democratic party of England'.[46] Democratic measures had become all the more necessary to the Tories since the 'state trick' of the Reform act, placing the power of the Commons in the hands of a narrow, 'sectarian' constituency fraudulently represented as the people, had deprived them of political power proportionate to their preponderance of social power: Disraeli wished the electorate were 'even more catholic, though certainly not more Papist'.[47] 'The more popular the constituency', he had told a Taunton supporter in July 1835, 'the stronger the Tories will become.'[48]

The re-invention of the Tory party was a spirited exercise in the transformational power of the romantic vision. In effecting to his satisfaction the intellectual rescue of the Tories from the state in which, he informed readers of *The Times*,[49] he had found them on his return to England from the Near East, without 'a single definite or intelligible idea as to their position or their duties, or the character of their party', Disraeli converted the party into a home which could accommodate his Radical furniture, booked its ticket on the democratic coach, and staked his claim to a leading role in its affairs as the man who could hold up to it the mirror of its true self. All the same, the *Vindication* both in its content and in its form, emphasized while it attempted to solve the problem of his insertion into high political life. It constructed a nation defined by law and institutions rather than by ancestry and blood, in which he could readily belong, but it recognized, almost against its intention, a society in which it was very hard for him to succeed. 'The country where the legislative and even the executive office may be constitutionally obtained by every subject of the land, is a democracy', he contended;[50] but, observing that, if equality of civil rights was the basis of English polity, then 'gradation' was the 'superstructure',[51] and that political influence was intimately related to landed property, he acknowledged a structure of power not easily to be penetrated by the 'tumultuous spirits' whose ability to rise out of their order he assumed. In vindicating the legislative authority of the House of Lords, he recognized, too, a traditionary element in the nature of political authority unavailable by definition to any new aristocracy of mere merit: an upper chamber, he wrote, 'must be an order of individuals, whose personal importance crosses us in all the transactions of life, and pervades the remotest nook and corner of the country, an importance also which we find to arise as much from the hallowed associations, or even the inveterate prejudices of society, as from their mere public privileges and constitutional and territorial importance'.[52] If that close-textured and long-matured mentality could not easily be fashioned to suit the aspirant self, the self would have to adapt to its exigencies, and if Englishmen indeed loved lords, Disraeli would have to cultivate their patronage.

The search for a seat in parliament had already led him to canvass Lord Durham, when he thought the latter likely to lead radicalism to victory. The *Vindication* appeared under the aegis of two aristocratic patrons. One of them was dead. Disraeli mitigated the audacity of his tweaking of the Tory mind by invoking the authority of Bolingbroke, also charged in his time with inconsistency because he maintained 'that vigilant and meditative independence which is the privilege of an original and determined spirit', equally tempted to 'the formation of a new party, that dream of youthful ambition in a perplexed and discordant age, but destined in English politics to be never more substantial than a vision', and also forced in the end to choose between Whigs and Tories, and, in the analysis of their 'interior and essential qualities', to recognize that they stood respectively for oligarchy and democracy.[53] The livelier patron was Lyndhurst, lord chancellor in Peel's brief ministry of 1834–5 and leader of opposition in the Lords to the Municipal Corporations bill, to whom the *Vindication* was addressed. In adopting the already somewhat archaic form of 'A Letter to a Noble and Learned Lord', Disraeli cannot have been unaware of the echo of Burke's *Letter to a Noble Lord*, written after Burke's acceptance of a ministerial pension had, as Frans de Bruyn puts it, 'exposed a labyrinth of tensions and contradictions through which he had thrashed his way from the beginning of his career, most notably, the vexed relationship of patron and client, the virtues imputed to independence and the indignities associated with dependence, the prestige of the gentleman-amateur versus the stigma of professionalism, and the disparity between hereditary privilege and hard-won personal accomplishment'.[54] Lyndhurst, in fact, had risen by talent, as Disraeli hoped to do, but that hardly diminished the latter's sense of incongruity between the exhilarating manifestation of his powerful self in the exercise of the right which the English constitution conferred of 'expressing my free thoughts to a free people',[55] and the patient application of his suppliant self to the humiliating business of working his passage in an aristocratic structure of power. In the *Vindication*, Disraeli was the new Bolingbroke, 'the ablest writer and the most accomplished orator of his age, that rare union that in a country of free parliaments and a free press, insures to its possessor the privilege of exercising a constant influence over the mind of his country, that rare union that has rendered Burke so memorable'.[56] But he was equally the new Burke, the marginal genius, 'not, like his Grace of Bedford, swaddled, and rocked, and dandled into a Legislator', as Burke had bitterly remarked,[57] but obliged to exhibit the jewels and seek the reward of 'vigilant and meditative independence' in letters to lords.

Disraeli was nothing if not proud, and it is not surprising that he became increasingly frustrated when the lords failed to deliver the rewards. Though he secured a seat at Maidstone in 1837, as 'an uncompromising Adherent to that ancient Constitution, which once was the boast of our Fathers, and is still the Blessing of their Children',[58] his start in parliament was undistinguished, and he was not carried into office on Lyndhurst's coat-tails when Peel formed his Conservative ministry in 1841. Indeed, he now faced the frigidity of the tightly-buttoned, meritocratic group of official men that Peel headed, disinclined, perhaps unable, to take seriously an exotic of his type. If he was not much more of a *parvenu* professional in politics than Gladstone, he was nonetheless the wrong sort of *parvenu* for Peel's Conservative party and, by the beginning of 1844, when he failed to receive the whip at the opening of the session, his disaffection had placed him virtually outside it. His immediate response to neglect was to act as pied piper to a handful of aristocratic young hopefuls in the Young England group, harassing the leader who had refused him office with what Peel explicitly recognized as a version of the 'patriot' opposition tactics of the previous century.[59] Young England's parliamentary weight was trivial, but it marked a transition, appropriate to Disraeli's age and situation, from the swashbuckling parade of his own youth towards the intellectual formation of the youth that was coming up behind, an escape from a mortifying political present with a bid to pre-empt the political future by capturing the minds of those who would shape it. The exercise was carried out principally through the trilogy of novels published between 1844 and 1847, the protagonist of each a young nobleman in search of a cause, in which Disraeli set out to educate the well-born youth of England in their social and political duties. *Coningsby or: The New Generation* (1844) invited them to recognize their country's authentic political traditions and to assume their great political responsi-bilities; *Sybil or: The Two Nations* (1845) summoned them to the task of ending that alienation between rich and poor which threatened to disin-tegrate the nation, announcing in its closing sentence that 'the Youth of a Nation are the trustees of posterity'; and *Tancred or: The New Crusade* (1847) beckoned them to the reinvigoration of national faith through the rediscovery of its pristine sources. But if this sounded like a new series of letters to noble lords, with Disraeli in the role of domestic tutor to the rising generation of aristocracy, the format thinly masked a more grand-iose project, questioning the foundations of aristocratic politics altogether and conceptually transforming Disraeli's relation to them.

The transformation came from the remarkable force and form of Disraeli's reassertion, once baulked of parliamentary success, of the role of the supereminent genius who could command the mind, by expressing the spirit, of his age. Endeavouring, in the closing pages of the *Literary Character*, to define the role of the intellectual in society, Isaac D'Israeli had concluded that 'true genius is the organ of its nation ... it is also that of the state of the times'. 'The public mind' was 'the creation of the Master-Writers'.[60] In the *Vindication*, Disraeli had developed the idea that nations had characters, like individuals, and, like individuals, ascertained by self-examination their principles of right conduct.[61] In the trilogy he set himself the task of directing that self-examination. The technique of integrating and realizing the individual nature through the exploration of its psycho-history as a prelude to creative action, with which he had bid for fame in *Contarini Fleming*, was now to be applied to the nation: the trilogy was Disraeli's *Bildungsroman*, his attempted psychotherapy, of the English people.[62] He meant to be the author of England in more senses than one, and the externality of his authorial standpoint was now more open than in the *Vindication*, partly because his bid for political power had emphasized the difficulty of discreet advance, but still more because he now found the means to represent it unequivocally, not merely as conferring preternatural insight, but as deriving from his membership of a worldwide racial aristocracy, and the choicest portion of it at that, which made him not the equal but the superior of any breed of nobility in a northern isle. Where once he had reduced English politics to scale against the background of the continental clash of aristocratic and democratic principles, he did so now in the context of the great tides of history which he represented as determined by race, and especially by the creative genius of the Hebrew race, which had incubated the religion and moulded the consciousness of the West.[63] If, in the *Vindication*, the English were credited with being in politics 'as the old Hebrews in religion, "a favoured and peculiar people"', in the trilogy even their politics, or at least their conservative politics, are pressed in the Hebrew mould: toryism itself, Coningsby learns, is only the local manifestation of the inherent attachment of the Jews to conservative values, 'copied from the mighty prototype which has fashioned Europe'.[64] When exulting in the power of the Hebrew spirit, mediated in the trilogy through the figure of Sidonia, Disraeli no longer sought for aristocratic patrons, he patronized the aristocracy.

If, formally, the novels of the 1840s looked to a regenerated aristocracy to heal the nation's traumas by renovating politics, appeasing social strife and revitalizing faith, they showed little confidence in its ability to do so. The ambiguity of Disraeli's attitude to the aristocratic political system, as to the aristocratic society upon the successful penetration of which, he knew, political advancement largely depended, was barely disguised. The three young aristocratic 'heroes' are all innocents, if not boobies, needing to be hand-reared by the author. The moral and intellectual resources of their class are constantly called into question by Disraeli's acid portrayal of specimens like Lord Monmouth in *Coningsby* or Lords Marney and De Mowbray in *Sybil*. The fitness of their stock to maintain its position in a challenging environment is impugned, their need to draw on fresh reservoirs of energy and talent forcibly underlined. 'Brains every day become more precious than blood', Coningsby is obliged to understand (*Coningsby*, IX, iv). Only transfusions of new ideas and new blood from outside its narrow landed and Anglican world can preserve the influence of his kind. Jane Ridley notes that his political education is conducted by Lyle, a Roman Catholic, Millbank, a manufacturer, and above all Sidonia, a Jew.[65] Millbank's daughter Edith, who marries Coningsby, and Sybil, from a family of dispossessed gentry professing the Catholic faith, who marries Egremont, pump in the blood. But Millbank argues in *Coningsby* (IV, iv) that the 'formal' aristocracy has already lost its sway to a 'natural' or 'essential' aristocracy constituted by 'those men whom a nation recognises as the most eminent for virtue, talents and property, and if you please, birth and standing in the land. They guide opinion; and therefore they govern.'

It was through the guidance of opinion that Disraeli was once more aiming at the top. His return to novel-writing was his means of bypassing a Conservative party and a House of Commons too slow to recognize his pre-eminence and appealing directly to a public opinion conceived as more powerful than an effete aristocratic elite. The existing system of parliamentary and party politics was pushed aside. Disraeli had made his first, false start in politics in the affair of the *Representative* newspaper by seeking power through the influence of print. Now he returned to the charge. In the *Vindication*, he had dismissed the claims of the House of Commons to represent the nation, responsible as it was not to the 'general body of the people' but only to the narrow 'estate' constituted by the electorate.[66] Developing the point in *Coningsby*, he pressed the claims of an alternative national forum more attuned to his talents. 'Public opinion', Sidonia declares (*Coningsby*, V, viii) 'has a more direct, a more comprehensive, a more efficient organ for its utterance, than a body of men sectionally chosen. The printing press is a political element unknown to classic or feudal times. It absorbs in a great degree the duties of the sovereign, the priest, the parliament; it controls, it educates, it discusses.' Coningsby dutifully parrots his guru's views: 'Opinion now is supreme, and opinion speaks in print. The representation of the press is far more complete than the representation of parliament' (*Coningsby*, VII, ii).

It has been well argued that the mid-nineteenth-century party system functioned to sustain parliamentary government and executive authority against the Crown on the one hand and the 'people' on the other.[67] Disraeli said something similar, in more polemical terms, at the end of *Sybil* (VI, xiii): 'absolute power has been wielded by those who profess themselves the servants of the People. In the selfish strife of factions, two great existences have been blotted out of the history of England – the Monarch and the Multitude; as the power of the Crown has diminished, the privileges of the People have disappeared; till at length the sceptre has become a pageant, and its subject has degenerated again into a serf.' It was natural that Disraeli, unable to penetrate or to overawe the parliamentary elite, should savour the possibility of constituting himself the champion of the two forces which it held at bay. In so doing, he necessarily challenged the legitimacy of parliamentary sovereignty and placed himself outside Peel's Conservative party, which he charged scathingly in *Coningsby* (II, v–vi; V, ii) with failing effectively to conserve the national institutions and arrangements on which the people relied for their protection. Yet if *Coningsby* was in that sense an anti-Conservative novel, it was not, *pace* John Vincent,[68] an 'anti-Tory novel'. The Disraeli who detected in *Sybil* (VI, xiii) 'a whisper rising in this country that Loyalty is not a phrase, Faith not a delusion, and Popular Liberty something more diffusive and substantial than the profane exercise of the sacred rights of sovereignty by political classes', was launched into a new exercise in the interpretation of popular constitutionalism in a Tory key.

His rendering of the theme in the mid-1840s was, in the widest perspective, another manifestation of his grand strategy of imposing himself on England by placing its problems in the frame of continental historical development and illuminating them as only a master spirit untrammelled by native prejudices could. In his vivid dramatization in *Sybil* of the threat posed to the stability and progress of the country by the social chasm represented in his famous metaphor of the two alienated nations of rich and poor, he linked the 'condition of England' question into the chain of European debate stemming largely from the Hegelian vision of 'civil society', under the influence of unchecked acquisitive individualism, generating its own nemesis in the form of a fatal conflict between a wealthy few and a deprived and alienated proletariat. The language of his discourse renewed the Hegelian echoes already faintly heard in the *Vindication*. England exhibited no 'community', but only 'aggregation' (*Sybil*, II, v); its people had 'ceased to be a nation' and were merely 'a crowd' (*Tancred*, II, i). Disraeli was modernizing Tory politics by bringing them to bear on the looming problem for the governments of the industrializing and urbanizing societies of the West, the protection of social cohesion and community in face of the atomistic individualism encouraged by what conservatives saw as the liberal emphasis on freedom from restraints. It was Tory commitment to the preservation of community that led logically to his defence of protection for the landed interest against Peel's decision to repeal the Corn Laws, even though he had no sympathy for protective duties as such and regarded liberalization of trade as part of the authentic Pittite tradition of the modern Tory party. It was

Tory commitment to the idea of community also which enabled him to tap the powerful strain in popular constitutionalism which shared the desire to see class identities transcended in the interest of the nation as a whole.[69]

Even while still in hope of Peel's favours, Disraeli had not relinquished his option on the idea of a national party uniting Tory and popular elements. He admired Oastler's Tory radicalism, and wrote to the Radical chairman of the Northern Political Union, Charles Attwood, in June 1840: 'I entirely agree with you, that "an union between the Conservative party and the Radical Masses" offers the only means by which we can preserve the Empire. Their interests are identical; united they form the Nation.'[70] He openly sympathized with the Chartists' contention that an 'ancient constitution' which had protected popular privileges was being subverted by such innovations as the new poor law and the new police, under the auspices of the 'monarchy of the middle classes' entrenched in an unrepresentative House of Commons and more interested in cheap, centralized government than in popular welfare.[71] He was clearly intrigued by the methods of mass political mobilization employed by the bodies which were making the running in extra-parliamentary politics, the Anti-Corn Law League and the Chartist movement, using the still new means of mass communication, the steam printing press, the railway, the penny post and the telegraph. His project of capturing the public mind by print chimed with the rapid expansion of newspaper circulation and printed propaganda, but he did not think print the only way to reach opinion. His fascinated descriptions in *Sybil* (IV, iv; V, x) of the great torchlight meeting on Mowbray Moor, the monster but impeccably disciplined procession to welcome the Chartist delegates back to Mowbray, and the ritual of Dandy Mick's initiation into a trade union, witnessed to his interest in the social psychology of the people, his grasp of the influence which form and ceremonial exerted over it, and his sense of the appeal which the theatricalization of politics for mass consumption could exert. He had always known that politics was, in one dimension, theatre: recreating in *Hartlebury* (II, i) his Red Lion speech of June 1832 at Wycombe, he had commended his hero, Bohun, as 'a perfect master of stage effect'. He had always sensed that the sources of political conviction were as much visceral as cerebral, and that tapping them might involve gripping the imagination of multitudes as well as compelling the reason of readers. 'Man', as Sidonia has it in *Coningsby* (IV, xiii) 'is only truly great when he acts from the passions, never irresistible but when he appeals to the imagination.'

Yet, though (evidently on his very best behaviour) he impressed with his 'friendliness and lack of affectation' the Chartist Thomas Cooper, just out of gaol, in May 1845, and in the following July stressed the need for a popular base for political reform while starring at the festival of the North London Odd Fellows,[72] Disraeli was not about to link up with any mass political movement. Like other versions of Tory radicalism, his was bent more on the cultural inclusion of the working classes in the nation than on encouraging or even countenancing them in independent political activity.[73] Disraeli's democratic principle was not hostile to the development of political consciousness among the working classes – he even looked indulgently in *Sybil* (VI, viii) on the involvement of working-class women in political discussion – but it was hostile to their separating out their political force and identity from the rest of the nation and trying to change society on their own. 'The people are not strong', Egremont declares (*Sybil*, IV, xv), 'the people never can be strong. Their attempts at self-vindication will end only in their suffering and confusion.' A movement like Chartism was thus ultimately futile; not least because, instead of asking Disraeli for guidance, it had the temerity to suppose it could guide him: Feargus O'Connor (whose correspondence Disraeli apparently consulted in writing *Sybil*), regarding Young England as 'coadjutors to a certain extent', thought in December 1844 that some of the Chartists' best speakers might 'meet them in a friendly spirit, and instruct them'.[74]

Disraeli sought the inspirational focus of his popular politics not in any charter of reforms but in a monarchy which could free the people from the domination of a parliament perverted by sectional interests. Sidonia looks to the action of public opinion through 'one who has no class interests ... the monarch on the throne, free from the vulgar prejudices and the corrupt interests of the subject, becomes again divine' (*Coningsby*, V, viii). Coningsby repeats the lesson (*ibid.*, VII, ii): 'the only way to terminate what in the language of the present day is called class legislation is not to entrust power to classes ... The only power that has no class sympathy is the sovereign ... The House of Commons is the house of a few; the sovereign is the sovereign of all.' The notion of a revitalized monarchy as the means of subduing the chaos of competing sectional claims and embodying the will of the nation as an organic community might almost have been an answer to Hegel's concern about the powerlessness of the British Crown before a parliament which, as the cockpit of private interests, was incapable of regulating social conflicts;[75] but, more importantly, it appealed readily to the strain of popular constitutionalist belief that saw the monarchy as the natural protector of the subject from aristocratic oppression. Cobbett had supported William IV's dismissal of the Whig ministry in 1834 by the use of the royal prerogative 'which has been given for our security'.[76] The Oldham Radical leader, John Knight, had told the town's working people in 1827 that an 'absolute monarchy' under a liberal and kind-hearted king would relieve the people's sufferings. 'With such a Monarch they would be much better without a House of Commons (Loud cries of "Aye, we would!" "We dunnat want 'em").'[77] For Disraeli, there was the further speculation that genius denied by parliamentary politics might find its outlet within a 'free monarchy … ruling an educated people, represented by a free and intellectual press'. 'Under such a system', Coningsby muses, where qualification for high office 'would not be parliamentary but personal, even statesmen would be educated' (*Coningsby*, VII, ii).[78] Guiding an emancipated Crown in alliance with a free and enlightened people to make the nation whole was a tempting prospect, especially if its final form was to be the leadership of the nation in the fulfilment of an imperial destiny which Disraeli was coming to equate with the continuation of the civilizing mission of his race, a notion not unrecognizable to the sense strong in popular constitutionalism, as in militant Protestantism, of the English as a chosen people, appointed to diffuse freedom and Christianity over the globe. It was the ultimate heroic role, in which Disraeli's genius could achieve not simply political greatness but its supreme reconciliation with its place of settlement.

It could not be performed. Britain was not embarked, any more than in 1831, on the path of social and political convulsion which might have shattered the aristocratic system of government and precipitated new political constellations and new forms of political leadership. Perhaps Disraeli knew that the vein of subversion running through *Coningsby* and *Sybil* could have no effective political expression. At any rate, at the same time as he sapped the foundations of aristocratic politics, he kept an eye on the chances they might yet offer, in *Coningsby* (IV, iv) conspicuously flattering the Whig leader, Lord John Russell, at an epoch when it seemed possible that the Whigs would turn Peel out.[79] Perhaps he knew, too, that he did not really possess the temperament and technique for a politics of mass communication and excitation. He was a revolutionary of the study rather than the streets, a paladin of the pen, not the platform, and his natural stage was in the intimacy of the debating chamber, not the hurly-burly of the mass meeting. Gradually, society and politics opened up for him. By July 1845, he was able to report to his sister the 'great social revol[uti]on' which had 'suddenly' carried him and his wife into the 'highest circles', with invitations in one week to the Lansdownes, the Salisburys and the Palmerstons.[80] The next year Peel, in repealing the Corn Laws, simultaneously cut the ground from under an approach based on exploiting popular resentment of parliament as an instrument of class legislation, and gave Disraeli the opportunity to leap by his power of philippic into the front rank of the protectionist party, left sorely bereft of debating talent when it rejected Peel and his adherents. Henceforth his political progress was ground out in the innards of the parliamentary system of which he had despaired.

The freebooting days were over, and genius had to compound with aristocracy and party. Disraeli's ascent to the leadership of the protectionists in the Commons, which he effectively achieved in 1849, depended on patronage as well as talent, at first the support of Lord George Bentinck, then the sufferance of Lord Stanley. It was Bentinck money that set him up as a country landowner at Hughenden and gave him the qualification to acquire the Buckinghamshire county seat which he would hold for nearly thirty years. The sense of being hired to conduct the protectionists' business in the Commons required the salve which he provided in *Tancred* in 1847 and in his biography of *Lord George Bentinck* in 1851, with a truculent re-assertion of the self of racial aristocracy and superior vision. But if he was demonstrating that he was entering service on his own terms, it was service nonetheless. Bulwer had remarked that 'a plebeian in high station is usually valet to the whole peerage'.[81] In *Sybil* (I, iii) Disraeli himself had portrayed with some asperity through the example of Burke the sort of shabby treatment that the intellect that supplied the deficiencies of aristocratic politicians might expect from those who used it. It was not until May 1850 that his party leader, Stanley, shifted from 'My dear sir' to 'Dear Disraeli' in writing to him.[82] The change was by no means a complete thaw. Derby (as Stanley became in 1851) did not invite Disraeli to his country seat at Knowsley until 1853, and still in 1856 Disraeli suspected that he 'only employed without trusting him'.[83]

Disraeli would never be wholly comfortable with his party or with the system of aristocratic parliamentary politics, the ritual of which he helped it perform, and there were occasional faint gestures of sentimental reversion to the creative and corrosive views of his early days, which relieved some of the tension generated by servitude to men inclined to slight his origins at the same time as they exploited his abilities. The vision of a new politics initiated by a revivified Crown was prompted to life again in the 1850s by the energy of the Prince Consort, 'establishing court-influence on ruins of political party ... with perseverance equal to that of George the Third, and talent infinitely greater', as Disraeli expressed it, ruing Albert's premature death. 'A few years more, and we should have had, in practice, an absolute monarchy: now all that is changed, and we shall go back to the old thing – the Venetian constitution – a Doge.'[84] The idea of a popular constitutionalist toryism remained, and even after the second Reform act Disraeli would defend the representative character of the Lords as against a House of Commons which was the mouthpiece only of a limited estate.[85] But there was no systematic intention to subvert the scheme of things within which Disraeli was obliged to work. By the mid-1850s, he had fashioned the identity with which he was to operate for the rest of his career, and defined the terms of its tenure in England. If he could not impose those terms on party or country, he had at least made them clear enough for self-respect and for him to be able to interpret the progress of his public career as implying, if not precisely recognition of them, at least an acquiescence in them sufficient for the satisfaction of pride. The politics of denization were necessarily politics of compromise. 'The Spirit of the Age', Sidonia declares in *Coningsby* (III, i), 'is the very thing that a great man changes ... prophets, great legislators, great conquerors. They destroy and they create.' That pre-Nietzschean smashing of old law-tables and the forging of new ones could not be accomplished even by a continental and revolutionary mind in a country so governed by traditionary influences as Disraeli recognized England to be. The ambiguities of his position would remain. He would always be what the English called 'different'.[86] But he had chosen to make difference the source of his inner strength and the justification of his public claims. If that different self could not be entirely fulfilled or unequivocally honoured in its destined place of settlement, it could validate the claim of the *Vindication* that there was no position to which the subject might not aspire. A little ungratefully, but consistently with his idea of his nature, Disraeli would complain that life as prime minister was 'not a complete existence. It gives me neither the highest development of the intellect or the heart; neither Poetry nor Love.'[87] It was something, all the same.

Notes

Blake   Robert Blake, *Disraeli* (London, 1966) (Chapter 5 uses the Anchor Books edition (Garden City, NY, 1968))

DL   *Benjamin Disraeli Letters*, ed. M. G. Wiebe *et al.* (6 vols. to date, Toronto, 1982–97)

M&B   William Flavelle Monypenny and George Earle Buckle, *The Life of Benjamin Disraeli, Earl of Beaconsfield* (6 vols., London, 1910–20)

INTRODUCTION

1 The major stimulus to renewed examination of the first half of Disraeli's career has been supplied by the work of the Disraeli Project at Queen's University, Kingston, which has so far published six volumes, covering 1815–56, of *Benjamin Disraeli Letters*, ed. M. G. Wiebe *et al.* (Toronto, 1982–97) (hereafter *DL*), as well as identifying an early novel co-authored by Disraeli and his sister, Sarah, *A Year at Hartlebury or The Election* (London, 1834; re-issued by John Murray, London, 1983). The references in the ensuing chapters provide a guide to recent work on Disraeli's earlier years. See also the review article by Anthony S. Wohl, 'Will the Real Benjamin Disraeli Please Stand Up? Or the Importance of Being Earnest', in *Nineteenth Century Studies* 11 (1997), 133–56. Recent contributions have by no means rendered obsolete the classic volumes on Disraeli by Monypenny and Buckle, B. R. Jerman and Robert Blake, but they have enlarged the field of enquiry and analysis, especially on the early years, which Jerman, in particular, did so much to open up to exploration.

2 See below, p. 25.

3 See James Ogden, *Isaac D'Israeli* (Oxford, 1969), pp. 106–13.

4 *DL*, iv.378, Appendix V.

5 'On the Life and Writings of Mr Disraeli, By His Son'; preface to Isaac Disraeli, *Curiosities of Literature*, fourteenth edn (3 vols., London, 1849), i.xliii.

6 See below, p. 38.

7 See below, p. 40.

8 Johann Gottlieb Fichte, *Addresses to the German Nation*, trans. Richard F. Jones and George H. Turnbull (Chicago and London, 1922; first published 1808), p. 42.

9 Christopher Sykes, *Evelyn Waugh: A Biography* (London, 1975), p. 49.

10 Paul J. Eakin, *Fictions in Autobiography. Studies in the Art of Self-Invention* (Princeton, 1985), p. 3. See also Eakin, *Touching the World. Reference in Autobiography* (Princeton, 1992).

11 Below, p. 50.

12 Below, pp. 45, 48, 51.

13 *DL*, i.447, Appendix III.

14 *Ibid.*

15 Jonathan Parry, 'Holborn at Heart', *London Review of Books*, 23 January 1997.

16 *DL*, iv.378, Appendix V (*c.* 1842).

17 Mary Anne Wyndham Lewis to Major Viney Evans, 8 September 1837, in M&B, i.379.

18 *DL*, 111, i.190, 28 May 1831; Clay quoted in M&B, i.175.

19 Eric J. Hobsbawm, *The Age of Revolution. Europe, 1789–1848* (London, 1962), p. 268.

20 See below, p. 154.

21 *DL*, 78, i.117, Benjamin Disraeli to Sara Austen, 7 March 1830, for the reference to greying hair, 'which I can unfeignedly declare – occasions me more anguish than even the prospect of death'.

22 See below, p. 74.

23 Hobsbawm, *Age of Revolution*, p. 261.

24 *Ibid.*

25 Cf. also Isaac D'Israeli's description of the nearness to delirium of the enthusiasm of creative genius. When the mind was overpowered by the imagination, he wrote: 'Often in the deep silence around us, we seek to relieve ourselves by some voluntary noise or action which may direct our attention to an exterior object, and bring us back to the world, which we had, as it were, left behind us.' *The Literary Character; or The History of Men of Genius*, fourth edn (2 vols., London, 1828), ii.25–6.

26 John Dryden, *Absalom and Achitophel* (1681–2). Dryden's reference to Achitophel's 'fiery Soul, which working out its way / Fretted the Pigmy-Body to decay' has its relevance to the diagnosis of Disraeli's illness. Cf. below, pp. 87–8.

27 Isaac D'Israeli, *The Literary Character*, ii.2–3.

28 See his reference ('On the Life and Writings of Mr Disraeli', pp. xliii–xliv) to Isaac's 'Mejnoun and Leila. A Persian Romance' in his *Romances* of 1799;

Ogden, *Isaac D'Israeli*, pp. 54–6. Isaac was advised by the oriental scholars Sir John Kennaway and Major William Ouseley and used the work of another noted orientalist, Sir William Jones.

29 Blake, pp. 10, 49.

30 *Ibid.*, pp. 49, 204; and see also Lord Blake's subsequent recognition of Disraeli's need to integrate his Jewish identity into the role he aspired to play in English life, in *Disraeli's Grand Tour: Benjamin Disraeli and the Holy Land, 1830–31* (London, 1982). Buckle's statement that 'The fundamental fact about Disraeli was that he was a Jew' (M&B, vi.635) would not have startled the latter's contemporaries, including Gladstone, who believed that Disraeli's 'Judaic feeling' was, after his wife's death, 'the deepest and truest ... in his whole mind' (John Morley, *The Life of William Ewart Gladstone* (3 vols., London, 1903), ii.533, and cf. ii.558, iii.475–6).

31 Stanley Weintraub, *Disraeli* (London, 1993); Anthony S. Wohl, ' "Dizzy-Ben-Dizzy": Disraeli as Alien', *Journal of British Studies* 34 (1995), 375–411, and ' "Ben JuJu": Representations of Disraeli's Jewishness in the Victorian Political Cartoon', *Jewish History* 10 (1996), 89–135. See also R. W. Davis, 'Disraeli, the Rothschilds, and Anti-Semitism', *ibid.*, 9–21.

32 Joseph Snape at Broughton Constitutional Club, 22 March 1879, quoted in John A. Garrard, 'Parties, Members and Voters After 1867: A Local Study', *Historical Journal* 20 (1977), 157.

33 See below, pp. 113–14.

34 Weintraub, *Disraeli*, pp. 111–13; the quotation is from the preface to *The Revolutionary Epick* (1834).

35 Below, pp. 118–19. The example of Edwin Montagu, cited by Endelman, does not suggest that discretion was much of a talisman against English anti-Semitism, to judge by Neville Chamberlain's comment on finishing Monypenny and Buckle's *Life of Disraeli*: 'you cannot like him, he is too different, in the way that Montagu is different'. Keith Feiling, *The Life of Neville Chamberlain* (London, 1947), p. 121.

36 *DL*, 262, i.347, Benjamin Disraeli to Sarah Disraeli, 8 April 1833.

37 See Brantlinger, below, pp. 99–100. Disraeli's reference to 'the great Corsican, who, like most of the inhabitants of the Mediterranean isles, had probably Arab blood in his veins' (*Coningsby*, IV, x) has to be read with his use of the phrases 'Hebrew Arabs', 'Jewish Arabs' and 'Mosaic Arabs' (*ibid.*), Sidonia's reference to 'we Arabs' (*Coningsby*, IV, xv) and the observation that Arabs are 'only Jews on horseback' (*Tancred*, IV, iii).

38 On the face of it, this represented a slightly more indulgent racial rating of the northern peoples than Disraeli had been inclined to at the time of *Contarini Fleming*, in which he suggested that the 'flat-nosed Franks' might be 'as distinct a race from their models [the peoples of the Near East], as they undoubtedly are from the Kalmuck and the Negro' (V, xix).

39 'On the Life and Writings of Mr Disraeli', pp. xlix–l. Ogden (*Isaac D'Israeli*, p. 157) regards Isaac as 'a pioneer of modern research methods'.

40 *DL*, 1433, iv.180–4, Benjamin Disraeli to the editor of the *Morning Post*, 16 August 1845.

41 To Lennox, 8 August 1852, in M&B, iii.329.

42 See Timothy D. Barnes, *Tertullian. A Historical and Literary Study* (Oxford, 1971), p. 92.

43 *DL*, iv.404–5, Appendix X. See Jupp, below, p. 143.

44 Felix Gilbert, 'The Germany of "Contarini Fleming"', *Contemporary Review* 149 (1936), 74–80. There does not, however, appear to be any direct evidence for Disraeli's knowing of the work of C. O. Müller. He certainly used the *Universal History* of another Müller – Johannes von Müller.

45 See below, pp. 161, 168, 170, and Paul Smith, *Disraeli. A Brief Life* (Cambridge, 1996), pp. 62–3, 74, 87.

46 Below, p. 99.

47 Edith J. Morley, ed., *Henry Crabb Robinson on Books and Their Writers* (3 vols., London, 1938), ii.511 (5 February 1837).

48 John Vincent, ed., *Disraeli, Derby and the Conservative Party. Journals and Memoirs of Edward Henry, Lord Stanley, 1849–1869* (Hassocks, 1978), pp. 31, 33 (1851). It was to Stanley, in 1851 and again in 1853, that Disraeli confided his ambition to write a life of Christ 'from a national point of view' (*ibid.*, pp. 33, 107).

49 Others, however, might replicate parts of it for comparable purposes. Victor Gollancz, as he became a noticeable figure in English society and politics, discovered a pride in Jewish history which led him to stress the role of great Jews – Jesus, Marx, Freud, Einstein – in the spiritual leadership of the West, and argued, in 1948, that, in rejecting Christianity, the Jews had thrown away 'the culmination of their own philosophy'. Ruth Dudley Edwards, *Victor Gollancz: A Biography* (London, 1987), pp. 391–2, 470. Disraeli's example, however interpreted, was capable of providing inspiration in circles well beyond Anglo-Jewry. Recalling his Viennese father's fascination with Disraeli and England, George Steiner declares: 'For the eastern and central European Jewish intelligentsia, the career of Disraeli had assumed a mythical, talismanic aura.' Interview with Jason Cowley, *The Times*, 22 September 1997.

50 'English Politics and Parties', *Bentley's Quarterly Review* 1 (1859), 15. Bellamy was the caterer.

51 Fichte, *Addresses*, p. 44.

I DISRAELI'S EDUCATION

1 Quoted by James S. Hamilton, 'Disraeli and Heine', *Disraeli Newsletter* 2, no. 1 (1977), 8.

2 M&B, i.19.

3 Blake, p. 12.

4 See C. C. Nickerson, 'Disraeli and the Reverend Eli Cogan', *Disraeli Newsletter* 2, no. 2 (1977), 14–17; Thom Braun, 'Cogan and Disraeli', *ibid.*, 18–27.

5 John Morley, *The Life of William Ewart Gladstone* (2 vols., London, 1905), i.50.

6 M&B, i.24.

7 Morley, *Gladstone*, i.38–9.

8 See Endelman below, p. 110.

9 Todd M. Endelman, *Radical Assimilation in English Jewish History, 1656–1945* (Bloomington, IN, 1990), p. 99. It would appear that English schoolboys had little difficulty in identifying Jews. Robert Southey recalled in 1807 that public school boys sang on Easter Sunday that: 'He is risen, he is risen / All the Jews must go to prison'. Southey also recalled that one day some of these boys attacked a Jewish peddler. When asked by a master of the school for an explanation, one of them said, 'Why, sir, did they not crucify our Lord?' Todd M. Endelman, *The Jews in Georgian England, 1714–1830: Tradition and Change in a Liberal Society* (Philadelphia, 1979), p. 92. Cf. Blake, p. 13.

10 Endelman, *Radical Assimilation*, p. 139.

11 Disraeli's papers located in the Bodleian Library, Oxford are referred to hereafter as the Hughenden Papers. Box 231, E/V/A/10(1) misc. mss. The memorandum is watermarked 1821.

12 *Ibid.*, Box 11, A/III/E/8. The diary is hitherto unpublished. See also *ibid.*, Box 11, A/III/E/1, which is hitherto unpublished: 'The great grandson of a man who has suffered severely by religious persecution will probably be affected unconsciously. So of a nation who has worked out its liberty. See also ye Jews.' And see *ibid.*, Box 231, E/V/A/1, *Aylmer Papillon* (1824) in which the English pretence of toleration is ridiculed. A little boy is to be transported for killing the 'sacred hare'. 'Well I thought that they had sported toleration in this country', Aylmer Papillon exclaims.

13 See below, pp. 85–7.

14 There is a diary in his papers (Box 11, A/III/E/4), watermarked 1818, devoted to Wolsey and Henry VIII, which tends to suggest that, like Contarini Fleming (I, viii), Disraeli became ambitious at the age of fourteen. See below, pp. 21–2.

15 See below, pp. 66–8.

16 Quoted by Philip Rieff, 'Disraeli: The Chosen of History', *Commentary* 13 (1952), 26. 'I have related, in the beginning of this volume', Sir William Fraser wrote, 'that Disraeli said to me that the passion which gave pleasure longest was revenge.' *Disraeli and His Day* (London, 1891), p. 24. See below, pp. 81–2 for a discussion of the significance of vengefulness in Disraeli's narcissistic personality.

17 *DL*, 400, ii.39, Benjamin Disraeli to Morgan O'Connell, 6 May 1835.

18 *DL*, i.447, Appendix III.

19 *DL*, i.446, Appendix III.

20 Blake, p. 84.

21 Hughenden Papers, Box 11, A/III/E/4. Vivian Grey asserts that he 'got through an immense series of historical reading', prior to studying politics (I, viii). The diary devoted to Henry VIII is watermarked 1818, and the diaries devoted to Bacon and Bolingbroke are dated 1821. 'The Reign of Henry the Eighth' contains notes from: The Right Honourable Edward Lord Herbert of Cherbury, *The Life and Reign of King Henry the Eighth* (London, 1672); Raphael Holinshed, *Chronicle of England, Scotland and Ireland* (6 vols., London, 1808); Polydorus Vergilius, *Historiae Anglicae* (London, 1649); Edward Hall, *Hall's Chronicle* (London, 1809). These are the editions that Disraeli read. See also Hughenden Papers, Box 231, E/V/A/6/1 'Notes on the Statutes passed in the reign of Henry VIII'.

22 Winston S. Churchill, *A History of the English-Speaking Peoples* (4 vols., London, 1956), ii.18.

23 Hughenden Papers, Box 11, A/III/E/4. The diary is watermarked 1818.

24 *Ibid.*

25 *Ibid.*, Box 11, A/III/E/2. Kraut, Christian Friedrich (born *c.* 1650–60), rose from obscure origins in Magdeburg to become minister of finance in the Brandenburg-Prussian state. He amassed great wealth during his ascent and was repeatedly found guilty of peculation.

26 *Ibid.* Ilgen, Heinrich Rudiger v. (1654–1728), son of middle-class parents in Minden, rose in virtue of his brilliance in foreign politics to be secretary of state in the Brandenburg-Prussian state. Ilgen induced the young Frederick I to ennoble him – and one foreign observer claimed that Ilgen was the effective king of Prussia.

27 C. E. Chapman, *A History of Spain* (New York, 1918), p. 378.

28 F. M .L. Thompson, *English Landed Society in the Nineteenth Century* (London, 1963), pp. 8–12.

29 Norman Gash, *Politics in the Age of Peel* (London, 1953), p. 213.

30 *Ibid.*, pp. 132–3.

31 Blake, p. 3.

32 See Paul Smith, 'Disraeli's Politics', *Transactions of the Royal Historical Society*, fifth series, 37 (1987), 69.

33 *Ibid.*

34 See M&B, v.263–4. In his Rector's address to the students at Glasgow University in 1873 Disraeli said that it was 'only by severe introspection that they could obtain self-knowledge'.

35 See Smith, 'Disraeli's Politics', 72 in which Disraeli's education, based on the principle of *Bildung*, is contrasted with the Victorian ideal of 'character'.

36 M&B, i.25. The diaries devoted to classics which Disraeli kept in 1820 while at home are published in *ibid.*, i.25–7.

37 *Ibid.*, i.27.

38 Hughenden Papers, Box 11, A/III/A (ii).

39 *Ibid.*

40 *Ibid.*, Box 231, E/V/A/7-8A.

41 M. H. Abrams, *The Mirror and the Lamp: Romantic Theory and the Critical Tradition* (New York, 1976), pp. 42–3. See below pp. 38–41.

42 Blake, p. 7. See below, pp. 68–9, 73–4 for a discussion of Disraeli's relationship with his father.

43 'General Preface to the Novels' (1870), in the *Bradenham Edition of the Novels and Tales of Benjamin Disraeli, First Earl of Beaconsfield* (12 vols., London, 1926–7), i.x–xi. Hereafter referred to as the *Bradenham Edition of the Novels*.

44 Hughenden Papers, Box 231, E/V/A/10(1) misc. mss. The memorandum is hitherto unpublished.

45 James Ogden, *Isaac D'Israeli* (Oxford, 1969), pp. 157–8.

46 Hughenden Papers, Box 231, E/V/A/10(1) misc. mss. The memorandum is hitherto unpublished.

47 M&B, i.164.

48 John Prest, *Lord John Russell* (London, 1972), p. 23.

49 M&B, i.32.

50 Hughenden Papers, Box 11, A/III/E/8. The diary is hitherto unpublished. Also see *Vivian Grey*, I, x. Vivian Grey is an admirer of 'Lord' Bacon.

51 Hughenden Papers, Box 11, A/III/E/8.

52 *Ibid.* Quoted from Essay XXIII.

53 *Ibid.* Quoted from Essay XXVII.

54 *Ibid.*, Box 11, A/III/E/5.

55 See Essay XIII for Bacon's definitive statement of his agreement with Machiavelli. 'And one of the doctors of Italy, Nicolas Machiavel, had the confidence to put in writing, almost in plain terms, *that the Christian faith had given up good men in prey to those that are tyrannical and unjust.* Which he spoke, because indeed there never was law, or sect, or opinion, did so much to magnify goodness as the Christian religion doth. Therefore to avoid the scandal and the danger both, it is good to take knowledge of the errors of an habit so excellent.'

56 Felix Raab, *The English Face of Machiavelli* (London, 1964), p. 74, quoting N. Orsini, *Bacone e Machiavelli.*

57 Herbert Butterfield, *The Statecraft of Machiavelli* (London, 1955), p. 135.

58 Raab, *English Face of Machiavelli*, p. 1.

59 See Leo Strauss, *Thoughts on Machiavelli* (Chicago, 1958), p. 10.

60 As he was, for example, by Harold Macmillan.

61 Hughenden Papers, Box 231, E/V/A/10(2) misc. mss., n.d. 'Machiavel' is the form of the name used by Bacon and Bolingbroke.

62 *Ibid.*, Box 11, A/III/E/8.

63 Henry Saint-John, Viscount Bolingbroke, *Letters on the Spirit of Patriotism and on the Idea of a Patriot King*, ed. A. Hassall (Oxford, 1917), p. 46. And see *DL*, 406, ii.45–51, Benjamin Disraeli, 'Letter to the Electors and Inhabitants of the Borough of Taunton', 13 June 1835.

64 Hughenden Papers, Box 7, A/I/B/246. Sarah Disraeli to Benjamin Disraeli, 11 May 1832.

65 Butterfield, *Statecraft of Machiavelli*, pp. 145–6. In speaking of the goodness of civil society's foundation, Bolingbroke asserts, 'But this good degenerates, according to the natural course of things; and governments, like other mixed bodies, tend to dissolution by the changes which are wrought in the several parts, and by the unaptness and disproportion, which result from hence throughout the whole composition.' But the great man may restore the regime to its first principles: 'The examples which Machiavel cites to show that the virtue of particular men among the Romans did frequently draw that government back to its original principles, are so many proofs that the duration of liberty depends on keeping the spirit of it alive and warm.'

66 Niccolò Machiavelli, *The Prince and The Discourses*, trans. Luigi Ricci (New York, 1950), p. 397.

67 Blake, p. 278.

68 Robert Blake, 'The Rise of Disraeli', *Essays in British History*, ed. H. R. Trevor-Roper (London, 1964), p. 245.

69 Machiavelli, *Prince and Discourses*, p. 441 (*Discourses*, Bk. III, ch. 9).

70 Benjamin Disraeli, *Lord George Bentinck: A Political Biography* (London, 1881; first published 1851), ch. vii.

71 Machiavelli, *Prince and Discourses*, pp. 19–23.

72 *Ibid.*, p. 94 (*Prince*, ch. 25).

73 When Contarini Fleming wishes to have his father made prime minister, he 'would scruple at no means to ensure our end'(II, xi).

74 Machiavelli, *Prince and Discourses*, p. 66 (*Prince*, ch. 18).

75 *Ibid.*, p. 403 (*Discourses*, Bk. III, ch. 2).

76 Machiavelli, *Prince and Discourses*, pp. 63–6.

77 Hughenden Papers, Box 11, A/III/E/1; A/III/E/5. The latter contains what appear to be notations about German life which may have been made while travelling in Germany in 1824.

78 Baroness Holstein Stäel, *Germany* (3 vols., London, 1813). The work was edited by William Lamb and translated by Frances Hodgson. See Roberta J. Forsberg, *Madame De Staël and the English* (New York, 1967), pp. 71–91, for a discussion of Murray's friendship with Mme De Staël.

79 Hughenden Papers, Box 11, A/III/B. See *DL*, 10, i.9–16, i.18 for his letters.

80 Carlyle's famous translation of *Wilhelm Meister's Apprenticeship* appeared in 1824; and in the same year Disraeli's future publisher, Henry Colburn, printed a translation of Goethe's *Dichtung und Wahrheit* entitled *Memoirs of Goethe: Written by Himself*. See the 1845 Preface to *Contarini Fleming* in the *Bradenham Edition of the Novels*, iv.ix, in which Disraeli expresses his respect for, but intention to outdo, *Wilhelm Meister* and the *Memoirs*. And see *DL*, 346, i.426, Benjamin Disraeli to Lady Blessington, 15 August 1834, in which Disraeli complains of the translation of Christoph Wieland's *Agathon* that he was reading, and of his inability to read German. Critics like Heine (whom Disraeli later read) and Milman noticed the 'Teutonic' qualities in *Contarini Fleming*; and Disraeli's friend and intellectual confidant Bulwer-Lytton, who was one of the leading exponents and transmitters of German culture in England, and who began at around this time to write novels of personal development after the manner of *Wilhelm Meister*, thought the latter had been the inspiration for *Contarini Fleming*. See *DL*, 461, ii.124, Benjamin Disraeli to Isaac D'Israeli, 4 January 1836; F. C. Brewster, *Disraeli in Outline* (London, 1890), p. 118; Richard A. Zipser, *Edward Bulwer-Lytton and Germany* (Berne and Frankfurt, 1974), p. 22; *DL*, i.446, Appendix III. Subsequent critics have also perceived in *Contarini Fleming* − with its gospel of action, its use of mysterious philosophic strangers and talismanic utterances, its troupes of actors, theatre madness and wandering in search of self − the influence of *Wilhelm Meister*. Jean-Marie Carré, *Goethe en Angleterre* (Paris, 1920), pp. 205−24; Susan Howe, *Wilhelm Meister and His English Kinsmen* (New York, 1930), p. 195. It is probable that Disraeli's emphasis on self-knowledge, self-mastery and self-realization between 1827 and 1832 owes much to *Wilhelm Meister*, which remained one of the most important works of western literature for him until late in life. See M&B, v.474; vi.181.

81 Forsberg, *Madame De Staël and the English*, p. 128.

82 *Ibid.*, p. 51. There is also a tribute to *De l'Allemagne* in *The Bride of Abydos*, Canto I, stanza 6.

83 Morroe Berger, ed., *Madame De Staël on Politics, Literature and National Character* (London, 1964), pp. 30−60.

84 Hughenden Papers, Box 11, A/III/E/1. Disraeli notes this in his diary devoted to Mme De Staël.

85 Friedrich Nietzsche, 'Beyond Good and Evil', *Basic Writings of Nietzsche*, ed. Walter Kaufmann (New York, 1967), p. 407. This passage has had a central influence on my work. It continues as follows:

> often lost in the mud and almost in love with it, until they become like the will-o'-the wisps around swamps and *pose* as stars − the people may call them idealists − often fighting against a long nausea, with a recurring spectre of unbelief that chills and forces them to languish for *gloria* and to gobble their 'belief in themselves' from the hands of intoxicated flatterers ... It is easy to

understand that *these* men should so readily receive, from woman – clairvoyant in the world of suffering and, unfortunately, also desirous far beyond her strength to help and save – those eruptions of boundless and most devoted *pity* which the multitude, above all the venerating multitude, does not understand and on which it lavishes inquisitive and self-satisfied interpretations.

86 Compare this with Byron, *Don Juan*, Canto I, stanzas 212–15.

87 Robert Blake, 'Disraeli's Political Novels', *History Today* 16 (1966), 463.

88 I am grateful to Paul Smith for allowing me to read his unpublished seminar paper entitled 'Disraeli: A Continental and Revolutionary Mind', given at Oxford University on 28 February 1980, and his inaugural lecture entitled 'The Primrose Sphinx: Disraeli', given at the University of Southampton on 20 May 1980, in which this idea is expressed.

89 Siegbert S. Prawer, ed., *The Romantic Period in Germany* (London, 1970), p. 59.

90 *Ibid.*, p. 34.

91 *Ibid.*, pp. 229–30.

92 David Cecil, *The Young Melbourne* (London, 1939), p. 181.

93 Smith, 'Disraeli's Politics', 71.

94 See Disraeli's judgement of Sir Robert Peel in *Lord George Bentinck*, ch. xvii.

95 Prawer, *Romantic Period in Germany*, p. 306.

96 *Ibid.*, pp. 306–7.

97 Hughenden Papers, Box 11, A/III/E/1.

98 See Abrams, *Mirror and the Lamp*, p. 209 for a discussion of the German transcendental ideal.

99 Prawer, *Romantic Period in Germany*, p. 4.

100 Hughenden Papers, Box 11, A/III/E/5.

101 Abrams, *Mirror and the Lamp*, p. 93.

102 *Ibid.*

103 Hughenden Papers, Box 11, A/III/E/1.

104 See I, xii for a description of the effect of German music on Contarini Fleming.

105 Hughenden Papers, Box 11, A/III/E/5.

106 See, for example, *Contarini Fleming*, I, iii. And see below, pp. 85–7.

107 Abrams, *Mirror and the Lamp*, 'Preface'.

108 Prawer, *Romantic Period in Germany*, pp. 314–15.

109 *Ibid.*, p. 219.

110 *DL*, i.447, Appendix III.

111 See Smith, 'Disraeli's Politics', 74.

112 See Schwarz, below, p. 64.

113 The 1845 Preface to *Contarini Fleming* in the *Bradenham Edition of the Novels*, iv.ix.

114 Isaiah Berlin, 'Benjamin Disraeli, Karl Marx and the Search for Identity', *Against the Current* (London, 1979), p. 273.

2 DISRAELI'S ROMANTICISM: SELF-FASHIONING IN THE NOVELS

1 Harold Fisch, 'Disraeli's Hebraic Compulsions', in *Essays Presented to Chief Rabbi Israel Brodie on the Occasion of His Seventieth Birthday*, eds. H. J. Zimmels, J. Rabbinowitz and I. Finestein (London, 1967), p. 91.

2 M. H. Abrams, 'English Romanticism: The Spirit of the Age', in *Romanticism and Consciousness*, ed. Harold Bloom (New York, 1970), pp. 102–3.

3 Thomas Mann, *A Sketch of My Life*, trans. H. T. Lowe-Porter (1930; first American edn New York, 1960), pp. 43–4.

4 *DL*, i.447, Appendix III. Others who have commented on this crucial entry include: Blake; B. R. Jerman, *The Young Disraeli* (Princeton, NJ, 1960); M&B.

5 See *Vivian Grey*, VI, vii. I have used the readily accessible *Hughenden Edition of the Novels and Tales of the Earl of Beaconsfield* (11 vols., London, 1881–2). Hereafter referred to as the *Hughenden Edition*. My source for the original editions of *Vivian Grey* and *The Young Duke* is the less accessible but authoritative *Centenary Edition*, ed. Lucien Wolf (London, 1904–5). Unfortunately only two volumes ever appeared in this edition.

6 Jerman, *Young Disraeli*, p. 136.

7 See M&B, i.176.

8 *Encyclopedia Judaica* (New York, 1971), i.750–1.

9 Quoted in M&B, i.194.

10 See chapter xxiv entitled 'The Jewish Question' in *Lord George Bentinck: A Political Biography* (London, 1905; first published 1851).

11 The novel was originally entitled *Venetia or the Poet's Daughter*; for more on the Byron and Shelley parallel, see M&B, i.360–4.

12 See Blake, p. 288.

13 With characteristic immodesty, he speaks of the 'artist's difficulty in using such a style: '[This] style ... is a delicate and difficult instrument for an artist to handle ... He must alike beware the turgid and the bombastic, the meagre and the mean. He must be easy in his robes of state, and a degree of elegance and dignity must accompany him even in the camp and the market house. The language must rise gradually with the rising passions of the speakers and subside in harmonious unison with their sinking emotions.' Quoted in M&B, i.198. This preface was omitted in later editions.

14 A. S. B. Glover, ed., *Shelley* (London, 1951), p. 1030.

15 Nevertheless, Disraeli probably appreciated the review of *Henrietta Temple* in the *New Monthly Magazine* which observed: 'In any other age than the present, or even now, had he lived less in society, Mr Disraeli would have been a poet. He has essentially the poetic temperament – the intense self-consciousness, the impetuosity, and the eye for beautiful.' Quoted in R. W. Stewart, ed., *Disraeli's Novels Reviewed, 1836–1968* (Metuchen, NJ, 1975), p. 155.

16 Glover, *Shelley*, pp. 1026–7.

17 Wolf, Introduction to *The Young Duke*, p. xiv.

18 Blake, p. 171. Much of this paragraph is indebted to Blake's chapter 8, entitled 'Young England'.

19 *DL*, 1229, iv.31, Benjamin Disraeli to Mary Anne Disraeli, 11 March 1842.

20 The general preface precedes *Lothair* in the *Hughenden Edition*.

21 Stephen R. Graubard, *Burke, Disraeli and Churchill* (Cambridge, 1961), p. 115.

22 Quoted in Alice Chandler, *A Dream of Order* (Lincoln, 1970), p. 161.

23 See Sheila M. Smith, 'Willenhall and Wodgate: Disraeli's use of Blue Book Evidence', *Review of English Studies*, new series 13 (November, 1962), 368–84; and Sheila M. Smith, 'Blue Books and Victorian Novelists', *Review of English Studies*, new series 21 (February, 1970), 23–40.

24 Marquis of Zetland, ed., *The Letters of Disraeli to Lady Bradford and Lady Chesterfield* (2 vols., New York, 1929), i.372.

25 Blake, p. 265.

26 *Ibid.*, p. 202.

27 Disraeli, *Lord George Bentinck*, ch. xxiv.

28 Cecil Roth, *Benjamin Disraeli* (New York, 1952), p. 79.

29 See Blake, pp. 258–61.

30 For an extensive discussion of similarities between Disraeli and Carlyle, see Morris Edmund Speare, *The Political Novel* (New York, 1924; reissued New York, 1966), pp. 170–1.

31 See Walter E. Houghton, *The Victorian Frame of Mind* (New Haven, 1957), pp. 325–6.

32 Blake, p. 210.

33 Geoffrey H. Hartman, 'Romanticism and Anti-Self-Consciousness', in *Romanticism and Consciousness*, ed. Harold Bloom (New York, 1970), p. 54.

34 Robert Langbaum, *The Modern Spirit: Essays on the Continuity of Nineteenth and Twentieth Century Literature* (New York, 1970), p. 167.

35 Paul Smith, 'Disraeli's Politics', *Transactions of the Royal Historical Society*, fifth Series, 37 (1987), 71–2.

3 DISRAELI'S CRUCIAL ILLNESS

1 Quoted in Paul Bloomfield, *Disraeli* (London, 1961), p. 5.

2 Philip Magnus, *Gladstone* (New York, 1954), p. 280.

3 Stanley Weintraub, *Disraeli* (London, 1993), p. 70 *et seq.* and Jane Ridley, *The Young Disraeli, 1804–1846* (London, 1995), ch. 3 have improved our understanding by describing the illness as depressive.

4 'Narcissism' is used in the current psychoanalytic acceptation of the term. See Jerrold M. Post, 'Current Concepts of the Narcissistic Personality: Implications for Political Psychology', *Political Psychology* 14 (1993), 99–121, 101–2 for a brief historical review of the development of the concept of narcissism

from Freud's seminal essay in 1914 to the work of Heinz Kohut and Otto Kernberg during the last two decades. The concepts elaborated in Dr Post's paper, concerning the phenomenology, psychodynamics and psychogenesis of narcissism, serve as the foundation for our analysis.

5 Blake, p. 15.

6 M&B, i.12.

7 *DL*, i.447, Appendix III. We have used the unexpurgated *Centenary Editions* of *Vivian Grey* (1904) and *The Young Duke* (1905), edited by Lucien Wolf.

8 *DL*, 49 n. 4., i.64, Maria D'Israeli to John Murray, 21 May 1826. Blake, p. 16. See below, pp. 76–8.

9 See Blake pp. 16–17; cf. above, pp. 18–20 and below, p. 110.

10 See above, pp. 22–3; Contarini Fleming also suffers from feelings of inferiority prior to attending school (I, vii).

11 See above, pp. 21–2, for diary evidence that Disraeli became ambitious at around the age of fourteen.

12 M&B, i.32–3.

13 See above, pp. 25–7; James Ogden, *Isaac D'Israeli* (Oxford, 1969).

14 *DL*, i.446, Appendix III.

15 Quoted in B. R. Jerman, *The Young Disraeli* (Princeton, 1960), pp. 36–7.

16 *An Enquiry into the Plans, Progress and Policy of the American Mining Companies*, third edn (London, 1825). See the Advertisement.

17 M.& B., i.59.

18 Blake, p. 47.

19 *DL*, 38, i.52, 22 November 1825.

20 *DL*, 28, i.39, 21 September 1825.

21 *Ibid.*

22 John Vincent, *Disraeli* (Oxford, 1990), p. 58. See Wendy Burton, 'The Composition of *Vivian Grey*', *Disraeli Newsletter* 2, no. 2 (1977), 33–43.

23 Robert Blake, *Disraeli's Grand Tour: Benjamin Disraeli and the Holy Land, 1830–31* (London, 1982), p. 5.

24 M&B, i.115.

25 *Ibid.*, i.116.

26 Janet Oppenheim, *'Shattered Nerves': Doctors, Patients and Depression in Victorian England* (Oxford, 1991), p. 9.

27 See Ilza Veith, *Hysteria: The History of a Disease* (Chicago, 1965), ch. 9 for a discussion of the significance of Robert Brundenell Carter (1828–1918) in the history of psychiatry. Veith says of his *On the Pathology and Treatment of Hysteria* (1853) that he wrote about hysterical illness 'in terms and with ideas so strikingly similar to those of Freud – before the latter was even born – that mere coincidence of their ideas seems scarcely credible'. *Ibid.*, p. 199.

28 Oppenheim, *'Shattered Nerves'*, p. 30.

29 Audrey C. Peterson, 'Brain Fever in Nineteenth Century Literature: Fact and Fiction', *Victorian Studies* 19 (1976), 445–64.

30 *Ibid.*, p. 447.

31 *Ibid.*, p. 449.

32 See Oppenheim, *'Shattered Nerves'*, pp. 113, 128; Peterson, 'Brain Fever in Nineteenth Century Literature', 455–60. It is understandable that Disraeli may have been diagnosed in this way. He had sustained the emotional shocks and over-taxed his brain. The fainting fits, rapid pulse and headaches were also present. See below pp. 75–7. In his memoir of his father, in which he seems to be recollecting his own experience, Disraeli attributes the illness to which Isaac succumbed in his twenties to 'study and too sedentary habits'. Benjamin Disraeli, 'On the Life and Writings of Mr Disraeli by His Son', in Isaac Disraeli, *Curiosities of Literature*, new edn (3 vols., London, 1859), i.xxi. Moreover, Disraeli seems to have endured treatments with mercury and ammonia ('heavenly maid!' as he called the latter) together with copious bloodlettings. *DL*, 351, i.431, Benjamin Disraeli to Benjamin Austen, 24 October 1834; *DL*, 132, i.220, Benjamin Disraeli to Benjamin Austen, 6 January 1832; *DL*, 81, i.118–19, Benjamin Disraeli to Benjamin Austen, 13 April 1830. But given the physician's limited arsenal, some of these remedies were used in other cases. Bloodletting had broad application, and mercury was also a specific for, *inter alia*, venereal disease – possibly used for that purpose in Disraeli's case. See Blake, p. 73.

33 *DL*, 1521, iv.260–1, Benjamin Disraeli to Philip Rose, 25 October 1846.

34 Marie Bonaparte, *The Life and Works of Edgar Allan Poe: A Psycho-Analytic Interpretation*, trans. John Rodker (London, 1949), 'Foreword'.

35 This conduct might also be seen in hypomanic patients, except for hypersensitivity, which could well be manifest during an ensuing decline into depression.

36 See Ridley, *Young Disraeli*, pp. 63, 191.

37 M&B, i.67.

38 *DL*, 66, i.103, 10 March 1828.

39 Blake, p. 54.

40 Otto Kernberg, *Borderline Conditions and Pathological Narcissism* (London, 1985), p. 234.

41 See, for example, *DL*, 84, i.122, Benjamin Disraeli to Thomas Evans, 9 May 1830; *Contarini Fleming*, IV, vi.

42 *DL*, 67, i.106, Benjamin Disraeli to T. J. Pettigrew, 19 March 1828.

43 Jerman, *Young Disraeli*, pp. 89–90.

44 *DL*, 91, i.132, Benjamin Disraeli to Isaac D'Israeli, 1 July 1830; *DL*, 92, i.136, Benjamin Disraeli to Isaac D'Israeli, 14 July 1830.

45 *DL*, 94, i.142, 1 August 1830.

46 Christopher M. Bass, ed., *Somatization: Physical Symptoms and Psychological Illness* (Oxford, 1990), p. 104; Oppenheim, *'Shattered Nerves'*, pp. 12, 101.

47 Weintraub, *Disraeli*, pp. 83–4.

48 *DL*, 81, i.119, 13 April 1830.

49 *DL*, 94, i.142, Benjamin Disraeli to Maria D'Israeli, 1 August 1830; *DL*, 50, i.66, Benjamin Disraeli to Isaac D'Israeli, 9 August 1826; *DL*, 92, i.136, Benjamin Disraeli to Isaac D'Israeli, 14 July 1830.

50 Blake, p. 99.

51 Jerman, *Young Disraeli*, p. 284. See below, p. 86.

52 M&B, iii.549.

53 John Vincent, ed., *Disraeli, Derby and the Conservative Party* (Hassocks, 1978), p. 72.

54 *DL*, 2048, v.359, Benjamin Disraeli to Sarah Disraeli, 12 October 1850. Blake, p. 746.

55 We are grateful to Dr Harold Merskey for his assistance in this portion of the diagnosis. It is interesting to note that Disraeli's father suffered from what seems to have been a depressive collapse at the age of twenty-nine, which lasted for about three years. Benjamin describes the illness as 'a failing of nervous energy, occasioned by study and too sedentary habits, early habitual reverie, restless and indefinite purpose'. The symptoms were 'lassitude and despondency'; and Benjamin stressed that Isaac was 'deficient in self-esteem' and that his symptoms needed to be comprehended in terms of his 'psychology'. Benjamin Disraeli, 'On the Life and Writings of Mr Disraeli by His Son', in *Curiosities of Literature*, i.xxi–xxiv. There is evidence that Isaac was 'rebellious' as a child and that early on he possessed the 'poetic temperament'. See Blake, pp. 7–8. Like his son, he became more stable after his major depressive illness. There is a strong hereditary contribution to the origins of 'bi-polar' affective (manic-depressive) illness; and the occurrence of a similar depressive complaint in Isaac fits very well with the idea that Benjamin manifested a hereditary pattern of depression.

56 Post, 'Current Concepts of the Narcissistic Personality', p. 107. The low self-esteem is conjoined to a sense of certainty about ultimate success, to which the narcissist feels entitled, and may lead to feelings of invulnerability. See *DL*, 84, i.123, Benjamin Disraeli to Thomas Evans, 9 May 1830; *Hartlebury*, II, vii. 'For the rest', Bohun the hero declares, 'if I live I *must* be a great man.' Alroy asserts, 'I cannot doubt my triumph. Triumph is part of my existence. I am born for glory' (V, xxvi). And see Robert Blake, 'The Rise of Disraeli', *Essays in British History*, ed. H. R. Trevor-Roper (London, 1964), p. 232.

57 Blake, p. 99.

58 Kernberg, *Borderline Conditions and Pathological Narcissism*, p. 257.

59 M&B, iii.464–5.

60 *DL*, 793, iii.73, 4 July 1838.

61 *DL*, 1316, iv.101, 21 July 1843.

62 M&B, i.180.

63 Blake, p. 326.

64 *DL*, i.446, Appendix III. See also M&B, iv.61; v.348.

65 Hughenden Papers, Box 26, A/X/A/26; A/X/A/39.

66 See Ridley, *The Young Disraeli*, ch. 8.

67 Kernberg, *Borderline Conditions and Pathological Narcissism*, p. 235. But the narcissist *is* dependent – as Disraeli was dependent on his wife for narcissistic supplies and for money.

68 See above, p. 28.

69 Ridley, *Young Disraeli*, p. 156.

70 M&B, i.124.

71 See above, p. 33.

72 Andrew Elfenbein, *Byron and the Victorians* (Cambridge, 1995), p. 206.

73 M&B, ii.245–6.

74 Quoted in Paul Smith, *Disraelian Conservatism and Social Reform* (London, 1967), p. 12.

75 See above, p. 32.

76 H. C. G. Matthew, *Gladstone, 1809–1874* (Oxford, 1991), p. 79.

77 M&B, iii.152.

78 P. W. Wilson, ed., *The Greville Diary* (2 vols., London, 1927), ii.396.

79 Benjamin Disraeli, 'What is He?', *The Radical Tory*, ed. H. W. J. Edwards (London, 1937), pp. 53–61. See also M&B, i.271, 282–3, 290, 313.

80 See below, pp. 85–7.

81 Todd M. Endelman, *Radical Assimilation in English Jewish History, 1656–1945* (Bloomington, IN, 1990), p. 138.

82 *DL*, i.447, Appendix III.

83 M&B, iii.442.

84 G. H. Francis, *Disraeli* (London, 1852), p. 115.

85 Blake, p. 175.

86 *DL*, 1725, v.92, 12 October 1848.

87 Francis, *Disraeli*, pp. 20–1. This presumption was also evident in his maiden speech.

88 *DL*, 219, i.308, Benjamin Disraeli to the editor of *The Times*, 11 November 1832. Disraeli asserted in a letter to *The Times* that he had said: 'The Whigs have opposed me, not I them, and they shall repent it.'

89 *DL*, 400, ii.39, Benjamin Disraeli to Morgan O'Connell, 6 May 1835.

90 Blake, p. 184.

91 Post, 'Current Concepts of the Narcissistic Personality', p. 115.

92 Walter Bagehot, *Biographical Studies* (London, 1881), p. 365.

93 Blake, p. 543.

94 Quoted in Smith, *Disraelian Conservatism and Social Reform*, p. 16, n. 4.

95 John Morley, *The Life of Richard Cobden* (2 vols., London, 1881), i.297.

96 Quoted in Blake, p. 220.

97 *DL*, i.447, Appendix III.

98 Cf. Robert Blake, *Disraeli's Grand Tour: Benjamin Disraeli and the Holy Land, 1830–31* (London, 1982), p. 113; M&B, i.196.

99 *DL*, i.447, Appendix III. This is Vivian Grey's ambition.

100 See Vincent, *Disraeli, Derby and the Conservative Party*, pp. 31–3.

101 Vamik D. Volkan, 'Narcissistic Personality Organization and Reparative Leadership', *International Journal of Group Psychotherapy* 30 (1980), 131–52.

102 *Ibid.*, p. 138.

103 *Ibid.*, p. 139.

104 *DL*, 57, i.92, Benjamin Disraeli to Isaac D'Israeli, 10 October 1826.

105 M&B, vi.1.

106 Isaiah Berlin, 'Benjamin Disraeli, Karl Marx and the Search for Identity', *Against the Current* (London, 1979), p. 258.

107 The narcissistic and hysterical personalities, like death and sleep, are brother and sister. Kernberg describes hysterical character structure as '[a]n exaggeration of narcissistic traits, especially those linked with exhibitionistic trends'. *Borderline Conditions and Pathological Narcissism*, p. 238. The hysterical personality, in response to parental 'wounding', is egocentric, attention-seeking, deceitful, shallow, childish, with vivid fantasy life and labile emotions, dependent, easily hurt and prone to identity confusion and depression. But the hysterical personality is 'warmer' and more 'emotionally involved' than the 'cold, shrewdly calculating' narcissistic personality. *Ibid.* The hysteric sometimes manifests 'double-sided' sexual behaviour, which is interesting in view of recent educated guesses that Disraeli was homo- or bi-sexual. See Ridley, *The Young Disraeli*, p. 131; Elfenbein, *Byron and the Victorians*, p. 216.

108 Disraeli may have suffered from a childhood variant of depression. In August 1816, at the age of eleven, toward the end of the summer vacation, and prior to his attendance at Potticary's school, Disraeli's grandfather wrote that Benjamin was 'very ill' and that he was 'very much alarmed by the account I have from Isaac & very much afeard [*sic*]'. M&B, i.21. Disraeli's grandfather gives no description of the illness; but it may have been depressive. It is thought that children with hysteroid features sometimes have the capacity unconsciously to induce illness in themselves 'to evade situations which are … frightening, or potentially humiliating' such as attendance at school. Anthony Storr, *The Art of Psychotherapy* (London, 1979), p. 85. From its contiguity to the first term, it is possible that Disraeli's illness was based upon a fear of school. Contarini Fleming recalls that he was seized by 'horror' when he was about to repair to 'College' at the end of his eleventh year. He was impressed at that time by 'a keen conviction of inferiority', and as a result he 'thought of the vicissitude that was about to occur with the same apprehen-

sion that men look forward to the indefinite horror of a terrible operation' (I, vii).

109 See above, pp. 18–19, 21–2, 37.

110 See generally, Richard Faber, *Beaconsfield and Bolingbroke* (London, 1961).

111 Blake, p. 764.

112 See, for example, A. J. P. Taylor, *Essays in English History* (Harmondsworth, 1950), p. 119; Vincent, *Disraeli*, p. 16.

113. Blake, p. 66.

114 It is not surprising that one who had troubled relations with his mother; came from 'lukewarm' Jewish circumstances; left school at sixteen and the law at twenty, and who, like Contarini Fleming, was a kind of friendless sojourner in his country of adoption, should feel compelled to act roles because of a lack of secure foundations in his personality.

115 See Harold Merskey, 'Anna O. Had a Severe Depressive Illness', *British Journal of Psychiatry* 161 (1992), 185–94. We are grateful to Dr Merskey for his comments on these symptoms.

116 M&B, i.357.

117 *DL*, 351, i.431, Benjamin Disraeli to Benjamin Austen, 24 October 1834.

118 Irving Layton, *A Red Carpet For the Sun* (Toronto, 1959), 'Foreword'.

119 Quoted in Eleanor Perényi, *Liszt* (London, 1974), p. 23. See above, pp. 37–41.

120 See, for example, *The Young Duke* (IV, viii); *Alroy* (I, i).

121 *DL*, 94, i.142, Benjamin Disraeli to Maria D'Israeli, 1 August 1830.

122 Kay Redfield Jamison, *Touched With Fire: Manic Depressive Illness and the Artistic Temperament* (New York, 1993), p. 4. We know that the mania was real in the cases of Disraeli's heroes Byron and Shelley, and also in Poe, Coleridge and Berlioz, who are shown in this work to have been manic depressive.

123 Quoted in Theodore Ziolkowski, *German Romanticism and Its Institutions* (Princeton, 1990), p. 205.

124 Friedrich Nietzsche, 'Beyond Good and Evil', *Basic Writings of Nietzsche*, ed. Walter Kaufmann (New York, 1967), p. 407.

125 Lord Macaulay, *Critical and Historical Essays* (London, 1883), p. 159.

126 Oppenheim, '*Shattered Nerves*', p. 145.

127 *Ibid.*

128 *Ibid.*, p. 147.

129 Cf. C. E. Rosenberg, 'Body and Mind in Nineteenth-Century Medicine: Some Clinical Origins of the Neurosis Construct', *Bulletin of the History of Medicine* 63 (1989), 185–97.

130 See, for example, the judgement of Lord Randolph Churchill and his wife in 1875. Winston S. Churchill, *Lord Randolph Churchill* (2 vols., London, 1906), i.73. Robert Blake suggests that 'it is quite easy to envisage Disraeli living either today or in the era of Lord North': Blake, p. 765. It is true that Disraeli's detachment and love of power have a timeless quality; but the

emotional aridity of classicism on the one hand, and of relativism on the other, would probably have left him 'sighing for moonlight'. See M&B, v.283.

131 Ilza Veith, *Hysteria: The History of a Disease* (Chicago, 1965), p. 209.

132 Sacheverell Sitwell, *Liszt* (New York, 1967), p. 30; cf. Alan Walker, *Liszt, 'The Virtuoso Years', 1811–1847* (London, 1983), p. 203, n. 22.

133 See, for example, David Punter, *The Romantic Unconscious: A Study in Narcissism and Patriarchy* (London, 1989); N. Bryllion Fagin, *The Histrionic Mr Poe* (Baltimore, 1949); Matthew Arnold, 'Byron', *Poetry and Criticism of Matthew Arnold*, ed. A. Dwight Culler (Boston, 1961), pp. 347–62. Romantic artists tended to theatricality in their lives and art, a tendency which Goethe – one of the great early psychiatric thinkers – believed to be 'sick'. A central premise of his *Wilhelm Meister's Apprenticeship* is that the post-Cartesian subject and object split had made the isolated subject self-dramatizing and excessively imaginative. See Ernst Behler, *German Romantic Literary Theory* (Cambridge, 1993), p. 32; Ziolkowski, *German Romanticism*, ch. 4; Gloria Flaherty, 'The Stage Struck Wilhelm Meister and Eighteenth-Century Psychiatric Medicine', *Modern Language Notes* 101 (1986), 493–515.

134 Richard Holmes, *Shelley: The Pursuit* (London, 1987), pp. 98, 106, 117, 127, 131, 140, 198; Kenneth Silverman, *Edgar A. Poe: Mournful and Never-ending Remembrance* (New York, 1991), pp. 59–68; Leslie A. Marchand, *Byron: A Portrait* (London, 1993; first published 1970), pp. 28–9, 112–13; Christopher Small, *Ariel Like A Harpy: Shelley, Mary and Frankenstein* (London, 1972), p. 122.

135 Walter Allen, *The English Novel* (Harmondsworth, 1958), p. 158. At the end of his twenty-third year (1815), Shelley went through a rare period of psychological introspection, during which he caught a glimpse of his narcissistic predicament, and unsuccessfully attempted to attain self-knowledge through his art – even embarking upon an analysis of his dreams. In 'Alastor; or, the Spirit of Solitude', the story of which is shaped by the myth of Narcissus and Echo, 'the Poet' searches for an ideal vision of beauty, but finds himself instead gazing at his own image in a pool: 'His eyes beheld / Their own wan light through the reflected lines / Of his thin hair, distinct in the dark depth / Of that still fountain; as the human heart, / Gazing in dreams over the gloomy grave, / Sees its own treacherous likeness there.' Harry Buxton Forman, ed., *The Works of Percy Bysshe Shelley* (8 vols., London, 1880), i.36–7; Holmes, *Shelley*, pp. 287–306.

136 *Contarini Fleming* was supposed to depict 'the development and formation of the poetic character', but turned into a consideration as to whether its hero was better suited to active life. 1845 'Preface to *Contarini Fleming*' in the *Bradenham Edition of the Novels and Tales of Benjamin Disraeli, First Earl of Beaconsfield* (12 vols., London, 1926–7), iv.ix. Contarini declares in the last chapter that it is 'doubtful' whether poetry 'will be my career. My interest in the happiness of my race is too keen to permit me for a moment to be blind to

the storms that lour on the horizon of society. Perchance also the political regeneration of that country to which I am devoted may not be distant, and in that great work I am resolved to participate' (VII, ii). In the year following the publication of the novel, having tested this inclination on the political stage, Disraeli confided with certainty to his 'Mutilated Diary' that he was 'only truly great in action'. *DL*, i.447, Appendix III. Notwithstanding the failure of his poem *The Revolutionary Epick* in the following year, he continued to cultivate both his political and artistic gifts – realizing that this unique combination of talents constituted his true genius. In *Hartlebury* the narrator observes that, 'Aubrey Bohun combined a fine poetical temperament, with a great love of action. The combination was rare. He was a man of genius' (I, xiv).

4 DISRAELI AND ORIENTALISM

1 Edward Said, *Orientalism* (New York, 1978), p. 5.

2 *Ibid.*, p. 166.

3 *Ibid.*, p. 169.

4 Homi K. Bhabha, *The Location of Culture* (London, 1994), pp. 71–5. Said's *Orientalism* (1978) was a founding moment for what is now called 'postcolonial' cultural studies. See, for example, Michael Sprinker, ed., *Edward Said: A Critical Reader* (Oxford, 1992).

5 Nigel Leask, *British Romantic Writers and the East: Anxieties of Empire* (Cambridge, 1992), p. 2; Lisa Lowe, *Critical Terrains: French and British Orientalisms* (Ithaca, NY, 1991), p. 80.

6 Said, *Orientalism*, p. 26.

7 *Ibid.*, p. 102.

8 Cecil Roth, *Benjamin Disraeli, Earl of Beaconsfield* (New York, 1952), p. 67.

9 See Disraeli's letter of 1 January 1834 to Benjamin Austen, in *DL*, 301, i.385. Nothing came of this proposal; Edward Lane's translation of *The Arabian Nights* began to appear in 1838.

10 Robert Blake, *Disraeli's Grand Tour: Benjamin Disraeli and the Holy Land, 1830–31* (London, 1982), p. 31.

11 For Edward Lane, see Said, *Orientalism*, pp. 158–64. For Burton's celebration of Arabic 'chivalry' in relation to Disraeli, see my *Rule of Darkness: British Literature and Imperialism, 1830–1914* (Ithaca, NY, 1988), pp. 158–71. On the general fascination with Arabia, see Kathryn Tidrick, *Heart-beguiling Araby* (Cambridge, 1981).

12 *DL*, 103, i.173, Benjamin Disraeli to Benjamin Austen, 18 November 1830; Blake, *Disraeli's Grand Tour*, p. 29.

13 Blake, *Disraeli's Grand Tour*, p. 30.

14 There were frequent discussions about restoring the Jews to Palestine both

before and during Disraeli's lifetime, partly inspired by Protestant interpretations of God's promises to the Hebrews in the Old Testament. As Mayir Vereté demonstrated in 'The Idea of the Restoration of the Jews in English Protestant Thought', this was especially well publicized in the 1790s, and included the idea that, according to biblical prophecy, Britain would be instrumental in the restoration. See Norman Rose, ed., *From Palmerston to Balfour: Collected Essays of Mayir Vereté* (London, 1992), pp. 78–140. Disraeli himself has been credited with various Zionist schemes and with penning the anonymous manuscripts published as *Unknown Documents on the Jewish Question: Disraeli's Plan for a Jewish State* (1947), though there is no evidence for his authorship. See Ann Pottinger Saab, 'Disraeli, Judaism, and the Eastern Question', *International History Review* 10 (1988), 575.

15   DL, 107, i.179, 27 December 1830.

16   *DL*, 109, i.183, Benjamin Disraeli to Isaac D'Israeli, 11 January 1831.

17   *DL*, 103, i.174, Benjamin Disraeli to Benjamin Austen, 18 November 1830.

18   This is a theme in Eric Hobsbawm and Terence Ranger, eds., *The Invention of Tradition* (Cambridge, 1983), especially Bernard Cohn, 'Representing Authority in Victorian India', pp. 165–209.

19   Blake, *Disraeli's Grand Tour*, p. 47. Disraeli was travelling after the Treaty of Adrianople, 1829, and the London Protocol of 1830, under which Greece was supposedly an independent kingdom. The crown was offered first to Prince John of Saxony (who refused it), then to Prince Leopold of Saxe-Coburg (who withdrew after first accepting it). In early 1833, the son of King Ludwig of Bavaria became Otto I of Greece.

20   Isaiah Berlin writes: 'When Disraeli presided over the elevation of Queen Victoria to the throne of the Empress of India, and all that went with it, the gorgeous trappings of empire, the elephants and durbars, and all those eastern splendours which had succeeded the realistic, hard-headed rule of the East India Company and inspired the vast and occasionally hollow periods of later imperialist rhetoric, it is difficult to resist the impression that something of this stemmed from Disraeli's genuine orientalism.' *Against the Current: Essays in the History of Ideas* (London, 1979), p. 271.

21   Roth, *Disraeli*, p. 66.

22   Benjamin Disraeli, *Lord George Bentinck: A Political Biography* (London, 1861; first published 1851), ch. xxiv.

23   Michael Ragussis, *Figures of Conversion: 'The Jewish Question' and English National Identity* (Durham, NC, 1995), p. 187. In his 16 August 1845 letter to the *Morning Post* on 'Young England Philosophy', Disraeli cites not only Blumenbach, 'the Newton of physiology', but James Cowles Pritchard, *Researches into the Physical History of Mankind* (which appeared in various expanded editions from 1813 to 1851) as providing the scientific basis for his own racial classification. *DL*, 1433, iv.180–4. I owe this point to Paul Smith.

24 It is ironic that George Eliot, author of the best-known pro-Semitic Victorian novel, *Daniel Deronda*, should have viewed Disraeli and Disraeli's novels through anti-Semitic lenses. In *Deronda*, Eliot was trying to counteract not just anti-Semitism, but also what she saw as Disraeli's erroneous and shallow beliefs. In an early letter, Eliot declared that Disraeli's 'theory of "races" ... has not a leg to stand on ... The fellowship of race, to which D'Israeli exultingly refers the munificence of Sidonia, is so evidently an inferior impulse which must ultimately be superseded that I wonder even he, Jew that he is, dares to boast of it.' Gordon S. Haight, ed., *Selections from George Eliot's Letters* (New Haven, 1985), p. 45. 'Boasting' is, perhaps, not inappropriate, because Disraeli's 'theory of "races"' was a compensatory attempt to fight racism with racism. 'No one can fail to notice that he boasted of his Jewish origins almost too insistently, and mentioned them in and out of season at some risk to his political career, and this despite his eccentric but genuine Christianity' (Berlin, *Against the Current*, p. 268). For an excellent account of Jews and Judaism in late Victorian and early modern English literature, see Bryan Cheyette, *Constructions of the 'Jew' in English Literature and Society: Racial Representations, 1875–1945* (Cambridge, 1993).

25 In *Disraeli* (Oxford, 1990), p. 27, John Vincent declares that 'Disraeli's racial doctrine went the whole hog. Not only was race the key to history, but some races were far superior to others. There were master races, and then there were the rest.' Perhaps it would be more accurate to say that for Disraeli there was *one* master race – the Hebrew, or at any rate the Semitic or Arabic – the only race, as Disraeli liked to emphasize, to whom God had directly revealed any of His grand truths. It would make little sense, however, to interpret Disraeli's racism as proto-fascist, as some scholars have done, both because racial explanations for history were the common currency of nineteenth-century intellectuals and because Disraeli was so obviously seeking, through his pro-Semitism, to trump versions of Anglo-Saxonism and Aryanism that necessarily involved anti-Semitism and that were themselves intellectual forebears of fascist and Nazi racism.

26 For Arnold and Disraeli see Ragussis, *Figures*, pp. 211–27.

27 Said, *Orientalism*, p. 102.

28 *Ibid.*, p. 43.

29 Disraeli, *Lord George Bentinck*, ch. xxiv.

30 *Ibid.*, p. 346.

31 Blake, *Disraeli's Grand Tour*, p. 128.

5 'A HEBREW TO THE END': THE EMERGENCE OF DISRAELI'S JEWISHNESS

I am grateful to my colleagues Zvi Gitelman and Miriam Bodian for their comments and advice on an earlier version of this essay.

1 James Anthony Froude, *The Life of the Earl of Beaconsfield*, Everyman's Library edn (London, [1914]), p. 262.

2 The best introduction to his life and work is still James Ogden, *Isaac D'Israeli* (Oxford, 1969).

3 For Isaac's break with Bevis Marks, see James Picciotto, *Sketches of Anglo-Jewish History*, ed. Israel Finestein (London, 1956), pp. 287–92. His letter of 3 December 1813 to the synagogue authorities is printed in full on pp. 289–90.

4 Todd M. Endelman, *Radical Assimilation in English Jewish History, 1656–1945* (Bloomington, IN, 1990), ch. 1.

5 Todd M. Endelman, 'L'impact de l'expérience *conversa* sur l'identité Sepharade en Angleterre', in *Mémoires juives d'Espagne et du Portugal*, eds. Aron Rodrigue and Esther Benbassa (Paris, 1996), pp. 79–90.

6 These comments were made in a letter to the elders of the Spanish and Portuguese Jewish congregation, which appears in Moses Margoliouth, *The History of the Jews in Great Britain* (3 vols., London, 1851), iii.78–86. It was later reprinted in Cecil Roth, ed., *Anglo-Jewish Letters (1158–1917)* (London, 1938), pp. 281–6.

7 Ogden, *Isaac D'Israeli*, pp. 195–7; Stanley Weintraub, *Disraeli: A Biography* (New York, 1993), pp. 141–2, 278; Jane Ridley, *The Young Disraeli, 1804–1846* (New York, 1995), p. 13.

8 Isaac did not own Mendelssohn's writings, with the one exception of a French edition of correspondence and essays by Mendelssohn and others related to the so-called Lavater affair – *Lettres juives du célèbre Mendelssohn ... avec les remarques et réponses de monsieur le docteur Kölble et autres savants hommes* (n.p., 1771). He also owned the second edition of Moses Samuel's *Memoirs of Moses Mendelssohn*, which was published in London in 1827, that is, long after his view of Mendelssohn had taken shape. For my reconstruction of the Judaica in Isaac's and then Benjamin's library, see note 13 below.

9 Benjamin Jaffe, 'A Reassessment of Benjamin Disraeli's Jewish Aspects', *Transactions of the Jewish Historical Society of England* 27 (1982), 116; Isaiah Berlin, 'Benjamin Disraeli, Karl Marx and the Search for Identity', *Against the Current: Essays in the History of Ideas*, ed. Henry Hardy (London, 1979), pp. 261–2.

10 Benjamin Disraeli, 'On the Life and Writings of Mr Disraeli', in Isaac Disraeli, *Curiosities of Literature*, new edn (3 vols., London, 1858).

11 Benjamin Disraeli to Sarah Brydges Willyams, 28 February 1853, quoted in Jaffe, 'Reassessment', 116.

12 M&B, i.19.

13 No catalogue of Isaac D'Israeli's extensive library exists. However, it is possible to reconstruct the Judaica in it – or, at least, a portion of it – on the basis of a handwritten list (DFam/E/1/9A) that has survived in the Rothschild Archive in London. Nathaniel de Rothschild, later the first Lord

Rothschild, was co-executor of Benjamin Disraeli's estate. After the latter's death, the estate sold a selection of fifty-four books from his library, all but two or three on Jewish subjects, a list of which remained in Lord Rothschild's keeping. Presumably the executors believed that Disraeli's sole heir, his nephew Coningsby, had no interest in them. While at least one of the books had to have been acquired by Benjamin himself, given its publication date, the bulk belonged, it would seem, to Isaac. On his father's death in January 1848, Benjamin inherited his 25,000 volume library; in serious debt, he sold most of it at Sotheby's, after having culled a number of works for his own collection at Hughenden. It seems doubtful that Benjamin would have purchased Judaica published in the eighteenth century or even before the late 1830s, when he first began to take an interest in his Jewish background. Thus, I believe it is reasonable to use this list as a guide, however imperfect, to the Judaica to which Isaac and later Benjamin turned for their knowledge of Jewish history and literature. It is, of course, likely that Isaac's collection of Judaica was more extensive and that Benjamin sold some volumes at Sotheby's after his death. The authors and titles on the list are printed, in alphabetical order, as an appendix to this chapter. I am grateful to Melanie Aspey of the Rothschild Archive for making it available to me.

14 M&B, i.19.

15 Todd M. Endelman, *The Jews of Georgian England, 1714–1830: Tradition and Change in a Liberal Society* (Philadelphia, 1979), ch. 3; Frank Felsenstein, *Anti-Semitic Stereotypes: A Paradigm of Otherness in English Popular Culture, 1660–1830* (Baltimore, 1995).

16 Above, p. 18.

17 Endelman, *Radical Assimilation*, pp. 128–9, 138–9.

18 Charles Lamb, 'Imperfect Sympathies', in *Essays of Elia*, first series (New York, 1845), pp. 75–6.

19 Picciotto, *Sketches*, p. 187.

20 The tour is described in Robert Blake, *Disraeli's Grand Tour, Benjamin Disraeli and the Holy Land, 1830–31* (New York, 1982).

21 *DL*, 56, i.86; 90, i.128–9, Benjamin Disraeli to Isaac D'Israeli, 29 September 1826 and 1 July 1830; 110, i.188, Isaac D'Israeli to Sarah Disraeli, 20 March 1831.

22 *DL*, 110, i.188, Benjamin Disraeli to Sarah Disraeli, 20 March 1831.

23 Blake, p. 80.

24 Nowell C. Smith, ed., *The Letters of Sydney Smith* (2 vols., Oxford, 1953), ii.614. Sydney Smith to Mrs Holland, 3 June 1835. In relating what happened at Taunton, Smith did not use Disraeli's name but referred to him as 'the Jew'.

25 *The Times*, 6 May 1835.

26 Ridley, *Young Disraeli*, p. 202.

27 William Fraser, *Disraeli and His Day*, second edn (London, 1891), pp. 473–4; Weintraub, *Disraeli*, p. 197.

28 See, for example, the illustrations reprinted in Weintraub, *Disraeli*, pp. 222, 291 and following p. 274; Ridley, *Young Disraeli*, following p. 278; Anne and Roger Cowen, *Victorian Jews through British Eyes* (Oxford, 1986), pp. 24–5.

29 Much about this messianic figure remains unknown. A short account of his life and the sources available for reconstructing it are in Salo W. Baron, *A Social and Religious History of the Jews* (18 vols., New York, 1952–83), vol. v, *Religious Controls and Dissensions* (New York, 1957), pp. 202–4, 385–6, n. 68 and n. 69. The sources on which Disraeli drew are listed in Charles B. Richmond, 'Benjamin Disraeli: A Psychological Biography, 1804–1832', unpublished M.Litt. thesis, University of Oxford, 1982, Appendix 4.

30 See above, p. 49.

31 *DL*, 683, ii.323–4, Benjamin Disraeli to Sarah Disraeli, 5 December 1837.

32 Abraham Gilam, 'Benjamin Disraeli and the Emancipation of the Jews', *Disraeli Newsletter* 5, no. 1 (1980), 26–46.

33 It is often suggested that Disraeli took Lionel de Rothschild as his model for Sidonia, but, according to Richard Davis, this is unlikely. The head of the Rothschild bank and the young politician were not close friends at the time Disraeli wrote the book, and Lionel's personality bore little resemblance to that of the fictional Sidonia. Davis adds, however: 'There can be little doubt that the fabulous financier with his mysterious international connections was Rothschild-inspired (though not by any particular Rothschild). This is as far as one can safely go.' *The English Rothschilds* (Chapel Hill, NC, 1983), p. 87.

34 Thomas Babington Macaulay, *Critical and Historical Essays Contributed to the Edinburgh Review* (2 vols., London, 1854), ii.141–3.

35 Rosa Luxemburg, *Briefe an Freunde*, ed. Benedikt Kautsky (Hamburg, 1950), pp. 48–9. Abraham Gilam argues that Disraeli had no other alternative, that he had to admit to his Jewishness if he wished to become leader of his party ('Disraeli and Emancipation', 35). While I agree that Disraeli would have been hard pressed not to acknowledge his origins, I do not agree that the alternative he chose – embracing racial chauvinism – was the only one available to him. There is, after all, a critical difference, which Gilam blurs, between acknowledging one's Jewishness and trumpeting the Jews' superiority. A range of alternate forms of behaviour exists between these two extremes. What I want to stress is the extremity of Disraeli's response.

36 Hannah Arendt, *The Origins of Totalitarianism*, pt. 1, *Antisemitism*, Harvest Books ed. (New York, 1968), pp. 72–5; Berlin, 'Disraeli, Marx and the Search for Identity'.

37 Berlin, 'Disraeli, Marx and the Search for Identity', p. 268.

38 The 'half-naked' phrase is quoted in Blake, *Disraeli's Grand Tour*, p. 126. According to Blake, the phrase comes from *Contarini Fleming*, but he does not

cite where in the novel it appears and neither I nor Nadia Valman, a student of Disraeli's novels, has been able to locate it.

39 Benjamin Disraeli, *Lord George Bentinck: A Political Biography* (London, 1851), ch. xxiv.

40 Quoted in T. Wemyss Reid, *The Life, Letters, and Friendships of Richard Monckton Milnes* (2 vols., London, 1890), i.436.

41 Arendt, *Antisemitism*, p. 75; Berlin, 'Disraeli, Marx and the Search for Identity', p. 270.

42 Paul Smith, '"How to be Top though Jewish": *Tancred, Lord George Bentinck* and the Protectionist Leadership, 1846–52', Conference on Disraeli's Jewishness, University of Southampton, 27–28 July 1994.

43 Blake, p. 243.

44 Constance Flower to Cyril Flower, 20 April 1881, Battersea Papers, Add. ms. 47,910/5, British Library, London.

45 The history of the myth and the uses to which both Jews and their critics put it have not received sufficient attention. For a short account, see Todd M. Endelman, 'Benjamin Disraeli and the Myth of Sephardi Superiority', *Jewish History* 10, no. 2 (1996), 1–15.

46 The most reliable account of Disraeli's ancestry is Cecil Roth, *Benjamin Disraeli, Earl of Beaconsfield* (New York, 1952), ch. 1. See also Michael Selzer, 'Benjamin Disraeli's Knowledge of his Ancestry', *Disraeli Newsletter* 1, no. 2 (1976), 8–17.

47 Benjamin Disraeli, 'Life and Writings of Mr Disraeli', pp. viii–ix.

48 John Vincent, ed., *Disraeli, Derby and the Conservative Party: Journals and Memoirs of Edward Henry, Lord Stanley, 1849–1869* (Hassocks, 1978), p. 32; *DL*, 1388, iv.153, Benjamin Disraeli to Richard Monckton Milnes, 29 December 1844; Weintraub, *Disraeli*, p. 377.

49 *DL*, 450, ii.109, Benjamin Disraeli to Isaac D'Israeli, 15 December 1835; *DL*, 1269, iv.68, Benjamin Disraeli to Sarah Disraeli, 2 December 1842.

50 Isaac D'Israeli, *The Genius of Judaism*, pp. 244–6.

51 Hugh A. MacDougall, *Racial Myth in English History: Trojans, Teutons, and Anglo-Saxons* (Hanover, NH, 1982), ch. 5.

52 Vincent, *Disraeli, Derby and the Conservative Party*, pp. 32–3. Cf. *DL*, vi.535–6, Appendix IA.

53 *Ibid.*; Gilam, 'Disraeli and Emancipation', 32.

54 Disraeli, *Lord George Bentinck*, ch. xxiv. Despite his hope that the Jewish people would one day embrace Christianity, Disraeli could be scornful about assimilation-minded Jews who tried to mute their Jewishness and 'pass through society without being discovered, or at least noticed'. See his witty demolition of the fictional social-climbing Laurella sisters, who were 'ashamed of their race, and not fanatically devoted to their religion, which might be true, but certainly was not fashionable'. *Tancred*, V, v.

55 Froude aptly characterized Disraeli's Christianity as 'something of his own', which 'would scarcely find acceptance in any Christian community'. *The Earl of Beaconsfield*, p. 108.

56 Smith, ' "How to be Top though Jewish" '.

57 Quoted in Blake, p. 248.

58 See, in general, Arthur H. Frietzsche, *Disraeli's Religion: The Treatment of Religion in Disraeli's Novels* (Logan, UT, 1961).

59 Vincent, *Disraeli, Derby and the Conservative Party*, p. 179; *DL*, 2166, v.459, Benjamin Disraeli to Sarah Disraeli, 1 August 1851.

60 M&B, iv.350.

61 Weintraub, *Disraeli*, p. 658.

62 Ridley claims that 'Disraeli rarely set foot in a church' (*Young Disraeli*, p. 268), but the evidence for this claim is not clear. Perhaps she is referring to that period in his life before he aspired to political leadership.

63 M&B, v.57−8.

64 The best treatments of the Jewish dimension of the Eastern crisis agitation are David Feldman, *Englishmen and Jews: Social Relations and Political Culture, 1840−1914* (New Haven, 1994), ch. 4, and Anthony S. Wohl, ' "Dizzi-Ben-Dizzi": Disraeli as Alien', *Journal of British Studies* 34 (1995), 375−411.

6 DISRAELI'S INTERPRETATION OF ENGLISH HISTORY

1 M&B, ii.295; John Vincent, *Disraeli* (Oxford, 1990), pp. 3, 21; Jane Ridley, *The Young Disraeli* (London, 1995), pp. 167, 298; Blake, p. 90.

2 Norman Gash, *Reaction and Reconstruction in English Politics, 1832−1852* (Oxford, 1965), ch. 1; Linda Colley, *Britons* (London, 1992), ch. 5.

3 Gash, *Reaction and Reconstruction*, ch. 2; E. A. Smith, *The House of Lords in British Politics and Society, 1815−1911* (London, 1992); also his and R. W. Davis' articles on Lord Grey and the duke of Wellington and the House of Lords in R. W. Davis, ed., *Lords of Parliament: Studies, 1714−1914* (Stanford, 1995). An article on the English peerage that appeared in the *Quarterly Review* in March 1830 (no. 84, pp. 281−332, hereafter *QR*, Peerage) is good evidence of the contemporary concern about the composition of the Lords.

4 See, for example, Wellington's contribution to the debate, the Duke of Wellington, ed., *Despatches, Correspondence, and Memoranda of Field Marshal Arthur, Duke of Wellington* (8 vols., London, 1867−80), ii.453.

5 Ian Newbould, 'Sir Robert Peel and the Conservative Party, 1832−41: A Study in Failure?', *English Historical Review* 98 (1983), 529−57.

6 Frank O'Gorman, *Voters, Patrons, and Parties. The Unreformed Electorate of Hanoverian England, 1734−1832* (Oxford, 1989), ch. 4.

7 This is a thesis I advance in my forthcoming *British Politics on the Eve of Reform: The Duke of Wellington's Administration, 1828−1830*.

8 John Belchem, 'Republicanism, Popular Constitutionalism and the Radical Platform in Early Nineteenth-Century England', *Social History* 6 (1981), 1–32.

9 Benjamin Disraeli, *Vindication of the English Constitution in a Letter to a Noble and Learned Lord* (London, 1835), pp. 20–5, 42–5.

10 *Ibid.*, pp. 87–9.

11 *Ibid.*, pp. 91–102; *Coningsby*, II, i; III, v.

12 Disraeli, *Vindication*, pp. 108–25; *Coningsby*, V, ii; *DL*, 409, ii.60–1, Benjamin Disraeli to Edwards Beadon, 2 July 1835.

13 Disraeli, *Vindication*, pp. 168–71.

14 *Ibid.*, pp. 166–97; *Sybil*, I, iii; *Coningsby*, II, i; Disraeli, *Lord George Bentinck*, ch. vii; Benjamin Disraeli, 'The Spirit of Whiggism', in *Whigs and Whiggism*, ed. William Hutcheon (London, 1913), pp. 334–5.

15 Disraeli, *Vindication*, pp. 166–97; *Coningsby*, V, ii; *Sybil*, I, iii; *DL*, ii.406–8, letter xix of 'The Letters of Runnymede', to Viscount Melbourne, 14 May 1836; *DL*, 1390, iv.155, Benjamin Disraeli to Lord Lansdowne, 25 January 1845.

16 Disraeli, *Vindication*, p. 197; *Coningsby*, II, i; *Sybil*, I, iii; Disraeli, *Lord George Bentinck*, ch. xvii; *Endymion*, I, vi; *DL*, ii.406–8, letter xix of 'The Letters of Runnymede', to Viscount Melbourne, 14 May 1836; *DL*, 458, ii.114–22, Benjamin Disraeli to the editor of *The Times*, 28 December 1835.

17 The view that his interpretation was steeped in what now appears to be perceptive observations on the politics of the pre- and post-Reform periods is strengthened by a quite astonishing example of prescience. *Vivian Grey* was published in 1826. In 1829–30 there was much talk in Ultra-Tory circles of their having more in common with the Whigs than their former colleagues and 'the men of business', Wellington and Peel. Sir Richard Vyvyan, who was four years older than Disraeli and had been returned to parliament in 1826, was one of the Ultra leaders; and Lord Grey was the Whig leader in waiting.

18 Thomas P. Peardon, *The Transition in English Historical Writing, 1760–1830* (New York, 1966), *passim*.

19 Edward Lytton Bulwer (subsequently Edward Bulwer-Lytton, first Baron Lytton), *England and the English* (3 vols., London, 1833), i.52–4. There is a remarkable similarity between Disraeli's political views and those expressed in this work. See also, N. H. Nicolas, *Observations on the State of Historical Literature* (London, 1830), *passim* but see particularly, pp. 3, 13 (for the quotation), 187–8.

20 Mark Francis and John Morrow, *English Political Thought in the Nineteenth Century* (London, 1994), ch. 1.

21 Above, pp. 179, n.21, 28.

22 Ridley, *Disraeli*, pp. 22–3, 26.

23 *DL*, iv.404–5, Appendix X.

24 Disraeli, *Vindication*, pp. 21–2, 25, 70.

25 *Ibid.*, p. 44; Disraeli, 'The Spirit of Whiggism' in *Whigs and Whiggism*, pp. 329, 341; *Sybil*, I, iii; *Coningsby*, II, vii. Disraeli met Sir Francis Palgrave in 1825, see *DL*, 44, i.60, n. 7, Benjamin Disraeli to John Gibson Lockhart, 28 November 1825.

26 *DL*, 306, i.392, n. 4, Benjamin Disraeli to Sarah Disraeli, 29 January 1834; *DL*, 332, i.415, n. 2, Benjamin Disraeli to Maria D'Israeli and Sarah Disraeli, 23 June 1834.

27 *Sybil*, I, iii.

28 Blake, p. 191.

29 Ridley, *The Young Disraeli*, p. 167; *The Works of Edmund Burke* (12 vols., London, 1899), iii.272-3.

30 John Miller, *An Historical View of English Government* (3 vols., London, 1803; first published 1768), ii.ch. 1.

31 Henry Hallam, *The Constitutional History of England from the Accession of Henry VII to the Death of George III* (3 vols., London, 1867; first published in 1827), iii.33-9; Sir James Mackintosh, *The History of England* (3 vols., London, 1830), i.239-44; John Lingard, *The History of England from the First Invasion by the Romans to the Revolution in 1688* (10 vols., London, 1854; first published 1819-30), ii.238ff. It was Hume who argued that the establishment of the Commons arose from the 'necessities' of the times, a word repeated by Disraeli: David Hume, *The History of England from the Invasion of Julius Caesar to the Revolution in 1688*, Liberty Classics edn (6 vols., New York, 1983), ii.99-109.

32 Mackintosh, *History*, i.266; Miller, *English Government*, ii.223.

33 Nicolas, *Observations*, p. 100.

34 Lingard, *History*, iv.66-8.

35 J. G. A. Pocock, ed., *The Political Works of James Harrington* (Cambridge, 1977), pp. 45, 50.

36 Hallam, *Constitutional History*, iii.38-9.

37 Pocock, *Harrington*, p. 57; *The Works of the Late Right Honourable Henry St John, Lord Viscount Bolingbroke* (8 vols., London, 1809), ii.233-4; Lingard, *History*, v.48-9, 108-13, and vi.324.

38 Hallam, *Constitutional History*, i.79. It was, of course, the reverse of Macaulay's view at the time. Hallam's thesis came under the scrutiny of the author of the article on the English peerage, *QR*, Peerage. In this, p. 330, the author says that Hallam's thesis was only partially accurate if all the families were considered, but that there was no doubt he was right in the cases of the Cavendish and Russell families.

39 I owe this point to John Burrow, *A Liberal Descent* (Cambridge, 1983), pp. 240-1 and Francis and Morrow, *Political Thought*, p. 117.

40 Bolingbroke, *Works*, ii.334-5; J. de Lolme, *The Constitution of England* (London, 1817; first published in English in 1784), p. 45.

41 Miller, *English Government*, iii.1–9; George Brodie, *A History of the British Empire, from the Accession of Charles I to the Restoration* (4 vols., Edinburgh, 1822), iii.4; Earl Russell, *The English Government and Constitution* (London, 1865; first published 1823), p. 79.

42 Hallam, *Constitutional History*, ii.94–102; Lingard, *History*, vii.267–8; Robert Bisset, *History of the Reign of George III*, second edn (6 vols., London, 1820), i.66.

43 Bolingbroke, *Works*, ii.94–5, 334–5, 408; Hume, *History*, vi.376–7, 381, 455, 528; Hallam, *Constitutional History*, ii.138–50; Isaac D'Israeli, *Commentaries on the Life and Reign of Charles the First, King of England*, ed. Benjamin Disraeli (2 vols., London, 1851; first published 1828–30), i.347.

44 Pocock, *Harrington*, pp. 136–7; Bolingbroke, *Works*, iii.11; David Hume and Tobias George Smollet, *The History of England from the Invasion of Julius Caesar to the End of the Reign of George II*, new edn (7 vols., London, 1865), vii.339.

45 Russell, *English Government*, pp. 172–80, 236; William, Archdeacon Coxe, *Memoirs of Lord Walpole* (London, 1802), pp. 439ff where he portrays post-Pelhamite politics as a jostling for office.

46 Francis and Morrow, *Political Thought*, p. 37; Hallam, *Constitutional History*, ii.427–8.

47 Pocock, *Harrington*, pp. 92–3.

48 Hallam, *Constitutional History*, ii.93–102, and iii.199, 295–6. In the case of Bolingbroke, his *Works* were published in 1809 and in 1835, the same year as the *Vindication of the English Constitution* was published. George Wingrove Cooke appears to have responded to Hallam's suggestion of a reappraisal with the publication of a two-volume *Memoir of Lord Bolingbroke*. It was well reviewed in the periodicals. The view that the Tories were the majority at the Hanoverian succession is admitted by Russell, *English Government*, p. 171. It is also worth noting that the hero of R. Plumer Ward's *Tremaine*, on which Disraeli based *Vivian Grey*, was an admirer of Bolingbroke.

49 Miller, *English Government*, iv.304–10.

50 Lytton Bulwer, *England and the English*, i.62 and ii.293, 299–301, 307.

51 See, on this point, R. W. Stewart, ed., *Disraeli's Novels Reviewed, 1826–1968* (Metuchen, NJ, 1975).

52 The reference to Bolingbroke is in *Vindication*, p. 188.

53 Linda Colley, *In Defiance of Oligarchy* (Cambridge, 1982), pp. 195, 295; for a recent assessment of the Peerage bill see Clyve Jones, 'Venice Preserv'd; or A Plot Discovered', in Clyve Jones, ed., *A Pillar of the Constitution: The House of Lords in British Politics, 1640–1784* (London, 1989), pp. 79–113, particularly p. 105.

54 Colley, *In Defiance of Oligarchy*, pp. 95, 145, 290.

55 H. T. Dickinson, *Liberty and Property*, pb edn (London, 1979), pp. 164–5, 177–81.

56 *Sybil*, I, iii; *Coningsby*, II, i; *DL*, iv.xvi, 'Introduction'; *DL*, 1390, iv.155, Benjamin Disraeli to Lord Lansdowne, 25 January 1845.

57 On 19 March 1830, Alderman Waithman, MP for London, said in the Commons that a 'new word', 'reciprocity', had been invented by Lord Shelburne. On 17 May in the same year Brougham referred to Shelburne as the most powerful and influential orator ever to sit in the Commons but added: 'I do not know whether any Honourable Gentlemen in this House have heard of him', *The Mirror of Parliament* (1830), pp. 906, 1788.

58 R. Bisset's view was that 'He was … more noted for extent and exactness of intelligence, than for the formation of able and beneficial plans from the result', *History*, iii.226; John Norris, *Shelburne and Reform* (London, 1963), pp. 292–3; John Ehrman, *The Younger Pitt: The Years of Acclaim* (London, 1969), pp. 85–9.

59 Boyd Hilton, 'The Political Arts of Lord Liverpool', *Transactions of the Royal Historical Society*, fifth series, 38 (1988), pp. 141–70.

7 DISRAELI'S POLITICS

The author is grateful to the Royal Historical Society for permission to make use of some material first published in 'Disraeli's Politics', *Transactions of the Royal Historical Society*, fifth series, 37 (1987), 65–85.

1 *DL*, v.535, Appendix V.

2 Bright's diary, 15 December 1852, in R. A. J. Walling, ed., *The Diaries of John Bright* (London, 1930), p. 130; Jowett to Florence Nightingale, 3 May 1868, in Vincent Quinn and John Prest, eds., *Dear Miss Nightingale: A Selection of Benjamin Jowett's Letters to Florence Nightingale, 1860–1893* (Oxford, 1987), p. 143. For a recent rendition of the 'lovable rogue' interpretation of Disraeli, see Michael Portillo, 'An Icon for the Tories', *Daily Telegraph*, 21 August 1997.

3 Helen M. and Marvin Swartz, eds., *Disraeli's Reminiscences* (London, 1975), Introduction, pp. xxii–xxiii. On the reliability of Disraeli's account, see Blake, pp. 302–3. The version given by Stanley to his son, Edward Stanley, confirms only Disraeli's statement that the Queen required Stanley to go bail for him: see John Vincent, ed., *Disraeli, Derby and the Conservative Party. Journals and Memoirs of Edward Henry, Lord Stanley, 1849–1869* (Hassocks, 1978), pp. 46–7.

4 M&B, ii.245–6.

5 *DL*, i.447, Appendix III.

6 *Ibid.*

7 Siegbert S. Prawer, *Karl Marx and World Literature* (Oxford, 1976), p. 2.

8 'Mutilated Diary', 1833, in *DL*, i.447, Appendix III.

9 Benjamin and Sarah Disraeli (under the pseudonyms of 'Cherry and Fair

Star'), *A Year at Hartlebury or the Election* (2 vols., London, 1834; re-issued London, 1983), I, xiv.

10 To Sarah Disraeli, 9 August 1830, *DL*, 95, i.147.

11 *Ibid.*, 120, i.207, 3 November 1831.

12 Address to the electors, 1 October 1832, *ibid.*, 215, i.304.

13 *Ibid.*, 133–4, 141–2, 144, 163, 167–8, 173, 179, 184, 188, n. 1, 198–9, 202; i.221–2, 228–31, 232–3, 250–2, 254–6, 260, 265–6, 270, 272, 284–6, 289–90. The tactical considerations at Wycombe are well outlined in Richard W. Davis, *Disraeli* (London, 1976), pp. 28–34.

14 Above, pp. 133–4.

15 Disraeli to Austen, [2?] June 1832, *DL*, 198, i.285.

16 M&B, i.220.

17 *Ibid.*, i.219.

18 See his remarks to Sarah, 26 May 1832, in *DL*, 193, i.280–1.

19 Byron to Hobhouse, 26 June 1819, in Leslie A. Marchand, ed., *Byron's Letters and Journals* (12 vols., London, 1973–82), vi.166. Cf. Disraeli's 'the greatest gentleman I ever knew' (Swartz, *Reminiscences*, p. 37). See, on Burdett, John Dinwiddy, 'Sir Francis Burdett and Burdettite Radicalism', *History*, 65 (1980), 17–31.

20 Swartz, *Reminiscences*, p. 37. Disraeli canvassed for Burdett in the 1837 Westminster by-election, in which the latter was effectively the Tory candidate.

21 Above, p. 135. On the Tory version of popular constitutionalism, see James Vernon, *Politics and the People. A Study in English Political Culture, c. 1815–1867* (Cambridge, 1993), pp. 298–302.

22 Addresses of 27 June and 1 October 1832, in *DL*, 203, 215, i.290–2, 303–5.

23 Bright's diary, 15 December 1852, in Walling, ed., *Diaries of John Bright*, p. 130.

24 *England and France: A Cure for the Ministerial Gallomania* (London, 1832), p. 13.

25 *DL*, 141, i.228.

26 *Ibid.*, 215, i.305.

27 'Mutilated Diary', 1833, in *ibid.*, i.446, Appendix III.

28 *What is He?* (London, 1833), p. 16.

29 *England and France*, pp. 13, 50.

30 Draft address to the Buckinghamshire electors, 12 December 1832, in *DL*, 222, i.309.

31 Disraeli to Edwards Beadon, 2 July 1835, *ibid.*, 409, ii.62.

32 Address to the electors and inhabitants of Taunton, 13 June 1835, *ibid.*, 406, ii.46–7.

33 *Vindication of the English Constitution in a Letter to a Noble and Learned Lord* (London, 1835), p. 193.

34 Benjamin Disraeli, *The Crisis Examined* (London, 1834), p. 16.

35 Disraeli, *Vindication*, p. 16.

36 *Ibid.*, pp. 22, 23.

37 *Ibid.*, p. 23.

38 *Ibid.*, pp. 24–5.

39 *Ibid.*, p. 103.

40 *Ibid.*, pp. 204, 206. There seems to be no direct evidence that Disraeli knew of the ideas of Hegel and the Hegelians, but his phraseology suggests that he had acquired some notion of them at secondhand. See below, pp. 168, 170.

41 Disraeli, *Vindication*, p. 204.

42 *Ibid.*, p. 205.

43 *Ibid.*, p. 181.

44 *Ibid.*, p. 74.

45 *Ibid.*, pp. 129–30.

46 *Ibid.*, p. 183.

47 *Ibid.*, pp. 100–1, 199.

48 Disraeli to Edwards Beadon, 2 July 1835, *DL*, 409, ii.61. John Vincent's study of pollbooks finds that 'Disraeli's idea of an untapped Tory stratum lying beneath middle-class radicalism had a certain amount of justification over the period 1832–68', at least in the sense that town labourers were somewhat more likely than craftsmen or shopkeepers to vote Tory (though, in Vincent's view, this is largely accounted for by 'their fewness and their corruptibility'). It is worth noting that in the 1841 election at Maidstone, Disraeli's first seat, which he had just abandoned after representing it since 1837, labourers voted Conservative as against Liberal in the proportion of about three to one, considerably higher than for the Maidstone electorate as a whole. In Shrewsbury, the constituency to which Disraeli transferred in 1841, the labourers had split almost equally in the 1837 election. John Vincent, *Pollbooks: How Victorians Voted* (Cambridge, 1976), pp. 16–17, 142, 176. Unfortunately no poll book has been found for any of Disraeli's contests.

49 Disraeli to the editor of *The Times*, 28 December 1835, *DL*, 458, ii.117.

50 Disraeli, *Vindication*, p. 207.

51 *Ibid.*, p. 205.

52 *Ibid.*, pp. 160–1.

53 *Ibid.*, p. 187.

54 Frans de Bruyn, *The Literary Genres of Edmund Burke. The Political Uses of Literary Form* (Oxford, 1996), p. 19.

55 Disraeli, *Vindication*, p. 210.

56 *Ibid.*, p. 186.

57 'Letter to a Noble Lord' (1796), in Paul Langford, general ed., *The Writings and Speeches of Edmund Burke*, ix (ed. Robert Brendan McDowell, Oxford, 1991), 160.

58 Address to the Maidstone electors, 1 July 1837, *DL*, 629, ii.275–6.

59 Peel to Graham, 22 December 1843, in Charles Stuart Parker, *Sir Robert Peel From His Private Papers* (3 vols., London, 1891–9), iii.425.

60 'Authors', Isaac added, 'stand between the governors and the governed, and form the single organ of both.' Isaac D'Israeli, *The Literary Character: or The History of Men of Genius*, fourth edn (2 vols., London, 1828), ii.299, 300, 317, 321. Benjamin quoted the sentence about standing between the governors and the governed in the memoir of his father written at the end of 1848, declaring that the latter 'had vindicated the right position of authors in the social scale'. 'On the Life and Writings of Mr Disraeli. By His Son', preface to Isaac Disraeli, *Curiosities of Literature*, fourteenth edn (3 vols., London, 1849), i.lii.

61 Disraeli, *Vindication*, pp. 16–17.

62 It is significant that, as he pursued that collective self-scrutiny, he offered 'to the new generation' a new edition of his paradigm of the individual search, *Contarini Fleming*. See his preface of July 1845, *Bradenham Edition of the Novels and Tales of Benjamin Disraeli, 1st Earl of Beaconsfield* (12 vols., London, 1926–7), iv.xi.

63 On Disraeli's racial views, see above, pp. 97–105, 115–23.

64 Disraeli, *Vindication*, p. 204; *Coningsby*, IV, xv.

65 Jane Ridley, *The Young Disraeli* (London, 1995), p. 279.

66 Disraeli, *Vindication*, pp. 65–102, 128–9.

67 Angus Hawkins, '"Parliamentary Government" and Victorian Political Parties, c. 1830–c. 1880', *English Historical Review*, 104 (1989), 642–3.

68 John Vincent, *Disraeli* (Oxford, 1990), p. 84. Cf. Ridley, *Young Disraeli*, p. 279.

69 See Vernon, *Politics and the People*, p. 325.

70 Disraeli to Sarah Disraeli (3 May 1837), on Oastler; to Attwood, 7 June 1840. *DL*, 606, ii.261; 1065, iii.272.

71 M&B, ii.82–8.

72 *DL*, 1407, n. 5, iv.168 (Cooper), 1429, n. 1, iv.178–9 (Odd Fellows).

73 Cf. Vernon, *Politics and the People*, pp. 235ff.

74 O'Connor at Marylebone, 17 December 1844, in Frederick C. Mather, ed., *Chartism and Society: An Anthology of Documents* (London, 1980), p. 225. For Disraeli's use of O'Connor's correspondence, see *DL* 1379, n. 2, iv.146; M&B, ii.250–1.

75 In his last occasional piece, on 'The English Reform Bill'.

76 Quoted in Norman Gash, *Reaction and Reconstruction in English Politics, 1832–1852* (Oxford, 1965), p. 10.

77 Quoted in Vernon, *Politics and the People*, p. 319.

78 Cf. Bulwer: 'In despotic states, the plebeian has even a greater chance of rising than in free'. Edward Lytton Bulwer, *England and the English*, second edn (2 vols., London, 1833), i.20. Book V, ch. 2 of Bulwer's work made the case for monarchy as 'the most efficient check to the anti-popular interests' (ii.250), arguing that the best government was that 'in which the people and the king form one state', and citing Prussia as 'the best governed country in the world' (ii.252–3). Disraeli also lauded Prussian example (*Vindication*, pp. 46–56).

79 On Disraeli's relations with the Whigs just after the publication of *Coningsby*, see *DL*, Introduction to vol. iv, p. xxii, and 1358, n. 6, iv.130.

80 Disraeli to Sarah Disraeli (19 July 1845), *DL*, 1428, iv.178. The 'social revolution' consisted largely in the opening of the best circles to Mary Anne, who hitherto had perhaps been a handicap.

81 *England and the English*, i.20–1.

82 M&B, iii.298, n. 2.

83 Edward Stanley's journal, 22 November 1856, quoted in Angus Hawkins, *Parliament, Party and the Art of Politics in Britain, 1855–59* (London, 1987), p. 48.

84 Stanley's journal, 23 January and 23 February 1862, in Vincent, ed., *Disraeli, Derby and the Conservative Party*, pp. 182, 183.

85 He reminded the Lancashire Conservatives, in his Manchester speech of 3 April 1872, that the House of Commons was elected by some 2.2 million in a population of about 32 million, arguing that thus 30 million people were represented as much by the House of Lords as by the Commons. *The Times*, 4 April 1872, p. 5.

86 Above, p. 176, n.35.

87 Disraeli to Lady Bradford, 3 August 1874, in M&B, v.247.

Index